Luminous Mind

Luminous Mind

The Way of the Buddha

Kyabje Kalu Rinpoche

An Anthology of Teachings Compiled
Under the Direction of Lama Denis Töndrup

Foreword by His Holiness the Dalai Lama

Translated from the French by Maria Montenegro

Wisdom Publications • Boston

WISDOM PUBLICATIONS
361 Newbury Street
Boston, Massachusetts 02115

Original French version:
La Voie du Boudhha: selon la tradition tibétaine
© Éditions du Seuil 1993

© Wisdom Publications 1997

Library of Congress Cataloging-in-Publication Data
Karma-raṅ-byuṅ-kun-khyab-phrin-las, Khenpo Kalu.
    [Voie du Bouddha.   French]
    Luminous mind : the way of the Buddha / Kyabje Kalu Rinpoche ; compiled by Denis
Töndrup ; translated from the French by Maria Montenegro ; foreword by His Holiness
the Dalai Lama.
        p.   cm.
    Includes index.
    ISBN 0-86171-118-1 (alk. paper)
    1. Spiritual life—Buddhism.   2. Buddhism—China—Tibet—Doctrines.
I. Töndrup, Denis.   II. Title.
BQ7805.K37814   1996   96–24689
294.3'4—dc20

ISBN 0-86171-118-1

01 00 99 98 97
  6   5   4   3   2

Cover Art: Eleven-Faced, Thousand-Armed Avalokiteshvara; 15th c.; Western Tibet;
gouache on cotton; Robert Hatfield Ellsworth Private Collection.

Cover Photo: Courtesy of John Taylor Bigelow

All photographs of Kalu Rinpoche courtesy of Sanje Elliott

Designed by: LJ·SAWLiT

Contents

SECTION TWO:
THE TRANSFORMATIONS OF MIND: LIVES, DEATHS, REBIRTHS

SECTION THREE:
THE MAHĀYĀNA: PATH OF OPENING AND COMPASSION

SECTION FOUR:
THE VAJRAYĀNA: PATH OF TRANSMUTATION

SECTION FIVE:
MAHĀMUDRĀ AND DZOGCHEN: THE IMMEDIATE PATH

SECTION SIX:
DHARMA PRACTICE TODAY

Publisher's Acknowledgment

The publisher gratefully acknowledges the generous help of the Hershey Family Foundation in sponsoring the production of this book.

Foreword
by His Holiness the Dalai Lama

Thinking of the forefathers of the Kagyu tradition, we remember Marpa Lotsawa for the hardships he underwent in obtaining Buddhist teachings from India and his scholarship in translating them into Tibetan. We remember Gampopa for consolidating the tradition and launching the monastic order. But the great yogi Milarepa is renowned and admired above all for his sincere dedication to spiritual practice and his saintly way of life. He remains a vital example to us all, yet there have been few like him before or since.

In our own time, Kalu Rinpoche had a similar simplicity in his determination to practice. Distinguished for the dozen years of his youth spent in meditative retreat, he devoted the rest of his life to guiding others and preserving the variety of Buddhist traditions. Following the tragedy which befell Tibet in the 1950s and the flight of many Tibetans to exile in India and elsewhere, he was a beacon of inspiration, not only for the Kagyu order, but for all traditions of Tibetan Buddhism then struggling to preserve their spiritual heritage.

In his later years, energy undiminished, he also accepted a number of requests to travel abroad and teach in Western countries. Consequently, he attracted many disciples and established Dharma centers—especially retreat centers where he supervised a number of three year retreats.

This book, *Luminous Mind,* contains an anthology of instructions that Kalu Rinpoche gave from his own experience, covering the full range of Buddhist practice from the basic analysis of the nature of the mind up to its ultimate refinement in the teachings of Mahāmudrā. As the Buddhist saying goes, "Rely less on the person than on what he teaches." This book is an apt memorial to Kalu Rinpoche, who now is no longer among us. If readers follow the additional dictum, "Rely less on the words of the teaching than on the meaning they express," and actually put them into effect, his great-hearted purpose will have been fulfilled.

Kyabje Kalu Rinpoche

Biographical Note

Kyabje Kalu Rinpoche (1904–1989) was born in Kham province in eastern Tibet. His birth was accompanied by extraordinary signs which foretold a predisposition to become an exceptional being. As a child, he displayed an unusually altruistic and intellectual nature.

His father, an accomplished yogi and well-known doctor, was a direct disciple of the three great master initiators[1] of the nonsectarian movement— *Rime* in Tibetan—a spiritual current that flourished in nineteenth-century Tibet. Rime advocated the transcendence of intellectual discussion by returning to the source of all teachings through inner experience cultivated in meditative practice. Among these three great sages, Jamgön Kongtrul Lodrö Thaye (1813–1899) was unquestionably the principal architect of the vast spiritual revival that the Rime movement inspired throughout the entire Tibetan tradition. Kyabje Kalu Rinpoche was eventually recognized as one of his main spiritual emanations, or *tulkus,* and became one of Jamgön Kongtrul Lodrö Thaye's main spiritual heirs. This is what Kalu Rinpoche's life—his ecumenical and universal approach—came to fully exemplify.

At thirteen years of age, Kyabje Kalu Rinpoche was ordained a monk at Pelpung monastery, one of eastern Tibet's main Kagyu monasteries, seat of the Taï Situpa. At a very tender age he pursued his studies and earned the title of Doctor of Traditional Sciences.[2]

At sixteen, he undertook a three-year lama retreat and received from Lama Norbu Töndrup, a perfectly realized being who became his main spiritual master, or root lama, the different transmissions of the old and new schools and particularly of the Five Golden Teachings of the Shangpa lineage, of which he became the principal holder. After this retreat, while beginning to use his talents in the service of his fellow Tibetans, he continued to study and practice at the feet of many realized lamas of the different Tibetan lineages and traditions.

At twenty-five, he chose to devote himself completely to practice and became a wandering yogi, practicing in Himalayan retreats as a solitary hermit for twelve years.

Later, when he was thirty-seven years of age, the fame of his realization brought him the name "Meditation Master of Three-Year Retreats," or *drubpön* in Tibetan, of Pelpung monastery. He exerted himself in this capacity for many years, during which he gathered a large number of disciples.

At age forty, Kyabje Kalu Rinpoche made various trips and pilgrimages to central Tibet which provided the opportunity to transmit the Five Golden Teachings to many well-known lamas of central Tibet, as well as to revive the teachings and monasteries of the Jonang and Shangpa traditions in other areas. Later on, he pursued these activities in Kham in eastern Tibet.

In 1955, when he was fifty-one, political problems due to the Chinese invasion of Kham forced him to return to central Tibet, and in 1957 he left for Bhutan, invited to serve as abbot of a large monastery and chaplain for the royal family.

In 1966, Kyabje Kalu Rinpoche settled at Sonada, India, where he founded the monastery and retreat centers that became his principal residence and the seat of the Shangpa-Kagyu tradition. It was at this time, about 1968, that the first Westerners—his future disciples—encountered him.

As patriarch of the Shangpa tradition, he became one of the most revered spiritual masters in all Tibetan traditions; he was particularly acclaimed for his realization and for his teaching of the spiritual yogas and ultimate practices of mahāmudrā and dzogchen. In his later years, he was invited by His Holiness the Karmapa, head of the Kagyu lineage, to teach the tulku princes, the holders of his lineage. Prompted by His Holiness the Dalai Lama, he likewise taught a number of geshes of his monastic and tantric colleges.

At the encouragement of the Karmapa and the Dalai Lama, he left for the West. In 1971, he accepted an invitation from Western disciples and made his first trip to Europe and North America. In response to the great interest with which his teachings were met, he founded the first Dharma center in Canada and formed a meditation group in Paris.

At the time of his second trip in 1974, the same interest prompted the creation of numerous Dharma centers in Europe and America, responsibility for which he entrusted to his first group of lama-disciples.

During a third tour in 1976–1977, he founded the West's first three-year retreat center in France. At the same time, he brought fifteen lamas to teach in the different centers he had founded.

While on tour in 1980 and 1982–1983, and in the years that followed, Kalu Rinpoche founded other Dharma and retreat centers in southeast Asia and other countries. His activity had become worldwide.

Between 1971 and 1989, he made a total of about ten long trips, many of which were world tours; he founded a hundred or so Dharma centers and some twenty three-year retreat centers which he entrusted to the care of more than thirty lama-disciples who had themselves completed a three-year retreat.

Kyabje Kalu Rinpoche's kindness and simplicity, along with the depth of his teachings and his capacity to lead disciples toward realization, touched innumerable beings all over the world. He was a perfect master, holder of the ultimate realization within pure monastic discipline, altruist and *tantrika*, and tireless teacher of Dharma in general and of the Karma-Kagyu and Shangpa lineages in particular. His radiant blessing and widespread activities brought about the deep and broad expansion of Buddhism to the Western world.

On May 10, 1989, Kalu Rinpoche seated himself in the meditation posture. Though his breathing stopped and he was considered physically dead, he remained in *samādhi* for three days, his mind dissolving into the absolute clear light, the ultimate liberation. Kyabje Kalu Rinpoche left behind an immense spiritual heritage carried on by his principal disciples today.

Kyabje Kalu Rinpoche's reincarnation was recognized by His Holiness the Dalai Lama and the Taï Situpa in a young boy born on September 17, 1990.

The Quick Ripening of the Desired Fruit

*A prayer composed by His Holiness the Dalai Lama
for the swift return of Kyabje Kalu Rinpoche.*

All-powerful Vajradhara, Tilopa, Nāropa,
And Marpa, who was actually Hevajra,
You, the four great pillars and all the others,
Glorious masters of the lineages of practice,
Bear witness to my longing.

You, who from the bhūmi of awakened activity (*karma*)
Have spontaneously accomplished (*rangjung*) in this world
The profound deeds of a buddha (*trinley*),
Propagated for beings of all levels (*kunkhyab*),
Lord of all those who have good fortune (*sangpo*),
To you I direct my prayer:

You, Lord, who for ages have perfected bodhicitta,
Please return once again to be the Dharma guide,
Leading beings and giving them
The sap of your profound secret instructions
According to their infinite aspirations and capacities.

You, who could everywhere establish the victory banner
    of the practice of the teachings' ultimate meaning
And who have attained the mind of the great ancestors
    of the tradition of practice;
You, holder of the Shangpa tradition and in particular
    the lineage of the Seven Jewels;
You, the glory of the qualities of the teaching,
Please return without delay.

By the inconceivable power of the truth of those who give refuge;
Lamas, deities, and Dharma protectors;
By the power of the truth of suchness and dependent arising,
As well as by the strength of our devotion and aspiration,
May this wish quickly bear fruit!

The glory of the teaching and of beings, the holder of the Shangpa-Kagyu tradition, Kalu Rinpoche Karma Rangjung Trinley Kunkhyab Sangpo, being gone for a short period to the realm of peace, his nephew, the excellent Gyaltsen, with an offering of white silk, has expressed to me the need to compose a prayer for the prompt return to the world of his supreme emanation.

In response to his request, Śākyamuni's monk, Tenzin Gyatso (His Holiness the Dalai Lama), with aspiration and fervor, has composed this prayer for the sake of virtue, the second of August 1989, or, according to the Tibetan calendar, the first day of the sixth month of the earth-snake year.

Preface

Several years ago, I proposed to Kyabje Kalu Rinpoche the idea of gathering into one anthology the many documents I had accumulated since becoming his disciple. He gave this project his complete approval and blessing, and work on it began, but the sheer volume of the many other activities he entrusted to me in the Dharma delayed its accomplishment for a long time.

Today, I am happy to see the completion of about ten years of compilation and to be able to offer the completed book, *Luminous Mind: The Way of the Buddha*. Although Rinpoche is no longer among us in body, I hope this book will at least help to expand his spiritual presence. It contains teachings I heard directly from his lips over the years. Having translated and meditated on them and put them into practice under his guidance, I have found the development of this book to be an intense experience that revived the memory of his words and kindness.

With the responsibility of transmitting these teachings, I tried to translate them as faithfully as possible, in the hopes that they would be clearly understood and might convey the inspiration they first awakened.

May this work, which is dedicated to Kyabje Kalu Rinpoche with devotion and gratitude, illuminate the nature of mind and the lives of innumerable beings.

Lama Denis Töndrup
Institut Karma-Ling

Editor's Note

In spite of the growing interest in Buddhism in the West, relatively few of Kyabje Kalu Rinpoche's teachings have been published to date. Moreover, Dharma students have long wished for an integrated work that contains the essentials.

Rather than create a simple compilation of teachings given in certain specific circumstances, our objective was to produce a work that would serve two purposes simultaneously: a general introduction to Dharma which would be accessible to a wide, nonspecialized audience, and an instructional manual that would serve as the basis for study and reference for Dharma students in general and for students of Kalu Rinpoche in particular.

We proceeded, using a very important collection of archived teachings, compiled over some twenty years, between 1968 and 1989, and derived from various sources: miscellaneous personal notes taken down for the most part at Sonada, Rinpoche's monastery in India, prior to 1974; a book written by Kyabje Kalu Rinpoche entitled *Fundamentals of Spiritual Practice*; and transcriptions of public teachings given in the West.

The process of selecting and creating a detailed inventory of these documents yielded a plan corresponding to one that Rinpoche himself used in his public teachings: first, a statement on the nature of mind and its transformations, followed by a glimpse into the various aspects of the path to enlightenment. These outlines became the two parts of this book. Under these headings, we selected the essential themes that form the different chapters.

The disparity of the sources—oral and written, public teachings and private conversations, guided meditations, anecdotes, stories, and so forth— posed problems which added to the inherent difficulties of oral translation from the Tibetan. We tried to maintain a sense of coherence as well as to standardize the translation of Dharma terminology.

In the second part of the book, there are various traditional stories chosen from those Rinpoche frequently told; these are sprinkled throughout the text and illustrate the dynamic aspect of the oral teachings. Some of them may be a bit disconcerting, but as Rinpoche explained at the end of one such story, the inconceivable is real, "just as it is true that the inconceivable nature of phenomena escapes our understanding!"

The inscriptions at the beginning of the chapters are citations from the living tradition Rinpoche often referred to, and some of the illustrations were inspired by his own original drawings. Since several chapters complement one another, we have inserted cross-references. We have also added a detailed table of contents, a thematic index, and two glossaries (terms and proper names). To find information on a given subject, the reader can first consult the table of contents, which presents a list of the main subjects, and then follow up with cross-references provided in the endnotes, which refer to other chapters on the same topic. To research particular terms, or subjects that do not appear in the table of contents, the reader can refer to the index (page 299). The pages listed in bold in these entries refer to the main passage where a definition or general explanation of the concept may be found. The glossary of terms lists only English-Tibetan-Sanskrit equivalents, since the reader can use the index to locate a term's definition in the text. The main proper names are indexed and explained in the glossary of proper names (page 285); they also appear in the index. Terms that appear only in the prayers and chants are not included in the index.

In addition to commonly used Sanskrit or Tibetan terms, we have kept some technical terms in their original language. This prevents the creation of strange neologisms, the use of descriptive paraphrasing, or the use of common words as technical terms, which often encourages hasty assimilations of ideas that are mistakenly interpreted. This solution has the advantage of enriching the English terminology while encouraging the discovery and correct understanding of new concepts. Except in special cases, we have preferred the use of the Sanskrit over Tibetan; this has the advantage of being more legible in transliteration as well as understood outside the circle of Tibetologists. The Sanskrit is spelled according to the way it is transliterated, with diacritical marks, and for the sake of pronunciation, Tibetan words are given in English phonetic transliteration. We have chosen these options because they seemed to reconcile precision with readability.

Acknowledgments

We would like to extend our gratitude first and foremost, of course, to Kyabje Kalu Rinpoche, whose wisdom and compassion are the source of these teachings and of this work, and also to His Holiness the Dalai Lama, who has honored it with a foreword.

Lama Denis Töndrup inspired and directed each stage of this anthology's preparation. He is one of Kyabje Kalu Rinpoche's senior Western students and was his personal translator. We owe him a great deal of thanks for translations and source materials.

Many others, over the years, have participated in the development of this collective effort. We will cite here those who contributed to the preliminary sources by their translations and notes: Sylvie Carteron, Dominique Gallot, A. Sonam Lhakyi, L. Chokyi, A. Zangmo. Rose-Marie Mengual in particular, along with Daniel Gerrer, and Marc and Monique Frion participated in the first edition of *Fundamentals of Spiritual Practice*. François Chenique, A. Dechen, N. Drolma, Marcelle Eysseric-Vacher, Jean Lessieux, N. Mingyour, Jean-Pierre Schnetzler, L. Sonam, and others already mentioned above reread the manuscript at different stages and made suggestions.

We would also like to acknowledge all those who painstakingly transcribed the recordings, among them Dominique Bouchez Mongardé, whose writing often appears in the early manuscripts, as well as Christine Drai and Madeleine Santi, who had the weighty responsibility of the archives at Institut Karma-Ling and who made various typewritten manuscripts with N. Chophel and Catherine Ratinier.

Illustrations, derived from traditional original works, were prepared by Cecile Boullet, N. Tenma, N. Phuntsok, and J.M. Soule; J. C. de Verneuil also contributed.

The book owes a tremendous gratitude to Maliana Perrey-Perrier for preparing a list of its sources and to Elisabeth Dayot and Christine Brunet for putting together the first part. The second part of the book was completed by Françoise Bonardel, who also made a vital contribution in the revision of the entire manuscript, offering numerous suggestions that greatly added to the quality of the finished product.

Finally, it is thanks to Claire Sicard's patience that a great many corrections were made and the definitive version produced, complete with glossaries and index.

His Holiness's foreword was arranged through the help of Alain Blisson, and the final version was attentively reread by Michel Drai, Georgette Rudigoz, and Anne and Michel Berry.

We would like to thank them all, as well as all those who, from near and far, anonymously made generous contributions to the realization of the original French edition, not to mention the Institut Karma-Ling and all its responsible benefactors, without whose support the original book could not have been completed.

We have decided that proceeds from this book will be given as an offering to Kyabje Kalu Rinpoche's monastery in Sonada, India. As to the spiritual benefits of our modest contributions, we would like to dedicate them to the welfare of all sentient beings.

General Introduction

The Unity of the Different Traditions

I

The Spirit of All Traditions

Every major religion of the world—
Buddhism, Christianity, Confucianism, Hinduism, Islam, Jainism,
Judaism, Sikhism, Taoism, Zoroastrianism—
has similar ideals of love, the same goal of benefiting humanity
through spiritual practice, and the same effect
of making their followers into better human beings.

—His Holiness the Dalai Lama, *Ocean of Wisdom*

Westerners have achieved an astonishingly high level of technological sophistication. Mass-produced machines allow us to travel through the air at great speed, explore the depths of the ocean, and witness instantly whatever is happening in any corner of the world and even beyond our own planet.

Yet our own mind, which is so close to us, remains impenetrable: we do not understand what our own mind really is. This is a paradox because, even though we have extremely refined telescopes to see light-years away and microscopes powerful enough to distinguish the atomic details of matter, the mind, which is the most basic and intimate aspect of our being, remains the most unrecognized, mysterious, and unknown.

Scientific developments and control over our material conditions have brought us a relatively high level of comfort and physical well-being. This is certainly wonderful, but even so, progress in science and technology does not prevent the mind from remaining in ignorance about itself and therefore conditioned and afflicted by suffering, frustration, and anguish. To alleviate these problems, it is crucial to discover and understand the actual nature of our own mind.

UNDERSTANDING OUR ACTUAL NATURE

The main point here is to understand our real nature, or what we actually are. Many of you know many things; you are educated. Try to use your capacities to study the mind.

You mustn't think this kind of investigation applies only to a small elite. Each of us has a mind whose nature is the same as everyone else's. We are all alike; we all have the feeling of existing with an ego which is subjected to all kinds of hardships and suffering, anxieties and fears. All of this results from ignorance about our basic nature. If we can reach the understanding of what we actually are, there is no better remedy for eliminating all suffering. This is the heart of all spiritual practices.

All spiritual traditions, whether Christian, Hindu, Judaic, Islamic, or Buddhist, teach that the understanding of what we are at the deepest level is the main point. This understanding of the nature of mind sheds light from within and illuminates the teachings of all traditions. In every tradition, whoever gains firsthand, experiential understanding of mind and retains that kind of awareness, is led to a worldview that would not have been possible prior to this direct experience. Knowledge of the nature of mind is the key that yields an understanding of all teachings; it sheds light on what we are, the nature of all our experiences, and reveals the deepest form of love and compassion.

The actual realization of the nature of mind opens onto a complete understanding of Dharma and all the traditions. To have a good theoretical knowledge of Dharma or any other spiritual tradition and to effectively realize the ultimate nature of mind, however, are profoundly different. Even a realized being who is not involved in a particular spiritual tradition would have, while living in the ordinary world, an extremely beneficial influence.

I would like to emphasize that this is true regardless of the spiritual tradition. Every tradition is illuminated by this awareness. But it is especially the case in the Buddha's teachings, in which this knowledge constitutes the heart and goal of all his instruction.

2

The Basic Unity of All Traditions

All spiritual traditions, whether Buddhist
or non-Buddhist, differ in their forms in order
to adapt to the abilities and faculties
of different kinds of people;
all of them, however,
work toward establishing beings on the path
of well-being and liberation.
Since they all derive from perfectly enlightened
activity, without exception they merit our trust.

—Kyabje Kalu Rinpoche

REALIZATION OF MIND AS THE ORIGIN OF ALL TRADITIONS

Several hundred religious traditions have manifested in the world. All of them issue from enlightened spiritual activity arising from the complete realization of the nature of mind. Every tradition works for the welfare of beings, according to their particular needs.

Certain religious traditions allow us to regain birth in the first stages of a higher realm; others, in the divine realms of the world of pure form or in the formless realms. Finally, some lead to the ultimate spiritual realization. But all of them teach us the necessary practices to prevent us from falling into lower realms of existence and to rise toward higher realms. All traditions offer spiritual strength and transformative power. In this sense, I have faith in all of them.

It is helpful to recognize that Christianity is a similar path to Buddhism because of the importance Christianity accords to faith, compassion, offerings, prayer, generosity, and disciplined behavior. I think those who aspire to the Christian teachings and have faith in them are fortunate beings who can thereby give true meaning to the human existence they have obtained.

In Buddhism, whether in Japan, Laos, Cambodia, Vietnam, Thailand, Burma, Sri Lanka, Korea, China, or Tibet, all the teachings and Dharma practices have the same foundations, so the practitioners of the various schools are all brothers and sisters.

In Tibet, more specifically, eight major lineages coexist, but today four principal lineages remain as schools. These are the Sakya, Gelug, Nyingma, and Kagyu traditions. Each of these lineages transmits the peerless word of Buddha by way of lineages of sages and adepts who are like pure gold. They transmit uncorrupted authentic Dharma that can lead beings to liberation from cyclic existence, to ultimate spiritual realization.

THE COMPLEMENTARITY OF DIFFERENT TRADITIONS

Since each Tibetan tradition and lineage constitutes an authentic, complete teaching, we might ask, "Then why are there so many of them?" In general, their variety corresponds to beings' varied capacities and inclinations. Each system exists to meet the particular needs and abilities of different people endowed with different mentalities.

Personally, I was the disciple of many masters of the four Tibetan traditions. With each of them, I established excellent connections and nurtured great faith in their different teachings. Among my disciples, there are many practitioners, lamas, and monks of these four Tibetan schools. Furthermore, I would like those who follow my teachings to have faith in all the traditions. I consider them impartially, since they are all beneficial to different people having specific affinities derived from their previous connections. All of the traditions insist on discipline proceeding from an understanding of karma as a way of radically changing our conditioned thinking and as a basis for proceeding toward the state of buddhahood. In addition, each tradition possesses its own collection of teachings and practical instructions arising from the personal experiences of each lineage's masters.

In general, to have faith in all the traditions is a sign of profound understanding of the teachings. However, it is absolutely necessary to engage in one given tradition, to receive detailed instructions in it, and to be introduced to its essential practices; and then, it is proper to practice mainly those teachings.

So, regardless of the school or lama from whom we receive teachings, we should try to adopt an impartial[3] attitude and devote ourselves to practice with total aspiration. Otherwise, merely remembering some phrases here and there, taking in only certain aspects of the teachings, and playing at being practitioners will make it quite difficult for us to gain any significant benefit.

3
Buddhadharma

Not to do any harm,
To perfectly effect what is beneficial
To completely discipline one's mind:
That is the teaching of Buddha.

—Buddha Śākyamuni

Twenty-five hundred years ago, through the experience of meditation, Buddha Śākyamuni penetrated the essence of mind. By direct contemplation, he realized mind's profound nature and thereby attained enlightenment. This was his crowning experience. Having discovered the reality of what we are, he expressed his teaching and proposed a way for others to gain access to the experience he had realized. This teaching is called the Buddhadharma, the teaching of Buddha.

It is experiential knowledge that teaches us to recognize our fundamental nature and liberates us from falling prey to illusions, passions, and thoughts. This awareness grants real happiness during this life, at the time of death, and in future lives up to ultimate spiritual enlightenment—which is the state of buddhahood. This knowledge develops universal wisdom and compassion.

THE INNER SCIENCE

Buddhadharma, which concerns our deepest inner nature, is called the inner science. This is the traditional name of what in the West is called Buddhism. The Tibetan expression rendered in Western languages as "Buddhism" is *nangpa sangyepai chö*. The last two terms taken together, *sangyepai chö*, refer to Buddhadharma, or the Dharma of awakening. "Dharma" in this context means "teaching," and the word "Buddha" refers to the origin of these teachings—the historical Buddha—as well as to the spiritual realization he attained, or buddhahood. *Nangpa* means "inner" and emphasizes the fact that these teachings are concerned not so much with the physical body and the outer world as with the mind abiding there, since the teachings' main purpose is to provide mental peace, well-being, and liberation. Buddhadharma is therefore the inner science, or the science of the interior, understood as the science of mind.

THE TRANSMISSION OF SPEECH AND MIND

All the words of the Buddha were recorded in writing and have been preserved in the Tibetan tradition in a collection of 108 volumes called the *Kangyur*, which means "the translation of the Buddha's words." The *Kangyur* contains texts called sūtras which are the foundation of the first two levels of teachings, the Hīnayāna and the Mahāyāna. It also contains texts called tantras, which are the basis of the third level of teachings, the Vajrayāna.

In addition to the *Kangyur*, which forms the basic canon of the tradition, there are all the commentaries and treatises that India's leading sages, scholars, and adepts subsequently composed in order to clarify Buddha's teachings. This collection is called the *Tengyur*, which means "the translation of the commentaries." The entire collection originally contained 240 volumes, of which only 215 remain today. In addition to the *Kangyur* and *Tengyur*, there are the thousands of volumes of commentaries by Tibetan scholars and adepts. This collection is known as the *Sungbum*.

All these teachings of the Buddha offer a way of awakening, of liberation from the illusions of ignorance and the afflictions those illusions induce. They are the remedies for the three fundamental mental poisons of desire, hatred, and ignorance, and all the resulting afflictive emotions. In their many subdivisions and combinations, these three basic poisons can result in up to 84,000 types of mental afflictions.

The sūtra teachings are made up of three collections: the vinaya, or collection on discipline; the sūtras, or collection of sayings; and the abhidharma, or collection on reality. These three collections are considered remedies to be applied to each of the three basic mental poisons. The vinaya, which clarifies the spirit of discipline and its rules, is the remedy for the 21,000 types of desire. The sūtra collection is an account of the teachings given by Buddha Śākyamuni in different places and circumstances. It is the remedy for the 21,000 types of hatred. The abhidharma is an explanation of the nature of reality, existence, the world, and individuals; it remedies the 21,000 types of ignorance. The tantra ("continuity") teachings constitute the Vajrayāna and are considered the remedy for the 21,000 types of combinations of the three mental poisons.

It would be difficult to study all these teachings completely, but the lineage lamas transmit to us their essence in the easily understandable form of direct oral instructions. All Buddha's teachings have been transmitted in writing through these texts, but also in mind through the realization of the lineage lamas up to the present day by an uninterrupted transmission from master to disciple. In the Kagyu lineage ("the tradition of practice") alone, there has been an ocean of adepts over the centuries, a host of beings who arrived at supreme awakening. Even today, there are masters who have gained perfect realization of these teachings. The various aspects of their transmission and accomplishment have remained intact up to the present; their teachings are thereby accessible to us in their entirety, in theory as well as in practice. It is up to us to have the intelligence, courage, and energy to practice these masters' instructions.

In the two parts of this book, we will deal successively with the mind, which is the basis of all the traditions, and its transformations from birth to birth; and the different Dharma practices that constitute the path to liberation.

PART ONE

MIND AND ITS TRANSFORMATIONS

Calling the Lama from Afar

Namo Gurubya
Your guidance, because of the profound connections of my aspirations,
Disturbs to its depths the ocean of saṃsāra's suffering
And directs me on the path of liberation and lasting bliss.
You, whose kindness could never be returned,
Please, Lama, listen to me!

Interrupting the ceaseless passions and illusions of karma,
By the discipline of the three vows,
You turn me away from samsaric ways
And join my mind to Dharma by your instructions, which ripen and liberate.
Sublime king of guides,
Please, Lama, listen to me!

The blaze of your transcendent wisdom consumes the thicket of my confusion
And directly shows me the face of the self-knowing dharmakāya;
You, who raise me in this very life to the realm of nondual union,
Omnipresent master of all buddha families,
Please, Lama, listen to me!

Lord Lama, master of the sea of maṇḍalas,
Lord Lama, who confers on me all attainments,
Lord Lama, source of all that is useful and desired,
From the depths of my heart, I pray:

Bless me and all mother sentient beings of the six realms
To be delivered as soon as possible from the mire of samsara's suffering,
And then bless us that in the cessation and realization of the myriad Kagyu
    adepts,
Our minds may indissolubly mingle with yours.

This prayer, calling from afar the loving lama who guides us on the path to libera-
tion, was composed extemporaneously by Karma Rangjung Kunkhyab at the
monastery of Chang Chub Chö Ling, or Dar Ling, in Bhutan, upon the repeated
requests of a group of thirteen devoted practitioners.

Part One
Section One

Mind, Reality, and Illusion

I

What Is Mind?

Just realizing the meaning of mind
Encompasses all understanding;
Whereas knowing everything
Without realizing the meaning of mind
is the worst (ignorance).

—Jamgön Kongtrul Lodrö Thaye, *The Outline of Essential Points*

Although we all have the sense of having a mind and of existing, our understanding of our mind and how we exist is generally vague and confused. We rightly say, "I have a mind or consciousness," "I am," "I exist"; we identify ourselves with a "me," an "I" to which we attribute qualities. But we do not know the nature of this mind, nor of this "me." We do not know what they consist of, how they function, or who or what we really are.

THE FUNDAMENTAL PARADOX

In seeking out mind, initially the most important thing is to recognize mind's nature by questioning, at the deepest level, what we really are. Those who really examine their mind and consider what it is are extremely rare, and for those who try to, the search proves difficult. As we search and observe what our mind is, often we do not actually close in on it; we do not really arrive at an understanding of it.

A scientific perspective, no doubt, can offer many answers toward a definition of mind. But that is not the kind of knowledge we're referring to here. The basic issue is that it is not possible for the mind to know itself, because the one who searches, the subject, is the mind itself, and the object it wants to examine is also mind. There is a paradox here: I can look for myself everywhere, search the world over, without ever finding myself, because I am what I search for.

The problem is the same as trying to see our own face: our eyes are very close to it, but they cannot see it any more than they can see themselves. We do not come to know our own mind simply because it is too close. One Dharma proverb says, "The eye cannot see its own pupil." Likewise, our own mind does not have the capacity to see itself; it is so close, so intimate, that we cannot discern it.

We need to know how to shift perspectives. In order to see our face, we use a mirror. In order to study our own mind, we need a method that functions like a mirror, to allow us to recognize mind. This method is the Dharma as it is transmitted to us by a spiritual guide.

It is in relation to the teaching and this spiritual friend or guide that the mind will gradually be able to awaken to its true nature and finally go beyond the initial paradox by realizing another mode of knowledge. This discovery is effected by various practices known as meditation.

IN SEARCH OF MIND

Mind is a strange thing. Asians traditionally situate it at the center of the body, at the level of the heart. Westerners understand mind to be located in the head or brain. Although different viewpoints are justified, these designations are inadequate. Basically, mind is no more in the heart than it is in the brain. Mind inhabits the body, but it is only an illusion that mind can be localized in this or that place. Essentially, we cannot say that mind is found at a particular place in the person or any place at all.

The search for mind is not easy because, in addition to the paradox whereby the knower cannot know itself, mind's essential nature is indescribable. It has no form, no color, nor any other characteristic that could allow us to conclude: *That's* what it is.

Yet each of us can develop an experience of the nature of our mind by asking ourselves about what is doing the observing: the observer, the knower, the subject that experiences thoughts and different sensations. Where exactly can it be found? What is it? It is a question of observing our own mind: Where is it? Who am I? What am I? Are body and mind the same or different? Do my experiences unfold inside or outside my mind? Are mind and its thoughts distinct, or are they one and the same? If yes, how? If no, how? This search is carried out in meditation, in close connection with a qualified guide who can tell us what is correct and what is mistaken. The process can take several months or even several years.

As this quest deepens, the spiritual guide progressively directs us toward the experience of the actual nature of mind. It is difficult to understand and realize because it is not something that can be apprehended through concepts or representations. The main study of mind cannot be done through theory; we need the practical experience of meditation, observing the mind again and again, in order to penetrate its true nature.

In meditation practice, there is a twofold approach: we can say that one is analytical and the other contemplative. The first is made up of questions like those we asked earlier. If we carry out this type of search persistently, while being competently guided, a definite understanding develops.

In the second approach, mind simply remains at rest in its own lucidity, without forcing or contrivance. This practice goes beyond all preceding forms of analysis, by making us leave the sphere of concepts and opening us to an immediate experience.[4] At the end of these meditations, we discover the mind's essential emptiness. That is, it is devoid of determinations and characteristics such as form, color, or aspect, and its nature is beyond representations, concepts, names, and forms. In order to try to evoke recognition of emptiness, we could compare it to the indeterminateness of space: mind is empty like space. But this is just an image, and, as we will see, mind is not only empty.

For the time being, I would like to stress how important knowledge of mind is, as well as the fruits of such knowledge. Mind is what we are. It is what experiences happiness and suffering. Mind is what experiences different thoughts and sensations; it is what is subject to pleasant and unpleasant emotions, what experiences desire, aversion, and so forth. A real understanding of the nature of mind is liberating because it disengages us from all illusions and consequently from the source of the suffering, fears, and difficulties that make up our daily life.

Let's take an example. If we have the illusion that a harmful person is a helper, he can trick us, abuse us, and cause us harm. But as soon as we recognize him as harmful, we will not be duped; in unmasking him, we can avoid falling prey to his evil deeds. The harmful person here is the ignorance of what we really are, or, more precisely, the illusion of the ego, of a self. The knowledge that unmasks this is awareness of the nature of mind; it liberates us from illusions and painful conditioning. This understanding of mind is the foundation of Buddhadharma and all its teachings.

2

One Mind, Two States

As long as [mind] is not recognized,
the wheel of existence turns.
When this is understood, the state of Buddha
is nothing other than that.
There is nothing that can be described
as either existing or not existing.
May the nature of reality,
the true nature of the Buddha mind, be recognized.

—The Third Karmapa, *Mahāmudrā: Boundless Joy and Freedom*

ENLIGHTENMENT AND ILLUSION

Mind has two faces, two facets, which are two aspects of one reality. These are enlightenment and illusion.

Enlightenment is the state of pure mind. It is nondualistic knowing and is called primordial wisdom. Its experiences are authentic; that is, they are without illusion. Pure mind is free and endowed with numerous qualities.

Illusion is the state of impure mind. Its mode of knowledge is dichotomous or dualistic; it is the "conditioned consciousness." Its experiences are tainted by illusions. Impure mind is conditioned and endowed with much suffering.

Ordinary beings experience this state of impure, deluded mind as their habitual state. Pure, enlightened mind is a state in which mind realizes its own nature as free of habitual conditions and the suffering associated with them. This is the enlightened state of a buddha.

When our mind is in its impure, deluded state, we are ordinary beings who move through different realms of conditioned consciousness. The transmigrations of the mind within these realms make up their indefinite rounds in conditioned, cyclic existence, or the cycle of lives—*saṃsāra* in Sanskrit.

When it is purified of all samsaric illusion, the mind no longer transmigrates. This is the enlightened state of a buddha, which is experience of the essential purity of our own mind, of our buddha nature. All beings, whatever they happen to be, have buddha nature. This is the reason we can all realize buddha nature. It is because we each possess buddha nature that it is possible to attain enlightenment. If we did not already have buddha nature, we would never be able to realize it.

So, the ordinary state and the enlightened state are distinguished only by the impurity or purity of mind, by the presence or absence of illusions. Our present mind already has the qualities of buddhahood; those qualities abide in mind; they are mind's pure nature. Unfortunately, our enlightened qualities are invisible to us because they are masked by different shrouds, veils, and other kinds of stains.

Buddha Śākyamuni taught:

> Buddha nature is present in all beings,
> But shrouded by adventitious illusions.
> Purified, they are truly Buddha.

The distance between the ordinary state and the "enlightened" state is what separates ignorance from knowledge of this pure nature of mind. In the ordinary state, it is unknown. In the enlightened state, it is fully realized. The situation in which mind is ignorant of its actual nature is what we call fundamental ignorance. In realizing its profound nature, mind is liberated from this ignorance, from the illusions and conditioning that ignorance creates, and so enters the unconditioned enlightened state called liberation.

All Buddhadharma and its practices involve purifying, "dis-illusioning" this mind, and proceeding from a tainted to an untainted state, from illusion to enlightenment.

3

The Nature of Mind

All phenomena are projections of the mind.
Mind is not "a" mind; the mind is empty in essence.
Although empty, everything constantly arises in it.
Through the deepest examination of the mind
may we find its innermost root.

—The Third Karmapa, *Wishes of Mahāmudrā*

The actual experience of the essential nature of mind is beyond words. To wish to describe it is like the situation of a mute who wants to describe the flavor of a candy in his mouth: he lacks an adequate means of expression. Even so, I would like to offer some ideas that hint at this experience.

The nature of pure mind can be thought of as having three essential, complementary, and simultaneous aspects: openness, clarity, and sensitivity.

OPENNESS

Mind is what thinks: "I am, I want, I don't want"; it is the thinker, the observer, the subject of all experiences. I am the mind. From one point of view, this mind does exist, since *I* am and *I* have a capacity for action. If *I* want to see, *I* can look; if *I* want to hear, *I* can listen; if *I* decide to do something with my hands, *I* can command my body, and so on. In this sense, the mind and its faculties seem to exist.

But if we search for it, we cannot find any part of it in us, not in our head, our body, or anywhere else. So from this other perspective, it seems not to exist. Therefore, on the one hand, the mind seems to exist, but on the other, it is not something that truly exists.

However exhaustive our investigations, we will never be able to find any formal characteristics of mind: it has neither dimension, color, form, nor any tangible quality. It is in this sense that it is called open, because it is essentially indeterminate, unqualifiable, beyond concept, and thus comparable to space. This indefinable nature is openness, the first essential quality of mind. It is beyond illusory consciousness that causes us to experience mind as a "me" possessing characteristics we habitually attribute to ourselves.

But we must be careful here! Because to say mind is open like space is not to reduce it to something nonexistent in the sense of being nonfunctional. Like space, pure mind cannot be located, but it is omnipresent and all-penetrating;

it embraces and pervades all things. Moreover, it is beyond change, and its open nature is indestructible and atemporal.

CLARITY

If the mind is indeed essentially open, in the sense explained above, it is not only open or void, because if it were, it would be inert and would not experience or know anything, neither sensations nor joy and suffering. Mind is not only open—it possesses a second essential quality, which is its capacity for experiences, for cognition. This dynamic quality is called clarity. It is both the lucidity of mind's intelligence and the luminosity of its experiences.

To better our understanding of clarity, we can compare the openness of mind to the space in a room we are in. This formless space allows for our experience; it contains experience in its totality. It is where our experience takes place. Clarity, then, would be the light that illuminates the room and allows us to recognize different things. If there were only inert empty space, there would be no possibility for awareness. This is only an example, because clarity of mind is not like the ordinary light of the sun, the moon, or electricity. It is a clarity of mind that makes possible all cognition and experience.

The open and luminous nature of mind is what we call the "clear light"; it is an open clarity that, at the level of pure mind, is aware in and of itself; that is why we call it self-luminous cognition or clarity.

There is no truly adequate example to illustrate this clarity at a pure level. But at an ordinary level, which we could relate to more easily, we can get a glimpse of some of its aspects by understanding one of mind's manifestations—the dream state. Let's say it is a dark night, and in this total darkness we are dreaming, or experiencing a dream world. The mental space where the dream takes place—independent of the physical place where we are—could be compared to the openness of mind, while its capacity for experiencing, despite the external darkness, corresponds to its clarity. This lucidity encompasses all mind's knowledge and is the clarity inherent in these experiences. It is also the lucidity of what or who experiences them; knower and known, lucidity and luminosity are but two facets of the same quality. As the intelligence that experiences the dream, it is lucidity, and as the clarity present in its experiences, it is luminosity. But at the nondual level of pure mind, it is one and the same quality, "clarity," called *prabhasvara* in Sanskrit, or *selwa* in Tibetan. This example may be helpful in understanding, but bear in mind that it is just an illustration showing at a habitual level a particular manifestation of clarity. In the example, there is a difference between the lucidity of the knower and the luminosity of that subject's experiences. This is because the dream is a dualistic experience, differentiated in terms of subject and object, in which clarity manifests itself at once in the awareness or lucidity of the subject and in the luminosity of its objects. In fact, the example is limited, because fundamentally there is no duality in pure minds: it is the same quality of clarity that is essentially nondual.

SENSITIVITY

For a complete description of pure mind, a third aspect should be added to the first two qualities already discussed, which is sensitivity or unimpededness. The clarity of mind is its capacity to experience; everything can arise in the mind, so its possibilities for awareness or intelligence are limitless. The Tibetan term that designates this quality literally means "absence of impediment." This is the mind's freedom to experience without obstruction. At a pure level, these experiences have the qualities of enlightenment. At a conditioned level, they are the mind's perceptions of each thing as being this or that; that is, the ability to distinguish, perceive, and conceive of all things.

To return to the example of the dream, mind's inherent quality of sensitivity would be, because of its openness and clarity, its ability to experience the multiplicity of aspects of the dream, both the perceptions of the dreaming subject and the experiences of the dreamed world. Clarity is what allows experiences to arise, whereas sensitivity is the totality of all aspects distinctly experienced.

This sensitivity corresponds, at the habitual, dualistic level, to all the types of thoughts and emotions arising in the mind and, at the pure level of a buddha, to all the wisdom or enlightened qualities put into practice to help beings.

So, pure mind can be understood as follows: in essence, open; in nature, clear; and in its aspects, an unimpeded sensitivity. These three facets, openness, clarity, and sensitivity, are not separate but concomitant. They are the simultaneous and complementary qualities of the awakened mind.

At the pure level, these qualities are the state of a buddha; at the impure level of ignorance and delusion, they become all the states of conditioned awareness, all the experiences of samsara. But whether the mind is enlightened or deluded, there is nothing beyond it, and it is essentially the same in all beings, human or nonhuman. Buddha nature, with all its powers and enlightened qualities, is present in each being. All the qualities of a buddha are in our minds, though veiled and obscured, just as a windowpane is naturally transparent and translucent but made opaque by a dense coat of dirt.

Purification, or the removal of these impurities, allows all the enlightened qualities present in the mind to be revealed. Actually, our mind has little freedom and few positive qualities because it is conditioned by our karma, or our habitual imprints from the past. Little by little, however, the practices of

Dharma and meditation free the mind and awaken it to all the qualities of a buddha.

A Brief Meditation

At this point it would probably help to do a short experiential practice, a meditation to try to improve our understanding of what this is all about.

Sitting comfortably, we let the mind rest in its natural state. We relax ourselves, our tensions, and remain without strain, without any particular intention, without artifice.... We release our mind and allow it to be open, like space.... Spacious, the mind remains clear and lucid.... Relaxed, loose, the mind abides transparent and luminous.... We do not keep our mind locked up in ourselves.... It is not confined to our head, our body, the environment, or anywhere. Relaxed, it is vast like space and encompasses everything.... It encompasses everything, from the United States to India, the whole world and universe. It pervades our entire world.

We remain at rest, relaxed, in this state of openness, limitless, fully lucid, and transparent.

The openness and transparency of the mind, similar to endless space, are signs of what we have called its openness. Its free and clear awareness are what we have called its clarity.

There is also its sensitivity, which is the mind's capacity for all-experiencing in an unimpeded awareness of persons, places, and all other things. Mind can know all these things and can recognize them distinctly.

Once again, without orienting "the mind," the subject-knower, either toward the outside or the inside, we remain as is, at ease and relaxed.... Without sinking into a state of indifference or mental dullness, our mind remains alert and vigilant.... In this state, the mind is open and disengaged. This is its openness.... Its lucid awareness is its clarity.... All the aspects it knows distinctly and unimpededly are its sensitivity.

An important obstacle arises as a result of habitually confining mind to body, which we perceive as being *our* body; we identify with this body, we fixate on it, and we lock ourselves up in it. To counteract this, it is important to relax all tension, all fidgeting. Tense and fidgety, the mind remains shut in. These tensions will end up causing physical pains and headaches.

Let the mind remain at rest in its lucid vastness, open and relaxed.

We can begin to meditate in this way,[5] but it is critical to pursue the practice under the direction of a qualified guide who will lead us on the right path. With his or her help, we can realize the emptiness of mind, of thoughts and emotions, which is the best of all methods for freeing ourselves from delusion and suffering. Recognizing the nature of negative emotions allows them to be released; it is therefore essential to learn to recognize their emptiness as soon as they arise. If we remain ignorant of their empty nature, they will carry us away on their torrent, enslaving and overpowering us. They have control over us because we attribute to them a reality that they don't actually have. If we realize their emptiness, then their alienating power and the suffering they cause will vanish.

This ability to recognize the open, empty nature of mind and all its productions, projections, thoughts, and emotions is the panacea, the universal remedy that in and of itself cures all delusion, all negative emotion, and all suffering.

Our mind can be compared to a hand that is bound or tied up, as much by the representation of our "me," of the ego or self, as by the conceptions and fixations belonging to this idea. Little by little, Dharma practice eliminates these self-cherishing fixations and conceptions, and, just as an unbound hand can open, the mind opens and gains all kinds of possibilities for activity. It then discovers many qualities and skills, like the hand freed from its ties. The qualities that are slowly revealed are those of enlightenment, of pure mind.

4
Mind's Veils

Self-manifestation, which has never existed as such,
is erroneously seen as an object.
Through ignorance, self-awareness is mistakenly experienced as an "I."
Through attachment to this duality
we are caught in the conditioned world.
May the root of confusion be found.

—The Third Karmapa, *Mahāmudrā: Boundless Joy and Freedom*

If there is no essential difference between the mind of a buddha and our own mind, why does a buddha have so many qualities attributed to him, and we do not? The difference is that in our minds the buddha nature is obscured by all sorts of coverings.

Each of the three facets of pure mind discussed in the last chapter becomes, at the impure level—that is, in ignorance—one of the elements that constitute dualistic experience. To begin with, ignorance of the openness of mind leads to a conception of a subject, me, the observer; and ignorance of the essential clarity leads to ignorance of exterior objects. This is how the subject-object, me-other dichotomy arises.

Once the two poles of the dualistic view have been established, various relationships develop among them, which in turn motivate different activities.

The stages of this process comprise four veils that mask the pure mind or buddha nature. These are: the veil of ignorance, the veil of the basic propensity, the veil of mental afflictions, and the veil of karma. They are consecutive and structured one after the other.

THE VEIL OF IGNORANCE

The mind's ignorance of its true nature, that is, the simple fact that it does not recognize what it truly is, is called *fundamental ignorance*. It is the basic inability of the conditioned mind to perceive itself. We can compare the pure mind having the three previously discussed essential qualities to calm, transparent waters in which everything can be seen clearly. The veil of ignorance is a lack of intelligence, a kind of clouded state, as an opaque vase causes water to lose its transparent clarity. Such an obscured mind loses the experience of lucid openness and becomes ignorant of its essential nature.

Fundamental ignorance is said to be innate, because it is inherent to our existence; we are born with it. It is, in fact, the point of departure of duality, the root of all delusions and the source of all suffering.

THE VEIL OF THE BASIC PROPENSITY

Mind controlled by ignorance engages in delusions, among which the most basic, the root of all others, is dualistic grasping in terms of subject and object.[6]

When the mind does not know the extent of its openness, instead of experiencing without center or periphery, we perceive everything through one central point of reference. This point, the center that appropriates all experiences, is the observer, the ego-subject. It is in this way that the mind, ignorant of its openness, engenders the delusional experience of a "me" or an "I."

At the same time, when the nature of clarity goes unrecognized, we experience a sense of the "other" instead of the mind's self-aware quality. Thus, the subject-ego distinguishes things which become exterior objects. The I and other, the dichotomy of subject and object arises. Those "other" things have a dual form: the appearances of the outside world and mental phenomena.

This propensity of the mind to be ignorant of its own nature and to perceive all situations in a dichotomous way is the veil of the basic propensity. This second veil, from this perspective, can also be called the veil of dualistic grasping.

THE VEIL OF THE PASSIONS

As we have just seen, the mind ignorant of its openness and its clarity is immersed in duality. Then, ignorance of mind's sensitivity gives rise to all the relationships that exist between the two poles of this dichotomy's subject and object. At the pure level, sensitivity is the immediacy and multiplicity of enlightened qualities, but in ignorance, those qualities are replaced by endless dual relational possibilities. In ignorance, we start by taking external objects to be real things. We then experience attraction to pleasant objects, aversion to disagreeable objects, and indifference to objects that seem to be neutral. If an object is pleasing, we want to possess it. On the other hand, faced with unpleasant objects or situations, we have an attitude of rejection or avoidance. Finally, we do not relate at all with certain objects or situations because of indifference or mental dullness.

These three types of relationships—attraction, aversion, and indifference—correspond to desire, hatred, and ignorance. These are the three primary mental poisons, the three main mental afflictions that animate and condition habitual mind.

On the basis of these three types of poisoned relationships, numerous other mental or emotional afflictions multiply, notably pride, greed, and jealousy. Pride arises from this "I" which is born of ignorance; greed is an extension of desirous attachment; while jealousy proceeds from hatred and aversion. Thus the three primary poisons branch into the six passions:[7] hatred, greed, ignorance, desirous attachment, jealousy, and pride. They correspond to the six states of consciousness characteristic of the six realms of existence. Next, these are subdivided again and again, adding up to 84,000 different types of passions! All these dualistic and afflicted relationships make up the veil of the passions.

THE VEIL OF KARMA

The various passions lead to a large variety of dualistic actions that can be—in terms of karma—positive, negative, or neutral. They condition the mind and cause it to take birth in one of the six realms of conditioned existence. This is what we call the veil of conditioned activity, or the veil of karma.

DHARMA: A PRACTICE OF UNVEILING

These four veils that cloak the mind make us ordinary beings, tossed around by delusions in the six realms of samsara. We cannot be free from this condition except by eliminating the veils and unveiling the mind. The practice of Dharma offers numerous methods that allow these impurities to fall away bit by bit, thereby revealing the jewel of pure mind.

The pure nature of mind can be compared to a crystal ball and the four veils to four pieces of cloth that cover and conceal it more and more. According to another image, these veils can be compared to layers of clouds covering the sky of the mind. Just as the clouds obscure the sky, the veils mask the open space as well as the clarity of its lucidity. Dharma practice, and primarily meditation, gradually removes these different veils, from the grossest to the most subtle.

When all these veils or coverings have been removed, there is a complete unveiling, a state of purification called *sang* in Tibetan. The blossoming of all aspects of space and light such purification reveals is described by the term *gye*. These two syllables, *sang gye*, which literally mean "perfect purity and blossoming," or "completely pure and totally blossomed," together form the Tibetan word for "buddha." The state of a buddha is the manifestation of qualities inherent to the mind once it has been purified of the veils that obscured it.

This unveiling that reveals the mind's inherent pure qualities marks all progress on the path of Dharma practice.

5

The Game of Illusion

Samsara is created by karma.
It is a projection of karma.
Beings are created by karma.
Karma is their cause and what differentiates them.

—*Mahākaruṇāpuṇḍarīkasūtra*

Mind is the basis of everything, of enlightenment as well as illusion. As the basis for enlightenment, it is the fundamental primordial wisdom having the three qualities we detailed earlier. Shrouded by the four veils, it becomes the fundamental consciousness, which is the basis for all the illusions that make up the different aspects of cyclic existence or samsara.

KARMA

Fundamental consciousness can be compared to a ground that receives imprints or seeds left by our actions. Once planted, these seeds remain in the ground of fundamental consciousness until the conditions for their germination and ripening have come together. In this way, they actualize their potential by producing the plants and fruits that are the various experiences of samsara. The traces that actions leave in the fundamental consciousness are causes that, when favorable conditions present themselves, then result in a particular state of individual consciousness accompanied by its own specific experiences. In general, the collection of imprints left in this fundamental awareness by past actions serves to condition all states and experiences of individual consciousness, that is, what we are and everything we experience. The linking of the different steps of this process, from the causes, the initial acts, up to their consequences, present and future experiences, is called *karma*, or causation of actions.

Karma is a Sanskrit word that literally means "conditioned activity." This notion includes the entire gamut of activity, from the cause up to the consequence of an action. Karma is, therefore, activity understood as being the series of causes and results of actions.[8]

SAMSARA

Karma, or our actions and their imprints, conditions the mind. Because of karma, mind experiences the illusions that make up various beings and environments—in other words, consciousness and its different experiences.

Therefore, the different kinds of consciousness, all joy and suffering, are illusory appearances manifested by the power of karma. All their categories are grouped into the six realms.

The six realms or six classes of beings include all the states in which the mind can take birth. They make up the whole of *saṃsāra*, a Sanskrit term that literally means "cyclic existence," the "cycle of conditioned existences," or the "round of births," so called because karmically conditioned beings transmigrate endlessly in that cycle. Now and then, by the power of a positive influence or positive karma, the mind takes birth in a higher realm; next, by the power of a negative influence or negative karma, the mind takes birth in a lower realm. This round of births turns continuously, at one point leading the mind to a higher realm, then later to a lower realm. This uninterrupted alternation ends only upon attaining liberation—emerging from conditioned existence. This is the end of samsara, the awakening of a buddha. As long as we have not attained liberation, the mind will transmigrate in the various realms of samsara; we have already traveled them all.

Today we are human; later, we may be reborn in another state of existence. What actually transmigrates from one life to another is the mind conditioned by karma, which determines its happiness, its suffering, and its abilities. What we are today—the different realms we have gone through and will go through—results from karma that conditions the projections of the mind and thereby forms its illusions.

KARMA AND FREEDOM

From this perspective then, karma is positive when it serves as a cause for a happy state and brings us closer to freedom, and karma is negative when it results in painful states and distances us from liberation.

It is very important to understand clearly that although karma conditions our experiences and actions, we still enjoy a certain measure of freedom— what would be called free will in the West—which is always present in us in varying proportions. At every turn we find ourselves at a crossroads: one way leads to happiness and enlightenment, the other to unhappiness and suffering. We are continually confronted with a choice: the right choice generates karma favorable to positive development, while a bad choice produces negative karma, the cause for unhappiness in the future. The choice is ours, but the consequences are unavoidable.[9]

This freedom or free will is possible because, in the midst of samsara, despite its conditioned nature, we always have a degree of direct awareness and authentic experience. Our mind and its experiences participate simultaneously in the conditionings of ignorance and in the freedom of direct awareness.

From ignorance comes a dualistic way of experiencing things in terms of subject and object, and this creates the individual ego-centered consciousness, which manifests the different passions. From direct awareness, on the other hand, positive non-ego-centered qualities arise. It is from these afflictions or from these positive qualities that negative or positive karma, respectively, arises.

Thus, positive karma flows from virtuous mental attitudes, such as love, compassion, good will, altruism, modest desires, and contentment, while negative karma comes from nonvirtuous mental attitudes, along with their six main afflictions of anger, greed, stupidity, desirous attachment, jealousy, and pride.

There is said to exist a third kind of karma, called unmoving karma. It is produced by certain types of meditation that stabilize the mind and put it in a state of equanimity. This type of karma results in births in the divine realms,[10] or states of consciousness characterized by a stable mind.

In general, everything that exists in samsara is generated by these three types of contaminated karma. By "contaminated" we mean they are dualistic activities that make distinctions concerning subject, object, and action. In fact, all the activities of ordinary consciousness can be subsumed under these three types of karma.

Among the different types of karma, we can further distinguish *propelling karma* and *completing karma*. Propelling karma, as its name suggests, propels one into a state of existence, whatever that may be. Completing karma determines the specific circumstances within that state of existence; it fills in the basic outline produced by the propelling karma. These two types of karma can combine so that, for example, if the karma propelling a certain mode of existence were positive and the completing karma that fills in the particulars were negative, we may take birth in a higher state of consciousness, but we would experience unpleasant conditions in that lifetime. For example, although we might take birth as a human, we would be poor. Conversely, a negative propelling karma associated with a positive completing karma would cause us to take birth in a lower-realm existence in which we would enjoy good circumstances. For example, we might be born in the West as a domestic animal that would have very privileged living conditions.

There is also collective and individual karma. The beings of one state of existence have all developed similar karma, so the world appears to them in a similar manner. This karma is said to be collective. Nevertheless, each being's particular situation in terms of location, physical appearance, happiness, and suffering is the manifestation of that being's own unique karma. This is individual karma, because it produces specific experiences.

The suffering of the three classes of lower-realm beings and the happiness of the three classes of higher-realm beings result from different combinations of karma.[11] Together, they constitute all the fluctuating and varied conditions caused by the many varieties of karma.

Different effects come from different actions; different types of karma create the diversity of beings and states of existence. It is in this sense that karma is the creator of samsara.

The Wheel of Samsara

6

The Six Realms

By whom and how were the weapons of hell created?
Who made its blazing floors?
And from where are its flames?
Śākyamuni taught
"All these are born of the deluded mind."

—Śāntideva, *Bodhicaryāvatāra*

Qualitatively, each of the six mental afflictions engenders a certain type of birth: hatred leads to a hell realm, greed to a hungry ghost realm, stupidity to an animal realm, desirous attachment to the human condition, jealousy to the jealous god realm, and pride to the divine states.

Quantitatively, these different states result from the accumulation of karma. So, a lot of negative karma generates a hell realm; a little less negative karma, the hungry ghost realm; and less than that, an animal realm.

When generally positive karma is mixed with a few negative aspects, we are reborn in one of the three higher realms of existence, according to the respective strengths of these karmas.

THE HELL REALM

Mind in the grip of anger and hatred produces the karma of a life in hell. What suffers in that hellish state is the mind, our mind. Hellish appearances, beings who attack or kill us, the environment, and all the suffering that afflicts us in that realm are productions of our own mind conditioned by our karma.

In these infernal states, we are relentlessly tormented by inconceivable suffering: we are killed, and in some hell realms we experience being killed over and over; we are tortured by extreme heat or cold. And there is no freedom nor any possibility whatsoever to dedicate ourselves to spiritual practice.

THE HUNGRY GHOST REALM

If our mind falls prey to greed or covetousness, the karma that results is birth as a hungry ghost. In this state, we can never get what we want, nor can we enjoy food or drink, which we desperately crave as hungry ghosts. We are always lacking and wanting, yet completely unable to satisfy our desires, and we suffer from hunger, thirst, and constant intense frustrations. It is also a state produced by our own mind and, though a little less unfavorable than the hell realm, it is just as miserable.

THE ANIMAL REALM

The mind can also fall under the sway of blindness, mental dullness, and stupidity, which cause birth as an animal. There are a great many animal species: wild animals, domestic animals, and so on. All of them experience different forms of suffering, such as being eaten alive, struggling against one another, or being subservient and abused. All the suffering found in the animal realm is also the production of the mind and the manifestation of karma resulting from previous negative actions.

These three types of existence make up the lower-realm states. Among them, the most favorable is the animal state. But even in that state, it is very difficult to awaken love and compassion and impossible to practice Dharma.

In all of these lower realms, there is no possibility of practicing Dharma and attaining realization; the mind is constantly disturbed by anger, hatred, desire, and so on. Moreover, lower-realm beings tend to perform more negative actions, which create still more painful karma. In this way, they perpetuate the conditioning of lower-realm lifetimes, which, furthermore, last an extremely long time.

THE HUMAN REALM

The human condition is the first of the higher-realm existences. Humans are practically the only beings endowed with the necessary conditions for spiritual progress, as well as the faculties that allow the practice and understanding of Dharma. However, being human does not guarantee spiritual progress. The value of human life is variable, and only those who have obtained what we call the precious human existence[12] can practice Dharma; they are as rare as stars in the daytime! Although it is a less painful condition than lower-realm existences, the human condition still has many types of suffering, the four main kinds being birth, illness, aging, and death. Aside from these four great sources of suffering, humans suffer when separated from those they dearly love during their lifetimes or at death, or from having to deal with people whom they do not wish to deal with or who are hostile toward them. Humans suffer from losing their belongings, from not being able to keep what they've managed to acquire, and from not being able to get what they want.

THE JEALOUS GOD REALM

Karma that is very positive overall but mixed with jealousy causes birth in the jealous god realm. This is a happy state endowed with many powers and pleasures but, because of the force of jealousy, there are constant struggles and conflicts. Jealous gods oppose gods who are their superiors and quarrel among themselves.

THE DIVINE REALM

Positive karma combined with very little negative karma results in a rebirth in the divine states. There are different levels of divine existence. The first are the divine states of the desire realm, so called because mind in those realms is still subject to desires and attachment. These gods have an extremely long life: in one of the first god realms, one day lasts the equivalent of a hundred human years, and they live five hundred of *their* years. At the next level of the divine realms, one hundred of our years equal one of their days, and they live a thousand years! In these generally happy realms, there is nevertheless some suffering, caused by occasional struggles with the gods of the jealous god realm.

Desire-realm existences span from the most miserable realms—the hell realms—up to these first god realms; all these states are under the control of desire.

Beyond the desire realm, there is the subtle-form realm, which includes a hierarchy of seventeen successive divine levels. Beings in these states have a subtle form and extremely large, luminous bodies; their minds know few passions, few thoughts; and they enjoy incredible happiness. The predominant passion is subtle pride—beings in these realms think they have attained something higher, and they live in a sort of self-satisfaction.

These states of the form realm correspond to four levels of meditative concentration, characterized by the progressive transcendence of investigation, analysis, joy, and bliss.[13]

Finally, beyond even these four levels of concentration of the form realm, there can be birth in the formless realm. Formless-realm beings experience no harsh suffering and have virtually no passions; they remain only in a very subtle form. The impurity remaining in their minds is a kind of mental dullness that prevents the realization of the ultimate nature of mind. In the formless realm, the mind has access to four successive states of consciousness: absorption of infinite space, absorption of infinite consciousness, absorption of nothingness, and absorption of neither discrimination nor nondiscrimination. The gods of the formless realm have the feeling of having a body, but this body is imperceptible. They have only the fifth aggregate of individuality—consciousness—still present as a subtle ignorance which gives them the feeling of existing in this formless body. This consciousness finally acts as a mother who gives birth again to the other aggregates. In this way, the gods of the formless realm return to the lower realms. In order to be free from samsara, consciousness itself must ultimately be transformed into primordial wisdom, the wisdom of enlightenment.

These eight states of the form and formless realms belong to a positive, undistracted mind; their successive stages are progressively free of attachment. All of these states of the six realms of samsara are transitory and conditioned: they are all part of the wheel of samsara. Even though the gods of the form and formless realms are spared the harsher forms of suffering, they still undergo death and transmigration. They don't have the power to remain in their divine condition, and they suffer having to be reborn in a lower realm.

If we find it difficult to accept the notion of these different realms, let us simply remember that everyone's experience is his or her reality. When we are dreaming, our dreams become our reality, and so it is for the six realms. For example, water can be experienced in very different ways: for hell beings, it causes torture; for hungry ghosts, it is desperately craved; for some animals, it is a medium necessary for life; for people, it is a drink; for jealous gods, it is a weapon; and for gods, it is sublime nectar. The depths of the ocean are the fish's natural habitat, but humans cannot live there. Birds fly in the sky, but this is impossible for the human body. People who are blind cannot go where they want, while those who have normal vision can move around freely. Everyone lives in his or her own world or realm without perceiving the others.[14]

So, samsara is made up of three realms: the desire realm, the form realm, and the formless realm. All the possibilities of conditioned existence are included in it.

Becoming aware that all beings suffer in this cycle of existence will inspire us to free ourselves from ignorance and the delusion we are steeped in as a result, and thereby to free ourselves from samsara, which is an ocean of suffering, and to strive to attain the supreme happiness of perfect buddhahood.[15]

In the past, we have taken countless births in cyclic existence. Today we are human beings: if we use this opportunity wisely, it can be the point of departure for our liberation.

7

Two Truths

The Buddha's teaching rests on two truths:
Conventional truth and ultimate truth.
Those who do not understand the distinction between them
Do not understand Buddha's profound truth.
Ultimate truth cannot be taught without basis on relative truth;
Without realization of the meaning of ultimate truth
Enlightenment cannot be attained.

—Nāgārjuna, *Madhyamakakārikā*, Ch. 24, Vs. 8–10

The mistaken belief that painfully conditions all beings in cyclic existence arises from ignorance. That ignorance is an absence of awareness about the actual emptiness of the mind and its productions. In fact, the mistaken belief is ignorance about the actual mode of existence of all things.

All things, all phenomena, all objects of knowledge—that is, the external universe and all its beings, everything we experience in terms of forms, sounds, flavors, odors, tangible objects, and objects of mental awareness—all we are and everything we can know manifests by the power of the mind's propensities, which are essentially empty.

The mind is neither existent nor nonexistent.[16] Likewise, the phenomena it produces are neither completely illusory nor completely real. As we ordinarily experience them, they are relatively real, but from an ultimate perspective, that relative reality is illusory.

THE TWO TRUTHS

All things can be viewed according to two levels of reality: the relative or conventional level and the ultimate level. These two truths correspond to two points of view, two visions of reality: the relative truth or view is relatively or conventionally true but ultimately illusory, and the ultimate truth or view is definitively true, the authentic experience beyond all illusion.

All samsaric perceptions are experiences of relative truth. Nirvana, which is beyond illusions and samsara's suffering, is the level of ultimate truth. Therefore, for example, the experiences of a hell-realm being are quite real from a relative viewpoint, while from an ultimate perspective those perceptions are illusory. This means that a being who finds itself in a hell realm really does experience suffering there: from its perspective, its experiences and suffering are real and quite hellish. But from an ultimate viewpoint, hell does not exist at all; it is actually only a projection, a production of conditioned mind whose nature is emptiness.

Suffering comes from not recognizing the emptiness of things, which results in our attributing to them a reality that they don't actually have. This grasping at things as real subjects us to painful experiences.

We can get a better understanding of this by using the example of a dream. When someone has a nightmare, that person suffers. For the dreamer, the nightmare is real; in fact, it is the only reality the dreamer knows. And yet the dream has no tangible reality and is not actually "real"; it has no reality outside of the dreamer's own conditioned mind, outside of the dreamer's own karma. From an ultimate perspective, it is in fact an illusion. The dreamer's illusion is in failing to recognize the nature of his experiences. Ignorant of what they actually are, the dreamer takes his own productions—the creations of his own mind—to be an autonomous reality; thus deluded, he is frightened by his own projections and thereby creates suffering for himself. The delusion is to perceive as real what actually is not. Buddha Śākyamuni taught that all the realms of cyclic or conditioned existence, all things, all our experiences are, in general, illusory appearances that cannot be considered as either truly real or completely illusory. He demonstrated this dual nature using the example of the appearance of the moon on the surface of a body of water:

> The nature of all things and all appearances
> Is like the reflection of the moon on water.

The moon reflected on the surface of a pool is real insofar as it is visible there, but its reality is only a relative, illusory appearance, because the moon on the water is just a reflection. It is neither truly real nor completely illusory. From this perspective, we can refer to relative truth as the truth of appearances. Buddha Śākyamuni used other examples, saying that all things are like a projection, a hallucination, a rainbow, a shadow, a mirage, a mirror image, and an echo; outside of a simple appearance resulting from the "functionality" of interrelated factors, no thing has existence in, of, or by itself.

It can really help us to understand this, because, although they have no true existence, we attach to all of these things as though they were real. The objective of Buddha's teaching is to dissolve this fixation, which is the source of all illusions and is as tenacious as our own karmic conditioning.

KARMA, INTERDEPENDENCE, AND EMPTINESS

Within the concept of karma, there is no notion of destiny or fatalism; we only reap what we sow. We experience the results of our own actions.[17] The notion of karma is closely connected with that of dependent arising, or *tendrel* in Tibetan. The chain of karma is also the interaction of *tendrel*, or interdependent factors whose causes and results mutually give rise to one another.

The Tibetan word *tendrel* means interaction, interconnection, interrelation, interdependence, or interdependent factors. All things, all our experiences, are *tendrel*, which is to say that they are events that exist because of the relationship between interrelated factors. This idea is essential to the understanding of Dharma in general and, in particular, how the mind transmigrates in cyclic existence.

To understand what *tendrel* or dependent arising is, let's take an example. When you hear the sound of a bell, ask yourself, What makes the sound? Is it the body of the bell, the clapper, the hand that moves the bell to and fro, or the ears that hear the sound? None of these elements alone produce the sound; it results from the interaction of all these factors. All the elements are necessary for the sound of a bell to be perceived, and they are necessary not in succession but simultaneously. The sound is an event whose existence depends on the interaction of those elements; that is *tendrel*.

Similarly, all conditioned lives, all samsaric phenomena, result from a multiplicity of interactions which belong to the twelve links of dependent origination. These twelve factors give rise to each other mutually. It is not that each factor causes the one that occurs next in time; as with the bell example, they are simultaneous, coexistent. It is necessary that the twelve factors be present at the same moment in order to produce a conditioned existence.[18] The bondage of causes and results of these interdependent factors that generate illusion is the action of samsara. Everything within samsara is karmically conditioned interrelationship; all our experiences are tendrel. The truth of appearances created by the bondage of dependent arisings is conventional or dualistic truth. This is how we ordinarily live. It is ruled by karma. The empty nature of what exists at the relative level is what we call ultimate truth. Truly understanding dependent arising allows us to go beyond the conditioning of the relative or conventional level and to attain the peace and freedom of unconditionality. When you completely understand dependent arising, you also understand emptiness. And that is freedom.

Therefore, wisdom, or knowledge, is not fundamentally separate from illusion. That is why it is often said that samsara and nirvana are not different and that a form of wisdom is latent in ignorance. Logic and reasoning ultimately lead to such statements, which appear to be contradictory and illogical. Logic and reasoning can go on ad infinitum. They are part of the samsaric process and ultimately lead to contradictions. Even so, since they are tools that can bring about realization of the truth, they are useful and should not be rejected, even if they are eventually released at the time of realizing emptiness.

But be careful. The correct understanding of emptiness is in no way nihilistic.[19] If we decide that everything is empty and without reality, that the state of buddhahood has no real existence, that karmic causality is empty, and that therefore there is no reason to bother, this would be a nihilistic view, even worse than the view that takes relative things to be truly existent. Nihilistic conceptions are a more serious mistake than the realist conceptions that take phenomena to exist as they appear.

The correct understanding of emptiness lies between the two extremes of eternalism (believing things to be inherently or truly existent) and nihilism (believing them not to exist at all). This middle way view eliminates wrong ideas and ultimately allows us to go beyond conceptualized notions about reality. But beware: to conceive of emptiness closes the door to liberation.

The great lineage holder Saraha said:

> To consider the world as real is a brutish attitude.
> To consider it as empty is even more savage.

And Nāgārjuna said:

> Those who conceive of emptiness are incurable.

PART ONE
Section Two

The Transformations of Mind:

Lives, Deaths, Rebirths

I

Mind After Death

If I say there is a self,
you will think it's permanent.
If I say there isn't a self,
you will think that at death
it disappears completely.

—*Samyuttanikāya*

ONE LIFE OR MANY LIVES?

All spiritual and religious traditions agree on some type of existence beyond this life, and all of them prepare us for that future. If after death there was nothing, if our existence was limited to this lifetime, we could be satisfied with worldly knowledge and activities. A spiritual practice, no matter what it was, would be unnecessary.

The idea that death is a complete end followed by sheer nothingness is the product of an extremely narrow mind. It is as if someone who lived in France were to conclude that beyond the country's borders the human species ceased to exist!

While religions might be in general agreement about the existence of an afterlife, the various traditions do have distinct perspectives about the nature of that afterlife. Some teach that death is not followed by more lifetimes, but by one eternal life, while Dharma teaches that death is followed by many lifetimes until enlightenment.

On the surface, those views might appear to be contrary, but they actually aren't. It's really just a question of presentation. Let's say that you're in France and you ask someone what Switzerland is like, and the person replies that Switzerland is a nice place. That response may be accurate, but it is quite general. Another person might give the same positive response, but add a more detailed description, explaining what it is that gives each area and each city its charm. This detailed description does not invalidate the first person's response in the least.

Likewise, Christianity, for example, offers a general presentation of the afterlife, teaching that there is life after death and that the conditions of that life depend upon the way in which you live your present life. For a Christian, virtue leads to heaven and sinfulness leads to hell. That's the basic idea.

Dharma, on the other hand, teaches the possibility of many future lives, that negative actions in this life lead to suffering in future lives while positive actions lead to happy future lives and finally to enlightenment.

These two traditions are in perfect agreement about the need to abandon the negative or harmful and adopt the positive; they also agree on the results of negative or positive actions. There is no contradiction between them. The difference is that Christianity offers a briefer presentation, while Buddhism offers a more detailed one.

DEATH AND THE CONTINUITY OF MIND

Space is beyond time; we can't say that space began to exist at a given point in time or that it will cease to exist after a certain amount of time has passed. Similarly, the mind's emptiness is beyond time; mind is essentially atemporal. By nature, mind is eternal, beyond births and deaths. These exist only at the level of the mind's illusions.

When the mind does not know its nature and is therefore caught up in the path of illusions, it transmigrates endlessly in illusion, from life to life. Conditioned by ignorance and karma, we have had to live out innumerable previous lives. In the future, we will be forced to live out many more. The mind transmigrates from life to life, from one illusion to the next—as long as it has not attained enlightenment, the awakening of a buddha or great bodhisattva.

In our present state, we cannot recognize our previous lives; we don't know where we came from, where we'll go, or what condition we'll be reborn into. Meanwhile, what we experience is actually only a transition, one passage among an infinity of possible lives and worlds beyond our conception.

2

Birth and Death: Continuity of Illusion

A collection of parts
produces the concept of vehicle.
Likewise, the collection of heaps
gives rise to the notion of person.

—*Samyuttanikāya*

WHO DIES? WHO IS BORN?

Let's consider more specifically what death is and, in dying, *who* dies. Usually, our experience of ourselves is of an individual that exists with a body and a mind: we identify with these and say, "my body," "my mind." The mind and body seem to form a whole; mind identifies with body and lives as a "me." However, there comes a moment, called death, when mind and body separate. From that moment on, the body is nothing but a cadaver, destined to disappear: it is either buried, thrown into the water, or cremated. But mind continues to exist because other appearances manifest to it by the power of karma, propelling it toward other births. Death occurs only to the physical body; mind does not disappear.

To get a better understanding of the relationship between body and mind, and to demonstrate the degree to which they are different, we can return to the analogy of the dream. In a clear dream, our dream body acts; it sees forms, hears sounds, and experiences an imaginary world in exactly the same way our present body experiences the world we know in our waking state. When we awaken, the dream body disappears, but the mind continues to experience with another body—our physical body—in another world—that of our waking state. The phenomenon of death is similar to this, only this time it is our physical body—the body of our waking state—that disappears.

The different births that karmically conditioned mind can take are comparable to a series of dreams; the passage from one dream to the next is like a death at the end of each dream and a rebirth at the beginning of the next one. Karmic tendencies and imprints create one dream, then a second, then a third, until the moment of awakening, at which point the dream appearances disappear. Likewise, karma causes us to live out different births and deaths in samsara as long as enlightenment has not been realized.

THE FIVE AGGREGATES OF INDIVIDUALITY

Our feeling of existing, of being a "me," "my body," "my mind," is the experience of individuality. This individuality is made up of five heaps or aggregates—*skandha* in Sanskrit. The five heaps are:

1. Forms, including the five elements (earth, water, fire, air, and space) as well as the body, along with the sense consciousnesses (visual, auditory, olfactory, gustatory, tactile, and mental).
2. Feelings, which are basically of three types: pleasant, unpleasant, and neutral.
3. Perceptions, understood as representations, discriminations, or conceptions.
4. Compositional factors, including all the mental factors and habits that cause us to react and that motivate our actions.
5. Consciousness, which is the awareness of all experiences created by the five sense powers and mental sense powers; it is the support for their apprehension.

If all living beings are composed of these five heaps or aggregates, a corpse, by contrast, has only the form heap, composed of five elements. Its form can be seen and perceived by others, but it has no feeling or sensation, perception, compositional factors, or consciousness.

The last heap, consciousness, is essentially transparent, like sky, with no beginning or end. Recognizing its nature is nirvana, the ultimate enlightenment. But as long as this recognition does not occur, we continue to turn in the cycle of samsara, flowing from birth to birth like the waters of the river Ganges.

At death, the fifth constituent, consciousness—which is fundamentally mind—doesn't disappear completely. There is a phase of unconsciousness, like the deep, dreamless sleep we would have if we had not slept for several nights in a row. This phase is called the *bardo of emptiness*.

After a time, usually three or four days, the transmigrating being becomes conscious again. Once again, we are aware of existing; the experience of "I am" recurs. This period of return to individual consciousness and its experiences corresponds to luminous appearances that manifest at the end of the bardo of emptiness.

Then the *bardo of becoming* begins, which lasts until the next birth.[20] Mind and ego, or individual consciousness, are like mother and child, the mother being mind or fundamental consciousness and the child being the individual consciousness or ego. The individual ego dies, but the mother remains, giving birth to a new child. To use another image, fundamental consciousness is like the ocean, and the individual consciousness is like its waves, which are individualized by the winds of karma.

In any case, when the individual karma is reconstituted, the individual karmic tendencies and mental habits resume their activities, which is the return of the fourth constituent: compositional factors. The other heaps also gradually reappear.[21]

In this series of lives, the consciousness is like Tarzan in the movies, whom we have seen in many different scenes doing a lot of different things. But throughout all of those scenes, he is still always Tarzan! In our case, the film is the series of samsaric illusions, the series of lives that correspond to different states of awareness. When the film ends, the illusion stops, and Tarzan the consciousness is no more.

The illusion of individuality is pursued until enlightenment, which corresponds in our example to the end of the film, the end of samsara. At that point, the consciousness has been transformed into the pristine awareness of a buddha.

3

From Life to Life: Transitions and the Bardo

May I recognize all the manifestations
that appear to me in the bardo
as being my own projections;
emanations of my own mind.

—Padmasambhava, *The Tibetan Book of the Dead*

There would be no rebirth if, at the moment of death, we disappeared like a candle flame going out or water evaporating. But mind is emptiness, and the void does not know death. At death, body and mind, attached as they are to illusory appearances, separate; each goes its own way. Then once again, by the power of karma, basic tendencies and afflictions caused by various agents lead us to be reborn in one of the six realms.

BARDO

According to Dharma as well as other traditions, death is not an end. Beyond death, there is a continuous series of experiences in different states known collectively as the *bardo*. This Tibetan term literally means "between two," "interval," or "passage." These passages are all the states that the consciousness passes through. The series of bardos makes up cyclic existence, or samsara.

The series of bardos corresponds to the transmigration of the consciousness from life to life, but also to the transformations that occur moment by moment in our states of consciousness. The teachings relating to the different bardos are presented in particular in the well-known traditional text, the *Bardo Thödrol*, literally, "the understanding that frees from the bardos," better known in the West as *The Tibetan Book of the Dead*. It gives practical instructions on how to proceed through the bardos and offers a path for realizing the nature of those bardos and liberating ourselves from them.

Even though "the interval between death and rebirth" is its best-known meaning, the word "bardo" refers not only to that period between death and rebirth, but to all the existential states the consciousness goes through. Therefore, the word is also used to refer to life, which is the bardo between birth and death and is, in most cases, the longest of the bardos. There is also the bardo between two thoughts, or between two states of consciousness, which is the shortest of the bardos. The period from the moment of falling asleep to waking up is called the dream bardo, while the experience of death itself is the bardo of the moment of death. After respiration stops completely, there is a period when the mind remains in a state of total unconsciousness, called the bardo of emptiness. Finally, the bardo of becoming is the period that follows the bardo of emptiness, during which the consciousness has the experience of a postmortem world, which lasts up until the moment of rebirth.

THE FOUR GREAT BARDOS

Briefly, the four great bardos from the process of dying to being reborn are:

1. The bardo of birth to death, or, the state we are in right now.
2. The bardo of the moment of death, corresponding to the passage from life to death.
3. The bardo of emptiness, the period following death.
4. The bardo of becoming, the stage between the bardo of emptiness and another lifetime in which we begin a new bardo of birth to death.

The six bardos frequently referred to include two others in the bardo of birth to death: the dream bardo and the meditation bardo. They each correspond to states of consciousness lived out during this lifetime.

In the following chapters we will describe each of the four great bardos, which together make up cyclic or samsaric existence.

4

The Bardo of the Moment of Death

When the bardo of the moment of death appears
may I abandon attachments and mental fixations,
and engage without distraction in the
path which the instructions make clear.
Mind projected into the sphere of uncreated space,
separated from body, from flesh and blood,
I will know that which is impermanence and illusion.

—Padmasambhava, *The Tibetan Book of the Dead*

The different vital factors that sustain life deteriorate and disappear at the end of a lifetime. The extinguishing of life is described as the dissolution or outer reabsorption of the principal elements—earth, water, fire, and air—and the inner reabsorption of the different types of thoughts and cognitions. During this bardo, the various winds that animate the body are destroyed.

In general, our body is controlled by five main winds, called the life-bearing wind, the upward-moving wind, the pervasive wind, the fire-dwelling wind, and the downward-voiding wind. These winds animate the physical body, and their proper functioning assures good health. At the moment of death, another wind manifests, called the wind of karma and becoming. It is usually diffused throughout the whole body. When it manifests, it upsets and interferes with the other winds; different pathological symptoms appear as the body approaches death.

OUTER DISSOLUTION

The wind that regulates the absorption of nourishment, or the fire-dwelling wind, is the first wind to be disturbed. It leaves its location in the navel cakra and ceases to function, which means that we can no longer be nourished by food, nor can food that is absorbed be digested; nutrients are quickly rejected.

Next, the life-bearing wind is disturbed and leaves its location at the heart, which results in emotional distress and a lack of mental clarity. This disturbance next affects the downward voiding wind of the lower abdominal functions so that retention of feces and urine is disrupted, causing incontinence or intestinal obstruction.

Then the upward-moving wind is impaired, causing short, labored breathing and difficulty with swallowing. Finally, the pervasive wind is affected, which brings on unpleasant physical sensations as well as difficulty moving the limbs.

The disturbances of these winds cause them to leave their usual locations in the body. This migration brings about the destruction of the subtle channels through which the winds normally circulate, as well as their two main centers or wheels, *cakras* in Sanskrit.

The destruction of these channels and their centers occurs concomitantly with a deterioration of the body's principal elements and the physical aspects connected with them: physical body, respiration, body temperature, blood, and flesh, corresponding respectively to the elements of space, air, fire, water, and earth. The secondary winds, located in the five great centers already mentioned, migrate and disappear at the same time as the main winds. The destruction of these secondary winds causes the gradual disappearance of the sense perceptions.

The destruction of the five winds happens at the same time as the dissolution or reabsorption of the elements, which occurs from the grossest to the most subtle. So, the earth element absorbs into the water element, water into fire, then fire into air, and air into consciousness.

The dissolution begins with the reabsorption of the earth element into the water element. The physical or outer symptoms include the disappearance of physical strength, so that the head has a tendency to fall and the trunk of the body caves in; flexing and extending the limbs becomes difficult and remaining seated is no longer possible. Phlegm and saliva flow out.

Various inner signs correspond to sensations experienced by the dying person during this phase. The mind lacks clarity, as though it were plunged in great darkness. The dying person has the urge to move, to change position or rearrange the covers, but is physically unable to. In fact, the immobile body becomes very sluggish; the dying person feels heavy, as though knocked down and buried under a mountain. The eyes, which can no longer see straight, tend to roll up in the head.

The most subtle or secret symptoms are visual experiences or visions, which also begin to develop during the time of the outer and inner symptoms. During this first reabsorption, the dying person's vision is unstable, as if looking at a mirage, or there is a visual distortion, like the appearance of water in a scorching desert or under a blazing sun.

The outer symptom of the second phase, which corresponds to the reabsorption of the water element into the fire element, is the drying out of the nose, mouth, and nostrils, along with the eventual loss of sphincter control, which results in incontinence. Inner symptoms are extreme mental agitation; unpleasant thoughts disturb the mind. The dying person feels as though he or she is being carried away by a torrent and has the sense of falling and being swallowed up, and hears the sound of a violent waterfall. At the secret level, the dying person's vision is foggy and perceives everything as blending into clouds of smoke.

The third phase is the dissolution of the fire element into the air element. Outer symptoms are the chilling of the mouth and nostrils, shortened breathing, and a loss of feeling associated with decreased vital heat, which leaves the arms and legs starting from the extremities and reabsorbs from the exterior to the core of the body. Inner symptoms include the momentary loss of mental clarity and lucidity. Things are no longer seen clearly. Secret symptoms include visions of blazing light, as if the universe were on fire. This is combined with visions of sparkling lights resembling fireflies.

Next comes the reabsorption of the air element into consciousness. The outer symptoms are gasping for breath with long exhalations and short, labored inhalations. The eyes roll back; breathing slows and approaches its eventual cessation. Inner symptoms are the appearance of apparitions that correspond to the dying person's karma. At the moment of death, the body is extremely frail; however, the mind is very strong. This physical weakness combined with the strength of the mind produces very intense illusory appearances. If the dying person has performed many negative actions in his or her lifetime, these visions will reflect them and cause extreme fear. For example, a murderer who has killed many animals might see those animals chasing and devouring him. At that moment, his body and speech might show terror by emitting cries or moans. By contrast, a Dharma practitioner whose karma is positive could experience this phase very happily, meeting various luminous divine beings. Inner signs or symptoms at this phase are hearing the sound of an extremely violent wind, a throbbing hum, or a very loud rumble. Secret symptoms are the sense that one is vanishing or fading and the experience of an appearance similar to the glow of a candle.

INNER DISSOLUTION

The consciousness then dissolves into emptiness. At this point, the body takes on a bit of color, breathing stops completely, and heat gathers just above the heart. This is the final moment of death. Dissolution of the consciousness into emptiness is characterized by luminous experiences called white luminosity, red luminosity, and black luminosity. These correspond to the reabsorption of the masculine and feminine principles contained in the body.

Our subtle body is actually made up of two principles, masculine and feminine, located respectively at the crown of the head and at the level of the navel. At the moment of death, they reabsorb into each other at the level of the heart.

Initially, the white masculine principle descends from the crown of the head toward the heart. At this moment, the experience of white luminosity occurs, which is similar to the light of the moon.

The reabsorption of consciousness occurs with its thoughts. These can be reduced to eighty types of conceptions, of which thirty-three arise from aversion, forty from desire, and seven from mental dullness or stupidity. The thirty-three kinds of thoughts connected with aversion, hatred, and anger dissolve during this first phase. Even if our fiercest enemy or our parents' assassin were in front of us, we would have no more aversion toward him.

Next, the red feminine principle reabsorbs, ascending from the navel toward the heart; this is the experience of red luminosity much like the light of the sun. The forty types of thought connected with desire and attachment cease during this phase. Even if a gorgeous, charming god or goddess were to appear, we would no longer experience any desire.

When the two principles reabsorb in the heart, the consciousness loses its faculty of knowing. This is the experience of black luminosity, similar to a midnight blue or a dark night. In an ordinary being, the mind sinks into total darkness. At this moment the seven kinds of thought connected with mental dullness or stupidity cease. Any spectacle that might arise in the mind will no longer be considered good or bad.

This whole process of dissolution, from the beginning up to the experience of black luminosity, is called the bardo of the moment of death.

At the end of the dissolution, the clear light, or mind's basic nature, is revealed. All beings have an experience of the clear light, but the ordinary being does not recognize it. For him or her, that recognition is replaced by a period of absence of experience, or unconsciousness. It is the lack of realization, or ignorance, which obscures the ordinary being during this phase of complete unconsciousness that replaces the experience of the clear light. But even if it is extremely fleeting and goes unrecognized, this experience of the clear light occurs to every being.

On the other hand, if a person has recognized the true nature of mind within his or her lifetime—that is, has realized mahāmudrā—the mind can recognize the fundamental clear light at this final moment of the bardo of death and, to whatever degree this recognition is stable, can remain absorbed in it.

For such a yogi, the daughter clear light, which was experienced during his or her lifetime, and the fundamental mother clear light unite. This is the state of buddhahood.

5

The Bardo of Emptiness

When the moment is upon me
May I not be frightened
By the collection of peaceful and wrathful aspects:
Emanations of my own mind.

—Padmasambhava, *The Tibetan Book of the Dead*

This bardo is called the bardo of emptiness because, as we have just discussed, it is the moment at which the clear light, or the essential nature of mind, appears to an enlightened being. The period of unconsciousness that an ordinary being experiences instead generally lasts three and a half days, during which time the mind remains in a dark, impenetrable, and unconscious state.

LIGHTS AND DEITIES

After this period of unconsciousness, the consciousness and its illusions revive, and for a few moments the consciousness experiences five essential luminosities that are described as extremely subtle. These appear simultaneously with the peaceful and wrathful aspects of the bardo, manifesting as rainbows, points of light, clouds, and other luminous phenomena. The appearances at the end of the bardo of emptiness are very fleeting.

Although these manifestations vary, this state is similar to that between waking and sleeping. The phenomena we have just discussed, which characterize the boundary between these two bardos, are described in *The Tibetan Book of the Dead* as apparitions of various peaceful and wrathful deities. If we can recognize the divine nature of these appearances, we can unite with them and immediately and spontaneously gain liberation, as all experience or appearance becomes the deity itself.

During this period, we hear violent and terrifying sounds louder than a thousand thunderclaps exploding together. This deafening sound is the sound of emptiness.

Throughout space in all directions, many different points of light and brilliant flashes of light like rainbows appear, and we perceive the conditions of existence and a vision of the various pure buddha realms and their celestial spheres: all of samsara's and nirvana's different states become perceptible. The experience of all these things is much like the lively districts of Paris during rush hour. It is as though we were in the middle of a huge throng, with people bustling here and there endlessly, and streams of cars driving in every direction. For our example to be complete, we would have to add heavy train traffic along with many airplanes criss-crossing the sky above, and the whole chaotic spectacle throbbing.

People initiated into the practices of the bardo who have an authentic experience of them can recognize these various appearances and gain liberation during this phase. Otherwise, it gets a bit difficult. Not knowing the nature of the wrathful deities, a person is terrified and, paralyzed with fear, loses consciousness. And since the nature of the peaceful aspects goes unrecognized, it is impossible to tolerate their radiance, so people recoil as if blinded by the light of the sun or the moon.

At this moment, extremely brilliant white, yellow, red, green, and blue lights appear; they are the lights of the six pure buddha realms. At the same time, six lights corresponding to the six realms of samsara appear. These six are the same colors as the six buddha realms' but are much duller. The vivid clarity of the buddha lights is dazzling and difficult to tolerate, which makes us withdraw from them. By contrast, the pale lights of the six realms of samsara are attractive and seductive and propel us to take birth there.

The end of the bardo of emptiness is the period of the restructuring of consciousness. The winds that animate consciousness remanifest. The wind "that makes ignorance arise" returns at the same time as the air wind, which corresponds to visions of green lights. Then, the fire, the water, and the earth winds, corresponding respectively to red, white, and yellow lights, reappear. These five lights are the emanation of the five winds and the quintessence of the five elements. This remanifestation of the five elements is produced as the mental body of the bardo being and its outer experiences are created.

Upon the reappearance of the winds, the different types of conceptions return in the inverse order of their disappearance: first, the seven kinds of ignorance or stupidity, followed by the forty types of desire or attachment, and finally, the thirty-three kinds of hatred or aversion.[22] This is how the manifestation and experiences of the bardo of becoming appear, which will stop when rebirth occurs in one of the six realms of samsara.

6

The Bardo of Becoming

The beings of the irreversible bardo
wander in an unstable mental body,
Which looks like their previous carnal body.
They have all their faculties and senses
and the projection powers of karma.
Their bodies are not hindered by any obstacle.

—Jamgön Kongtrul Lodrö Thaye, *Text of Surcho*

During the bardo of becoming, the mind re-creates the experience of the various projections brought about by its karma; at the end of this bardo, conditioned by that karma, it takes rebirth in one of the six realms of samsara. Just as deep sleep gives rise to all kinds of dreamworld experiences, after the unconsciousness and the fleeting visions of the bardo of emptiness described in the last chapter, there appear the experiences of the bardo of becoming. This is a state in which experiences have a reality similar to those we are actually familiar with, but the conditions of existence are different.

THE BODY AND THE MENTAL WORLD

In this bardo, there is no gross physical body; instead, there is a mental body made up of four and a half aggregates which are: consciousness, compositional factors, perceptions, sensations, and half of the form aggregate. Beings in the bardo of becoming have a subtle form body, a mental body imperceptible to ordinary beings. Beings endowed with such a body perceive it as theirs and can also perceive others in the same state.

In general, we have three kinds of bodies. First there is the ordinary body, called the karmic body, because it is the result of fully matured karma; this is the body we currently have. The second is the habitual body. This is the dreamworld body, which results from the mind's tendency to identify itself with a physical form. It comes from imprints and habits accumulated during the waking state. The third, or mental body, is the one belonging to the being in the bardo of becoming. During the first part of the bardo of becoming, the mental body looks like the physical aspect of the life it just finished. The being in the bardo may, if threatened, fear for its life. It could also have the impression of being killed in confrontations with enemies or in other circumstances. But all these events and enemies are only illusory projections produced by latent impressions in the mind; the mental body cannot be killed by other projections, which are themselves mental. Even though it is indestructible, the mental body experiences all kinds of fears, terrors, and cravings because of the influence of habits and imprints from the past. In all of this, the experiences of the mental body and the appearances of the bardo of becoming are comparable to those of dreams, but much more intense.

The bardo being has five faculties corresponding to our ordinary five senses, as well as certain powers, such as clairvoyance, which allow it to perceive the world of the living. It also has the power to move around without being hindered by physical objects. In fact, nothing can impede the mental body. It only has to think, for example, about India, and it will immediately find itself there; if it thinks about the United States, it will instantly be there; if it thinks of its home prior to dying, it will be there right away. Just by thinking of a place, it will be there. Likewise, it has only to think about or wish for something for the experience to instantly arise.

Actually, our mind thinks a lot. When we are in the bardo of becoming, these different thoughts crystallize and appear as realities, producing a world in great flux. The huge multitude of thoughts, turning and shifting like a whirlwind, makes this situation extremely unstable and difficult.

Having arrived at this stage of the bardo, someone who has, for example, led a family life, will remember his home. He will see those who were dear to him, his wife, children, and so on. He yearns to talk to them, to communicate with them, but they cannot see him and are no longer interested in him; he addresses them, but there is no response, and this causes him tremendous suffering. Because he is unable to make contact, he realizes he is no longer in the world of the living. This inability to communicate provokes grief, suffering, and aggression.

At this point, he realizes that he has, in fact, left his body and can actually see the buried or incinerated corpse. These terrifying and distressing experiences lead him to believe that he is dead. He perceives those who were near and dear to him crying and grieving. Their emotions can revive his own attachment. Moreover, if his loved ones are not sad, or, worse, if they are happy about his death, he feels anger, and this causes him further suffering. It might be that his heirs are fighting among themselves over the division of the things he has left behind, which is still another source of frustration and anger.

Someone who was particularly attached to his home or possessions will see them again. He sees people seizing the things he had accumulated, which arouses his greed and attachment. He tries to hold on to them, but no one sees him, and he remains utterly powerless. Anger overcomes him and can cause him to take rebirth in a hell realm.

The various different experiences of the bardo of becoming depend upon the karma of the being in that state: negative karma produces terrifying and painful appearances, while positive karma is a source of pleasant, happy experiences.

The duration of the bardo of becoming varies; rebirth can occur at any time, but generally at the end of seven cycles of seven days. Rebirth can also take place after one, two, or three weeks. The maximum usually is forty-nine days, but a very long bardo could last up to a year.

If the mind is steeped in extremely negative tendencies, this bardo will last only a short while, because the being will immediately go the lower realms. Likewise, if the mind is saturated with positive tendencies, rebirth will occur just as quickly in a higher realm. On the other hand, if the karmic imprints are mitigated or weak, the bardo of becoming will be less certain and last longer.

Whatever its duration, the experiences and appearances that the deceased perceives in the first part of the bardo of becoming relate to the immediately preceding lifetime. Then, karma gradually causes those appearances to fade, while those of the next life begin to manifest. Then come the experiences that suggest what that next lifetime will be. Usually, during the first three weeks, the rebirth consciousness abides in a world where its experiences are much like those of its previous life. Then, at the beginning of the fourth week, it begins to perceive the world into which it will take birth.

In this phase of the bardo, six signs, in the form of various experiences, manifest in very fleeting and unpredictable ways, which suggest the karma and the rebirth that will be taken. These six signs are different habitats, environments, behaviors, foods, company, and mental experiences or perceptions that shift from moment to moment.

There are also four experiences that occur among all the beings in this bardo: these are the terrifying sounds called the four fearsomes: the collapse of a mountain, an engulfing ocean, a blazing inferno, and a gusting whirlwind. These experiences correspond to little deaths within that bardo, as certain winds are reversed. The reversal of the earth wind produces the impression of being buried under a gigantic mountain or under a house. At the reversal of the water wind, there is a feeling of losing one's footing and sinking in the ocean. At the reversal of the fire wind, there is the feeling of being grilled in an immense fire, and upon the reversal of the air wind, there is the feeling of being swept away, as if carried off by a tornado.

There is also the experience of the three abysses in this bardo. The bardo being has the impression of falling into a grayish white, reddish, or dark well or tunnel; this is produced by the manifestation of the tendencies toward hatred, desire, and ignorance, respectively.

The Moment of Rebirth

At this point, the moment of rebirth occurs. There are four possible kinds of rebirths: womb birth, apparitional birth, birth from heat and moisture, and birth from an egg; sometimes they are combined. Births in hell or divine realms are apparitional.

Rebirth is accompanied by different experiences:

The bardo being—the rebirth consciousness, or *bardoa* in Tibetan—that experiences arctic cold is attracted by a burning flame. This is how it ends up being born in a hot hell.

The bardoa may also be extremely terrified and, to feel secure, goes and hides in a hole. This is how it is reborn in an animal realm.

If the bardoa has positive karma, it can perceive a celestial place with a marvelous palace. Reaching that place, it is born in the divine realms of long life, in which it enjoys a radiant body for a very long time.

If the bardoa is to be born of a womb as a human, in addition to the necessary karma, three factors must come together: the bardo being, the father's sperm, and the mother's egg. The bardo being perceives the parents having sex. If the bardoa will be born as a male, he feels attraction for the mother and revulsion toward the father. If the bardo being will be born as a female, the opposite—attraction for the father and revulsion toward the mother—will occur. At the moment of conception, the father's semen, the mother's ovum, and the bardoa or rebirth consciousness unite. The gametes are the outer aspects of the male white substance and female red substance.[23] They contain the potential for the different elements—space, air, fire, water, and earth in their outer aspects. The bardoa, with its mental body, contains these elements in their inner aspects. At the moment of conception, there is a consolidation of the five outer elements and the five inner elements. This is how a new individual arises. With this fusion of the two gametes and the bardoa, there comes a period of unconsciousness. Little by little, at the beginning of embryogenesis, the consciousness will be found. At that time, without exception, all recollection of the bardo is lost.

Whether we are Buddhist or not, whether we are connected to one tradition or another, the most important thing for us at death is to know our mind and our nature well and to practice now to gain this understanding.

7

The Bardo of Birth to Death

When I am in the bardo of birth til death,
May I waste no time;
Abandoning laziness, may I engage without distraction
In the study, assimilation of,
And meditation on the teachings.
May I practice, integrating on the path
Appearance and mind.

—Padmasambhava, *The Tibetan Book of the Dead*

GESTATION

When the bardoa, or rebirth consciousness, unites with the mother's and father's substances, memories become confused and begin to disappear like the clouded dreams of deep sleep.

During the first week in the womb, the embryo looks like rice mush and suffers as though it were being cooked in a copper pot. In the second week, it is oblong, and looks like frozen butter; at this point, the pervasive wind differentiates the four elements (earth, water, fire, and air). In the third week, the embryo has a complete form, shaped like an ant, and, due to the activator wind, the manifestation of the four elements becomes evident.

The embryo continues to change until the seventh week, when the spiral wind forms the four limbs, creating the feeling of being forcefully stretched, as if across a stick. At the seventh week, the opening wind produces the nine bodily openings; to the embryo this feels as if an open wound were being poked with a finger.

From this point on, if the mother eats something cold, the embryo feels as though it is being thrown onto ice; if she eats a lot of food, the embryo feels pressed between rocks; if she eats too little, being whipped around in the air; if she runs violently or falls, it has the feeling of being hurled down the side of a cliff; if she has sex, for the embryo it is like being flogged with metal thorns.

After the thirty-seventh week, the fetus starts to perceive being in the mother's womb as being imprisoned in a dark, unpleasant place; it is unhappy and wants to get out. During the thirty-eighth week, the baby is directed toward the birth canal by the "joining to the flower" wind and suffers as though the body were being carried away by a moving wheel.

The fetus is thus animated by twenty-eight winds. It grows, nourished by the mother's blood and nutrients, until its body is completely formed.

Finally, turned over by the reversing wind, the baby emerges, arms folded, suffering as though being forced through a narrow tube. When the baby comes out of the womb, it has the sensation of being deposited onto thorns; when it is finally cleaned and dried, it feels like it is being burned alive. Considering all this suffering, who would want to return to the mother's womb? This is how we are born.

DURING LIFE

During this bardo of birth to death, which is ordinary life, the mind produces the primary delusion of existing as a body that it considers its own.

This delusion about our body also rests on the elements earth, water, fire, and air. These elements exist in us since conception, at the inner as well as the outer level. They mature in us like a flower that blooms. By their maturation, the body and mind develop, grow, and acquire their power.[24] This period of growth might last up to twenty-five years, after which, in the second part of a lifetime, the body and abilities weaken; a process of deterioration accompanies aging, followed finally by death. There are, therefore, two natural stages: evolution and involution. Nevertheless, this process can be interrupted by a sudden death, as if a flower had been cut.

In the bardo of birth to death, we also experience the dream bardo and maybe the bardo of meditation. Then once again, we pass on to the bardo of emptiness and the bardo of becoming, which lead us toward yet another birth.

8

The Eight Consciousnesses
and the Five Principal Elements

Buddha nature is accompanied by seven consciousnesses,
which we grasp at, resulting in duality.
When that is recognized it will stop spreading.

—*Laṅkāvatārasūtra*

In order to understand clearly the connection between the teachings on
mind and transmigration in the bardos, and to better understand these
bardo processes, it might be helpful to consider the transformations that the
mind undergoes throughout those phases.

Buddha nature or pure mind, that primordial wisdom,[25] is, after all,
emptiness, lucidity, and infinite possibility. It is the clear light, encountered
by all beings at the end of the dissolution of consciousness at the moment of
death, or, in the bardo of agony, followed by the bardo of emptiness.

This clear light or basic primordial wisdom has as its essence the five principal elements: space, air, fire, water, and earth. These transform when the
mind and its manifestations are modified, as we will see.

When buddha nature is obscured by ignorance, it becomes the universal
ground of samsara. As such, it is called the universal or fundamental consciousness, or the eighth consciousness. It encompasses and pervades everything, and from it arise all the illusions of individual consciousnesses.

The development of delusion begins with the appearance of duality. The nondual state of emptiness, lucidity, and unobstructedness splits up into subject-
object duality and acts out of that perception. From emptiness arises the me-sub-
ject, from lucidity arises the sense of otherness, and from unobstructedness arise
all relationships based on attraction, repulsion, and ignorance. With this split,
contaminated consciousness or dualistic consciousness occurs—the consciousness
that someone has something. It is referred to as contaminated because it is pol-
luted with dualism, which is the seventh consciousness. This contaminated consciousness has an entourage of six other consciousnesses, corresponding to the
different sense faculties: visual, auditory, olfactory, gustatory, tactile, and mental.

ALTERATION OF THE ELEMENTS IN THE MIND AND BARDOS

Empty, luminous, and infinite in potential, mind can be understood as having five
basic qualities: emptiness, mobility, clarity, continuity, and stability. Each of these

corresponds respectively to the five principal elements of space, air, fire, water, and earth. We have already described mind as not being a tangible thing: it is indeterminate, omnipresent, and immaterial; it is emptiness, with the nature of space. Thoughts and mental states constantly arise in the mind; this movement and fluctuation is the air element's nature. Furthermore, mind is clear; it can know, and that clear lucidity is the fire element's nature. And mind is continuous; its experiences are an uninterrupted flow of thoughts and perceptions. This continuity is the water element's nature. Finally, mind is the ground or basis from which arise all knowable things in samsara as well as nirvana, and this quality is the earth element's nature.

The five qualities of pure mind also have the nature of the five elements. Entering into illusions and duality, the mind is altered, but the productions of the mind preserve the nature of the five elements in different aspects. All manifestation is the play of mind in the transformations of the five principal elements. Moreover, there are subtle energies sustaining the mind and its mutations, traditionally called winds or airs. Mind, consciousness, and myriad diverse experiences are produced by these wind energies; they are indistinguishable from mind and are the energy that animates and influences them.

The five basic qualities of mind just described correspond to five very subtle winds, whose energy manifests in mind as the five essential luminosities which are referred to as extremely subtle. They are, respectively, blue, green, red, white, and yellow. These luminosities begin to manifest at the moment when the consciousness is reestablished at the end of the bardo of emptiness.[26] They make up part of the process of "birth," the emergence of dualistic consciousness. The experiences and projections of the consciousness subsequently arise from the five luminosities; they produce the appearances of the five elements which are perceived through illusion as the mental body and the outer world.

All illusory appearances that the consciousness experiences are basically emanations of mind, the manifestation of the five principal elements, initially occurring as essential qualities of mind, then in the winds and luminosities and finally as appearances. Each of these levels has the nature of the different elements: space, air, fire, water, and earth.

The process of structuring the consciousness occurs at every moment, in all our states of consciousness, but particularly at the beginning of the bardo of becoming. Then, during that bardo, by the interplay of the five elements, the consciousness projects the appearance of a mental body, a subtle form with which it identifies as a subject, while at the same time it projects these objects, perceived in an illusory way as the outer world.

So this consciousness subject, identified with its mental body, develops relationships with these form-projections that are gradually structured as the other aggregates: sensations, representations, and factors. The five aggregates that together form an individual (forms, sensations, representations, factors, and consciousness) are thus created. But at this stage of the bardo of becoming, the mental consciousness lives out all of its experiences only within itself, and the individual thus composed has only four and a half aggregates.[27] In this way, the experiences of the bardo of becoming will last up until conception. At the moment of conception, the migrating consciousness, made up of four and a half aggregates or heaps, combines with outer elements, present in the father's semen and the mother's ovum. So, the conceived embryo includes all five elements in their inner aspect—consciousness—and in their outer aspects, which come from the parent's gametes.

The five elements of space, air, fire, water, and earth exist in the embryo, and then in the physical body, as cavities, wind, heat, liquids, and solids on the one hand, and on the other, as the principles of stretching, mobility, energy, fluidity, and cohesion. The tangible form that the body acquires is the gross aspect of the form heap; an individual made up of five heaps is thus created, and slowly the six sense faculties develop—visual, auditory, olfactory, tactile, gustatory, and mental.

In the realm of these different sense faculties of the mental consciousness, two aspects, pure and impure, emerge. The first aspect proceeds from primordial awareness and the second from dualistic consciousness. The contaminated and afflicted mental consciousness proceeds from dualistic awareness along with everything negative, such as anger, greed, ignorance, attachment, jealousy, and pride. On the other hand, a positive mental consciousness arises from primordial wisdom with the qualities of wisdom, compassion, love, and faith. These two aspects of the mental consciousness extend throughout the six consciousnesses and sense faculties. This results in a variety of experiences of the six kinds of objects: forms, sounds, smells, flavors, tactile objects, and thoughts.

To draw an analogy, the fundamental consciousness is like the master or king; the mental consciousness is like his son, the prince; and the sense consciousnesses are like their emissaries. This is how we distinguish the eight consciousnesses. When the prince, or our contaminated mental consciousness, reigns over the six sense consciousnesses, they function in relation to their objects by way of the six sense faculties.

The interaction of the many elements within dependent arising or tendrel[28] gives rise to innumerable conceptions that control body, speech, and mind. The various karmas activated by these illusions leave imprints in the fundamental consciousness, much like seeds planted in the ground. And, like the various interdependent factors such as fertilizer, light, and moisture that cause the seeds to yield a harvest, karmic imprints left in fundamental consciousness yield the harvest of a mass of happy or miserable lives, depending upon whether those imprints are positive or negative.

The Wheel of Samsara and the Bardos

9

The Twelve Links of Dependent Origination

Monks, when this is, that comes.
When this is born, that appears.
And so it is from "ignorance causing the (formative) factors"
to "birth causing old age and death."

—*Śālistambhasūtra*

All samsaric existence depends on the conditions and factors that form it; nothing has any autonomous or independent existence whatsoever. As conditions change, the phenomena that make up these lives arise and pass away; they are neither permanent nor independent.

All states conditioned by samsara appear, abide, and disappear as the interaction and transition of interdependent factors. Appearance and disappearance, birth and death follow one another continuously. The traditional diagram presented here, called the wheel of samsara, wheel of birth, or wheel of life, illustrates the sequence of twelve components that make up the appearance and disappearance of the consciousness and its experiences, or samsara.

These twelve factors, which we already discussed,[29] parallel the series of bardos and the transformations of mind which were described in the preceding chapters. They are complementary presentations that overlap.

Each link in this chain of reactions arises by virtue of the others; each one produces the next. Therefore, for example, where there is becoming there will be birth, followed by deterioration and death.

For an ordinary person, death is followed by a period of unconsciousness or ignorance in the bardo of emptiness. This ignorance is the point of departure in the cycle of illusion, the first mental obscuration that gives rise to all the others.

In the outer links of the wheel of life, the first link, *ignorance*, is symbolized by a blind person groping for the way with a cane. That ignorance also appears in symbolic form at the center or hub around which the wheel of samsara constantly turns.

On the basis of ignorance, under the influence of latent formative elements in the fundamental consciousness, the experience of individual consciousness is reactivated. These elements are karmic imprints remaining in the fundamental consciousness after death and the disappearance of individual consciousness.

At the moment of death, the action of karma temporarily disappears. Then it returns as *formative factors*, the second link, reconditioning the mind in the individual consciousness along with mind's productions. These factors exist in the form of propensities and habits. The karma, or formative factors that cause the reappearance of the "I am" delusion, or sense of individual consciousness, are the point of departure here, but they continue their activity throughout the cycle. This rebirth of the individual consciousness is symbolized by a potter molding clay and corresponds to the end of the bardo of emptiness, the moment at which the consciousness reestablishes itself before beginning its migration into the bardo of becoming.

The "individual" *consciousness* is the third link, symbolized by the agitated monkey which is the cognitive mode that experiences everything in terms of subject and object, which in turn gives rise to all dualistic activity.

The fourth link is called *name and form*, depicted by a boat with two people representing, respectively, consciousness and the mental body in the bardo of becoming. The consciousness subject corresponds to name, while form is the body with which it is identified in the experience of "I am that," as in "I am that body."

The fifth link is the *six realms*, depicted by a house with six openings that correspond to six sense fields in which the bardo being's consciousness is developed.

The sixth link, *contact*, represents the connection formed between consciousness-subject and its projection, or projected objects, between the consciousness identified with the mental body and the world it mistakenly perceives as being "out there," or outside of it. Recall again the analogy of the dream.[30] This link is depicted by an arrow touching a man's eye.

The seventh link, *sensation*, shows a couple embracing; this represents the initial experience that arises as a result of the meeting of a subject and its objects.

The eighth link, *thirst*, depicted by a man drinking, is the urgency that provokes the subject to seize the thing as an object. The ninth link, *grasping*, is the subject's actual fixation upon an object, depicted by a man picking fruit from a tree. These links underlie our perceptions in general and those of the bardo of becoming in particular.

The tenth link, illustrated by a pregnant woman, is called *becoming*. Grasping, the fixation of the ninth link, concretizes into the birth of a new life.

The eleventh link is *birth* in the world created by this state of existence. It is represented by a woman giving birth. This is entry into the bardo of birth to death. All the preceding links are like an electrical current whose energy generates the birth of a given state of existence. The exhaustion of this current finally leads to the next state and its disappearance and death. After birth, life evolves, deteriorates into old age, and ends with death.

Aging and death, represented by a corpse being carried off to the charnel ground, is the twelfth and final link. After the bardo of the moment of death comes the bardo of emptiness, and so on. The wheel of samsara turns endlessly.

We take birth countless times in samsara's six realms; this is illustrated toward the center of the wheel of life by six Tibetan letters.[31] The entire wheel of samsara turns around the three mental poisons depicted at the center of the illustration: ignorance, symbolized by the pig; hatred, symbolized by the snake; and desire, symbolized by the cock.

10

Practices at the Moment of Death

Without thinking that death will come,
I am absorbed in plans for the future.
After having done the many and futile activities of this life
I will leave utterly empty-handed.
What a blunder;
as I will certainly need an understanding of the excellent Dharma.
So why not practice now?

—Padmasambhava, *Tibetan Book of the Dead*

We do not become free at death. Since karma conditions our mind, it determines the course of our bardo experience and the rebirth we will take. What is most important is our karma and our actual inner experience. This is why it is essential to become aware of the need for spiritual work from now on: study, devotion to practice, living according to discipline based on an understanding of karma, and cultivating the practices that will help us at the time of death.[32]

LIBERATING PRACTICES IN THE DIFFERENT BARDOS

The theoretical durations of the bardos are: for the bardo of death, the time it takes to finish a meal; for the bardo of emptiness, three and a half days; and for the bardo of becoming, forty-nine days.

These, however, are very general approximations. The duration of the different bardos varies according to the power of the positive and negative actions that make up the individual's karma; however, it is not calculated according to the twenty-four-hour day of the human realm. Liberation can also occur after an indeterminate period of time. It is also possible for there to be no bardo at all.

On the basis of Dharma practice in general, if certain practices are mastered during our lifetime, we can gain liberation while passing through the different bardos at the moment of death and after.

If we have realized mahāmudrā,[33] or the nature of mind, during our lifetime, we can, at the end of the bardo of death, recognize the clear light and achieve liberation. Instead of the state of ordinary unconsciousness, the luminous essence of the mind appears, which, like the light of a torch, completely dissipates the darkness of ignorance. If we practiced with a yidam[34] or meditational buddha such as Chenrezig, the buddha of compassion, recited his mantra, and developed a good meditation practice, this would be especially precious at the time of death. Such a practitioner might encounter Chenrezig's blessing as well as the mental habits and positive imprints left on the mind-stream from doing that practice. The stages of the sādhana have the power to liberate us during the bardos. We can gain liberation at any one of these stages, really become Chenrezig, and be born in his presence in a pure land.

There are also specific meditations and instructions on the bardos, such as those of *The Tibetan Book of the Dead*. These meditations and instructions allow for liberation at different stages of the bardos, by helping us to recognize the nature of the bardos and in particular the illusory nature of the appearances encountered in the bardo of becoming. These instructions are applied from the moment of total unconsciousness in the bardo of emptiness, when one awakens to fleeting manifestations of luminous forms and divinities, and for the entire duration of the bardo of becoming.

If we have not realized the clear light, meditated with a yidam, or practiced the bardo teachings, it is still possible to do a *phowa,* or transference of consciousness at the moment of death. Phowa allows the consciousness to be transferred to a state free from samsara. If it is practiced successfully during the bardo of the moment of death, the consciousness will not be carried through the bardos of emptiness or becoming. Instead, it will be immediately projected toward a higher realm. This is possible because of training in this life or through the compassion of a qualified lama who performs a phowa on our behalf.

In the best-case scenario, which would be complete mastery, this practice allows us to be reborn in what is known as a field of enlightenment, a spiritual state free from samsara and karmic propensities. It is as though we were catapulted directly to Sukhāvatī's pure land, Dewa Chen in Tibetan, the realm of great bliss, or if we were a bird able to fly straight to the firmament of enlightenment. Phowa is a meditation that we can do easily, and for that reason it is extremely precious.

Otherwise, if phowa is only halfway mastered, we will take a samsaric rebirth, but in a fortunate celestial realm favorable to liberation. In the worst case, we would take rebirth as a human endowed with conditions favorable for spiritual practice.

Through realization of phowa, liberation takes place without passing through the bardos. The absence of bardos, on the other hand, can also occur to people who have committed very serious negative actions whose force is so intense as to propel them straight to a hell realm right after they die, without the reprieve of other bardos.

In general, if we have developed the habit of praying to our lamas, to the Three Jewels, or to a particular aspect of Buddha, the impression on our minds establishes a connection with them and connects us with their blessing, which protects us and leads us to liberation in the bardo of becoming.

WISHES TO BE REBORN IN A PURE LAND

Even if we have not done the specific practices just described or received their instructions, it is still a given that the impressions on our mind determine our death and bardo experience; and prayers and wishes we have made during our lifetime which have saturated our mind can spontaneously lead our mind toward a pure land free from samsara's conditioning.

Among the many aspects of Buddha toward whom we can direct our minds are Amitābha, Chenrezig, and their enlightened field, Sukhāvatī. These are especially important.

Merely wishing to be reborn in Sukhāvatī while we're alive will cause us to be actually reborn there, rather than going to an ordinary physical place. In fact, this life's fully matured[35] "karmic body" is made of substantial elements with which we identify, and these prevent the mind from freely going where it wishes. On the contrary, in the bardo of becoming, there is no more physical body, but the mental body has the power to move like thought. This is why, by the power of wishes generated by Buddha Amitābha, Chenrezig, and ourselves, we can make a connection that leads our mind toward Sukhāvatī and causes it to truly be reborn there. This is particularly possible during the first week of the bardo of becoming, when we repeatedly become aware that we are dead, so by the power of the habits established during our lives, we pray to Amitābha and Chenrezig to be reborn in Sukhāvatī; by their power, we can instantly be reborn there. If we regularly utter sincere prayers to be reborn in Sukhāvatī, we carry with us the aspiration to go there when we die. This aspiration will act on our mind, becoming the means for being reborn there and for achieving liberation more quickly than if we had traveled by plane or rocket!

In the meantime, obstacles to being reborn in Sukhāvatī can arise. If, for example, our family or spouse weeps over us or demands that we come back to life, or if the attitude of our loved ones provokes our sadness, attachment, or anger, our mind will not be able to direct itself toward Sukhāvatī because it will be torn between two thoughts: the desire to go to Sukhāvatī and the memory of those held dear. The strings of attachment can therefore be so restrictive that they negate the impulse to aspire toward Sukhāvatī. It would be the same if we remained attached to the world we just left, to our possessions or our social status. These ties direct our mind once again toward what we just left behind and cause a detour away from Sukhāvatī. Luckily, though, there is a method for warding off this danger, and that is to develop the habit from this moment on of considering everyone and everything we are attached to as an actual offering for Amitābha and Chenrezig. The thought that beings and things do not belong to us anymore can neutralize the emotion that otherwise binds us to them. So we can offer to Amitābha and Chenrezig everything we may be attached to; having dedicated that totally, we will retain no attachment whatsoever.

Elderly people whose involvement in Dharma is recent may justifiably think they won't have time to tackle a lot of profound practices, such as mahāmudrā and others that lead to enlightenment in this life. They might also tell themselves that they no longer have the capacity or the time to devote themselves to long, difficult practices. This should not discourage them: to have great faith in Amitābha and Chenrezig, to pray sincerely to be born in Sukhāvatī's pure land, and to recite Chenrezig's mantra definitely result in being born there after death.

Birth in Sukhāvatī is apparitional, which is to say that a being who is reborn there instantly appears before Amitābha and Chenrezig. That direct vision causes us to reach the first bodhisattva bhūmi, Sublime Joy,[36] immediately. This state corresponds to initial awakening, after which there is no return to the bonds of samsara. The name of Amitābha's pure land, Sukhāvatī, means "great bliss" because the mind, free of all samsaric suffering and pain, knows nothing but happiness and joy. To be reborn in this spiritual state puts an end to the cycle of rebirths. There, the mind is freed from karmic obscurations and its enlightened qualities begin to reveal themselves and to work for the benefit of beings. But even if the mind is quite purified of the karmic veils and most of the veils of mental afflictions, subtle obscurations still remain. Nevertheless, it is a state in which we experience important enlightened qualities from which we can help those who remain in samsara. There are many ways to come to help them and guide them toward liberation. In general, there are many fields of enlightenment: at the level of the Truth Body, or dharmakāya; at the level of the Enjoyment Body, or sambhogakāya; or at the level of the Emanation Body, or nirmānakāya.[37] Sukhāvatī is an enlightened field with forms, at the level of the Emanation Body, or nirmānakāya. Because of this, it is still subject to certain limitations. For example, in Sukhāvatī, a certain type of change, or impermanence, remains. These are not the gross impermanence and change we know in our own plane of existence, but a subtler kind.

There are four factors that determine taking rebirth in Sukhāvatī. The first is to clearly imagine the presence of Sukhāvatī as well as that of Amitābha and Chenrezig; to develop an intense sense of their actual presence, their magnificence, and their realm, where all appearances are as bright and luminous as though they were made of jewels. The second is our practice of purification and the two accumulations:[38] the purification of negativity and the two accumulations of merit and wisdom. The third is the altruistic motivation of bodhicitta, or the mind of enlightenment.[39] Based on bodhicitta, the fourth factor is the aspiration arising from strong and sincere wishes to be reborn in Sukhāvatī. Of these four, aspiration is the most important determining factor.

These instructions on Sukhāvatī are not just a promise for the future; to be convinced of their validity and to put these teachings into practice dispels many kinds of suffering in this life. Old age is typically accompanied by a series of problems: eating too much causes trouble, while eating too little causes other problems; we're not comfortable in heavy warm clothes, but light ones do not keep us warm enough. On top of the physical inconveniences, our impending death weighs heavily on our mind. On the other hand, if we wish from now on to be born in Sukhāvatī, and if we have the conviction that our wishes will come true, old age, rather than tormenting us, becomes a source of joy thanks to the hope of quickly leaving this world for another, better one.

If you can neither do the practices nor generate the wish to be reborn in Sukhāvatī, you can at least acquaint yourself with the ten positive acts and the ten negative acts. You can strive to adopt those positive actions and abandon the negative ones. Ultimately, that will guide you to a happy human rebirth where you will meet with Dharma and gradually progress on the path to enlightenment.

11

Human Life and Its Problems

The joys of samsara,
Like dew on a blade of grass,
Disappear in a flash.
To aspire toward
Supreme and changeless liberation
Is the practice of bodhisattvas.

—Togme Sangpo, *Thirty-Seven Practices of Bodhisattvas*

In the world of humans, life can be relatively happy, though all humans always undergo the three kinds of suffering and are subject to many problems.

THE THREE KINDS OF SUFFERING

The first kind of suffering is quite subtle. It is the suffering inherent to individuality and is due to the imperfections and limitations inherent in the very fact of existing, the sole fact of being composed of the five heaps that make up an individual.

We have already discussed these heaps or aggregates: form, feeling, perception, compositional factors, and consciousness.[40] The being made up of these five heaps is conditioned and imperfect. That conditioning and those imperfections create the first kind of suffering inherent to the aggregates of individuality. They are inherent to it like butter is to milk. Merely by being made up of five heaps, we are subject to this subtle form of dissatisfaction. However, this type of suffering is so subtle that it is practically imperceptible, and, for the most part, we are not even aware of it. It can be compared to a speck of dust in our hand: when one attains an advanced level of realization at which most of the gross forms of suffering are dispelled, this kind of suffering becomes much more evident and so is perceived much more acutely, as if the speck of dust had lodged in our eye!

Influenced by a variety of factors, all other forms of suffering develop on the basis of the suffering of individuality. The second kind of suffering, which is more perceptible, is called the suffering of change. It is a form of suffering latent in what we ordinarily regard as happiness, pleasures, and comforts, whether mental or physical. It belongs to desires, attachments, and impermanence. It is the frustration or unhappiness experienced every time something we love or something that pleases us changes, deteriorates, or disappears.

The third kind of suffering is known simply as suffering because it causes pain and unhappiness. It is the suffering of suffering caused by pains and problems that lead from one to another in daily life.

THE MAIN KINDS OF HUMAN SUFFERING

Four main types of suffering affect humans: birth, old age, sickness, and death. Just thinking about these and being aware of their reality helps us to understand the unsatisfactory nature of samsaric or conditioned existence, allowing us to free ourselves from the attachments to ordinary existence and therefore to strive for liberation.

We have already mentioned the suffering of birth in the discussion on the bardo of birth to death.[41]

The suffering caused by illness is often intolerable. We are subject to the orders of doctors and have to undergo rigorous medical exams. We are dependent and become exhausted carrying out their instructions. We can't even sit up in bed, eat or drink, or satisfy our desires. At the end of the day, we still have to go through an interminable night of terrible pain and suffering.

The suffering caused by old age is equally great. Our body, once straight and strong, shrinks and becomes crooked, and we need a cane to hold ourselves up. Our hair turns gray and falls out; we become bald and lose our attractiveness. Our skin, once soft and smooth as Chinese silk, becomes a pile of deep, rough wrinkles, just as a lotus flower is pink immediately after blooming but becomes gray and creased when it fades. The body's strength wanes; whether standing or sitting, it becomes tired. Mind becomes weak, and we haven't the slightest bit of get-up-and-go for any activity. Senses lose their acuity: eyes no longer see clearly, ears cannot hear, the nose cannot smell, the tongue cannot distinguish flavors, and being touched no longer brings pleasure. Memories are unclear; what happens at one moment is forgotten in the next. We cannot adapt; we feel we no longer belong anywhere. Our company isn't appreciated, and no one thinks about us except with pity. Our former wealth dwindles, as does our authority. Our possibilities for this life are finished, and our energy declines and vanishes. We realize there is only one thing ahead of us: death, and the thought depresses us.

The suffering caused by death is such that when fear consumes us, we are utterly cut off from joy and seized by the torment of illness. Our mouth is dry, our face is distraught, and our shaky limbs can no longer move. We soil ourselves with saliva, sweat, urine, and vomit, and in our distress, we make harsh noises. After all their remedies have failed, the doctors give up on us. Horrifying fantasies arise in our mind, causing terror and panic. The movement of our breathing stops and then, with our mouth and nostrils gaping, we go beyond this world completely upset by the great migration of death. We then enter into the unknown, sink into the abyss, and are carried away by the vast ocean, swept away by the winds of karma.

At the inevitable moment of departure, we must leave everything behind, abandoning wealth, privilege, influence, home, family, and our treasured body. Beads of sweat form on our face, and the various signs of the bardo of the moment of death gradually manifest. After these bardo experiences, we take birth yet again in a realm consistent with our karma.

In addition to these four great sources of suffering, humans must also experience having to separate—because of life events or death—from loved ones: father, mother, children, grandchildren, spouse, all those they dearly love and are attached to. Humans also endure meeting with beings that are hostile to them, having their things taken away, and being subjugated, abused, battered, killed, or put on trial. As humans, we also suffer from not getting what we want and not being able to keep what we have.

Now more than ever, in this era of rampant desires, we are constantly tormented day and night by material worries and desires, by attachment and hatred. It is now so important that we recognize the harmfulness of desires for, and attachment to, material possessions and passions. If we understand that all samsaric phenomena are as fleeting as waves on the surface of the water, merely illusory appearances, insubstantial as hallucinations or dreams, we will not be attached to them, and we will be able to content ourselves with what we have and remain happy, our minds open and at peace.

In this way, by the practice of Dharma, we have the possibility of definitely becoming free from samsara and navigating beyond it to the supreme bliss of buddhahood.

12

Human Life: Using It Well

Right now I have this precious vessel,
Human life.
For the benefit of all beings, as well as myself,
Without distraction, day and night, I will practice,
Study, reflect, and meditate on the teachings.
That is the way of bodhisattvas.

—Togme Sangpo, *Thirty-Seven Practices of Bodhisattvas*

Among the myriad possible lives, only human life is endowed with the faculties that allow for an understanding and practice of Dharma. But merely
being human is not always enough for spiritual progress; the value of human
birth is actually quite variable. There are three kinds of human life: unfortunate human life, ordinary human life, and precious human life.

Unfortunate human life is one in which a person commits negative acts
because he or she is subject to mental afflictions that in turn create a painful
future.

Ordinary or banal human existence, while not used for negative ends, is
not particularly positive either. This is the type of life most people lead: not
doing anything particularly positive or negative.

Finally, there is the precious human rebirth: a human life in which a
connection with a spiritual path and a guide have been established and in
which, with faith in that path, it is possible to practice; all the favorable
circumstances for practice are in place. That kind of life is said to be precious
because it is the basis of spiritual realization. Through it we can reach
enlightenment, or buddhahood. It is also precious because of its extreme
rarity—like a star in the daytime. Consider its rarity among the numerous
nations on our planet: the civilizations of a great many nations make no
reference to the spiritual path. Hundreds of millions of people live in an
environment that completely lacks Dharma. Even in countries where
Dharma is accessible, look how few people actually study and practice it.

Notice how in our city, our town, our immediate surroundings, so few people
have the right circumstances for practice: freedom, motivation, the spiritual
inclination to really devote themselves to the path. This precious human life is
rare also because it is so hard to obtain. That we even have a precious human
life is no accident; it is the result of positive actions accomplished on the path

by morality, love, and compassion. All these acts left karmic imprints that have brought us to the present situation into which we were born: endowed with a precious human life. Among you there are some with faith in Dharma and others who are curious or sympathetic. Just by virtue of that, you possess the precious human rebirth.

In the past, we have been born and reborn an incalculable number of times in cyclic existence. Right now we have a precious human rebirth.[42] If we do not devote ourselves to Dharma practice, this will be a loss much worse than that of a poor man who won't take a treasure he has just come upon. Ultimately, we will continue to err indefinitely in the cycle of lives. If we know how to use this life, it can be the point of departure for our liberation.

We are at a fork in the road: one route ascends to higher realms and freedom; the other descends to lower realms. We have the choice of taking the high road or the low road. To use this precious human life as a support to Dharma practice and liberation is to give it its true meaning.

13

On the Urgency of Practice

You, young men and women here,
Don't think that death will come little by little;
It comes fast as lightning.

—Milarepa, *One Hundred Thousand Songs*

All phenomena are impermanent. Our body too is the result of a collection of different elements: good and bad karma, the father's semen and the mother's egg, the elements, and, of course, the primary consciousness. All beings in the universe are mortal. Those of the past have died; those of the present and future will also die. Year by year, day by day, hour by hour, moment by moment, we all move closer to the moment of our death, and, no matter how brave or strong we are, we cannot deter it. No matter how fast we run, we cannot flee from death. However vast our learning, our keen erudition changes nothing. Not the heroism of an army, the influence of the powerful, the best-trained troops, nor the ruses of clever people—nothing can stop death, just as nothing can keep the sun from sinking and disappearing behind the mountains.

No one knows how long they will live. Some die when they're still in the womb, others at birth or before they can even stand on their own two legs; some die in youth, others in old age. We also have no idea what the cause of our death will be; no one knows whether it will be by fire, water, wind, lightning, falling off a cliff, an avalanche or landslide, the collapse of a house, an army, poison, a sudden attack, or an illness. How fragile we are, like a candle in the wind, a bubble, or a dewdrop on a blade of grass.

When death comes, even though we don't want it, we have to let go of all desire and abandon absolutely everything: land, house, wealth, parents, children, family, spouse...leaving even our body, we go alone, with no freedom and no friends, to this fearsome place, which is the bardo. That is everyone's lot sooner or later. When we see someone die, hear of someone's death, or think about it, it should serve as a reminder that we too will definitely die. As long as we are strong, radiant, and happy, we don't think about it, but when a terminal illness descends upon us, we lose all strength, our color fades, we take on the peaked aspect of a corpse, and we become unhappy. Then, when all the medicines, treatments, and rites turn out to be ineffective and nothing else can stave off the torments of disease, we know we will die. We will be terrified of it and will suffer terribly, desperate at having to go alone, leaving everything behind.

When we whisper our final words, we realize at last that there is no escape from mortality. After we die, even those who loved us will not want to see our corpse remaining among them for even a day or two. Just looking at it disgusts and frightens them. Crossing the threshold of the house one last time, our body is removed by the undertakers and either deposited in a cemetery or incinerated. No one will ever see us again. When we see, hear, or think about death in our day-to-day life, however we may be exposed to it, we should apply these thoughts of death to ourselves, to remind us that we too are of the same nature.

Our life is like an hourglass that never stops. Each moment follows the next without respite. From minute to minute, life exhausts itself: we are babies, then adults, then old, then dead. One instant follows another relentlessly.

If we become conscious that death is inevitable for all of us, shouldn't we strive to practice Dharma from this very moment on?

This precious human body we have right now can communicate, can understand the teachings, is endowed with all the necessary faculties, and has met with Dharma. If we fritter it away, not only will we have to endure the reign of samsara's suffering, but we will not have a chance of finding a similar opportunity. That's why we must firmly resolve to use this life well, by practicing Dharma enthusiastically during the time that remains in this life—this quick, bright moment, like the sun piercing through clouds.

PART TWO

THE PATH OF LIBERATION

Beseeching the Lama to Shower Blessings

Song of the Manifestation Appearing as the Lama, written by Kyabje Kalu Rinpoche

Namo Guru Bya

Symbolic Lama, shining outwardly
Like the light of myriad forms and appearances
Of limitless dependent arisings,
Ineffable play of the array of illusory projections;
In the state of empty appearance naturally liberated,
I pray through your blessing to realize
That the display of appearance is nirmāṇakāya.

Mantra-Lama, arising in the interim
As the vibration of the multiple sounds and words
Of ceaseless causes and conditions,
Inconceivable pageant of harmonious song:
Within the sphere of empty sound naturally liberated,
I pray through your blessing to realize
That this ceaselessness is saṃbhogakāya.

Real Lama, revealed inwardly
As the self-knowing of the manifold
Thoughts and ideas of awareness
That is empty and free of speech.
Infinite range of mind:
Within the sphere of clarity and voidness
Of great bliss and emptiness
I pray through your blessing to perceive
That the unborn is dharmakāya.

All the various phenomena: appearances, sounds, and thoughts
Are thus but the glorious Lama's play;
His symbolic ways to show us the nature of reality.
Recalling your kindness I pray;
Bless me to realize the nature of all phenomena.

The immeasurable ocean of all aspects of the three roots
Is none other than the play of the Venerable Lama
Who manifests like the moon's reflection in water
According to the aspirations of each disciple.
Within the perfection of the totality of your qualities
I pray, bless me that my mind
May be inseparably mixed with yours.

Bless me to abandon belief in self-existence.
Bless me to develop absence of need in my mind.
Bless me to develop love and compassion.
Bless me to develop genuine respect and devotion.
Bless me to stop non-Dharmic thoughts.
Bless me to spontaneously pacify illusions.
Bless me to realize the state of mahāmudrā.
Bless me to attain buddhahood in this very life.

May I, from now until enlightenment,
Adorned with the ornament of perfect morality,
Master the awakening mind of equanimity
As well as the generation and completion stages,
Attain the enlightenment of a buddha, a state
In which the minds of Lama and disciple finally become one.

At the request of the practitioner, Lama Karma Sherab, this fervent song of the manifestation appearing as the lama was spontaneously composed by Karma Rangjung Kunkhyab. May it cause the blessing of the Glorious Lama to enter the hearts of all.

PART TWO
Section One

A General Overview:
The Different Approaches of Dharma

The Three Turnings of the Teaching

I taught a unique vehicle;
there's no need to distinguish others.
It is to guide students well that I taught
different approaches.

—*Laṅkāvatārasūtra*

We have already seen that mind is eclipsed by many different obscurations; if they are removed, mind's fundamental nature, like the sun shining brightly in the clear open sky, can manifest all the qualities of wisdom, compassion, and a buddha's abilities. The different Dharma paths that we'll discuss are all methods for removing various obscurations and attaining spiritual realization.[43]

Usually we are prisoners of dualistic fixation that makes us experience many deceptive appearances without being able to recognize their true nature. Seeing this, Buddha Śākyamuni, in his great compassion, taught many methods for becoming free. All of them are skillful means for helping different kinds of beings, accommodating each individual's abilities and needs.

The multiplicity of teachings that Buddha gave for the benefit of all beings is included in three vehicles, or means of advancing on the path. These are called the Hīnayāna, the Mahāyāna, and the Vajrayāna. The Dharma is spread in the world in these three forms.

From the perspective of any of these approaches, the idea is to go beyond the samsaric activities of conventional mind, which is self-centered, intent on personal interest and ego-centered ambitions, and which seeks individual interests in trying to selfishly acquire wealth, fame, or anything else.

From the Hīnayāna perspective, the strongly self-referent fixation is the origin of the 84,000 mental afflictions—pleasure, pain, indifference, higher or lower states of awareness—as well as all of samara's conditioning. The Hīnayāna method teaches us to overcome this fixation through meditation on the perfection of wisdom of nonego or nonself.

In the Mahāyāna, the point is not only to deliver oneself from self-reference, but to deliver all beings and help them to reach the bliss of enlightenment. Even so, the Mahāyāna practices, as well as those of the Hīnayāna, involve moving beyond the afflicted self-grasping attitudes of attraction, revulsion, and indifference.

The purpose of the Vajrayāna, like that of the Hīnayāna and the Mahāyāna, is to transcend the fixations of ego expressed in terms of attachment, revulsion, and indifference, along with all of the deluded states of mind that proceed from them. To free us from these, Vajrayāna methods use meditation on a deity and recitation of that deity's mantra.

All three of the yānas or vehicles allow for the complete elimination of the feeling of existing apart, as an individual, as well as our usual experience of attachment to things as permanent, which is to say all the fixations of subject-object grasping.

The Turnings and the Yānas

Given the reality of suffering, in order to help beings, Buddha Śākyamuni, in the first turning of the Wheel of Dharma, explained the Four Noble Truths, which are:

1. The Noble Truth of Suffering, or that life consists of suffering and limitation;
2. The Noble Truth of the Cause of Suffering, which is ignorance of the nature of mind and its afflictions;
3. The Noble Truth of Cessation, which is the end of all suffering by reaching enlightenment; and
4. The Noble Truth of the Path, or the way that leads to enlightenment, which is the practice of Dharma.

These Four Noble Truths form the first approach to Dharma; the origin of suffering is in the attitudes that disturb the mind, and the path that releases us from them involves restraining the mind, cultivating positive actions, and abandoning negative ones. Without this first cycle of teaching, beings would not have known how to distinguish between positive and negative actions, and they would not have been able to exert themselves on the path of practice, of cultivating the positive and abandoning the negative.

After that, Buddha Śākyamuni turned the Wheel of Dharma a second time, giving the teachings on emptiness, the indefinable nature of ultimate reality. At this point, he taught that all phenomena lack inherent existence; they do not exist independent of causes. Rather, they are projections of mind, whose nature is similar to space. This second cycle of teachings was given as an antidote to the tendency to grasp at things as real or permanent, as though they exist really and truly. Had Buddha not given these teachings, beings could not have freed themselves from their idea of the world as real or substantial.

Later on, Buddha Śākyamuni turned the Wheel of Dharma a third time, giving the teachings known as the complete and perfect explanation. In the third cycle, as in the second, Buddha taught that all things are projections of mind, empty of inherent existence, but furthermore, he elucidated the qualities of the clear light of emptiness and its potential for wisdom and infinite manifestations. The actual nature of pure mind is, therefore, a reality that can be experienced.

THE CHARACTERISTICS OF EACH VEHICLE

On the path toward enlightenment, these three cycles of teaching correspond to different approaches and types of practice designated as Hīnayāna, Mahāyāna, and Vajrayāna. All of these approaches are necessary and lead to the same goal: enlightenment. However, each might be more or less suited to our own particular situation.

The Hīnayāna is literally the "straight and narrow way," or individual vehicle. Its approach mainly requires renunciation of worldly passions; emphasis is on renunciation, detachment, and restraint.

The Mahāyāna is the open path, or the universal vehicle. It is an approach that might seem easier to apply and practice in our usual situations, because it does not require us to abandon the mundane things of the world, as in the Hīnayāna approach. It is, however, necessary to perceive their illusory nature through an experience of them as intangible, insubstantial, and unreal. This practice teaches us to cultivate the experience of emptiness—the profound nature of all phenomena—and to adopt an attitude of love and compassion toward all beings.

Overall, the Mahāyāna teaches the understanding of emptiness together with love and compassion, simultaneously. It teaches us to recognize all beings as having been our own parents in a previous life, so that we can generate the kind of love and compassion we feel for our own parents when they are in distress. One or another of these aspects—emptiness or compassion—may predominate within certain Mahāyāna traditions, but they are both indispensable. To practice love and transcendent wisdom simultaneously is to follow unwaveringly the flawless path that can truly lead to enlightenment.

From another angle, there is also a distinction between these two facets: love and compassion are the practice for the relative or conventional level, while experience of emptiness is the practice at the ultimate level. Relative and ultimate complement each other, and the ultimate rests on the relative. One well-known quote says:

> No one arrives at ultimate realization
> without depending on the relative.

The two develop together: compassion introduces us to an understanding of emptiness, and realization of emptiness is the realm of ultimate compassion. This Mahāyāna approach of joining love and emptiness emphasizes inner discipline: correct motivation along with meditative experience. It is a universally practical path in actual daily life.

Finally, there is the Vajrayāna, literally, the "adamantine way" or "lightning path," which is basically an even easier approach to practice, and much faster, because it is based on transmutation. The Vajrayāna has the same basis as the Mahāyāna, but it uses special spiritual methods adapted to different beings. When we speak of Vajrayāna, it is important to understand that this is not just one practice, but involves different levels of practice: outer, inner, secret, and most secret. The emphasis here is on the innermost discipline.

These approaches, Hīnayāna, Mahāyāna, and Vajrayāna, each accommodate the faculties, abilities, and aspirations of different kinds of people.

2

The Three Vehicles:
Complementarity and Unity

The cycle of the causal vehicle, or Pāramitāyāna,
was set in motion for those who aspire
to teachings on the basis of causality.
The fruition vehicle, the Vajrayāna,
was then taught as a short-cut.

—*rdo rje theg pa'i mtha' gnyis sel ba* of Jñānaśrī

All Buddha's teachings fall into three complementary categories or approaches: Hīnayāna, Mahāyāna, and Vajrayāna.

THREE METHODS

Our conditioning, our problems, and our suffering originate in negative mental habits: ignorance, egotism, and afflicted attitudes. The different aspects of Dharma are methods for eliminating this ignorance and resulting negativities, according to each being's needs and capacities: by protecting ourselves from what gives rise to those deluded states of mind, transforming them, or liberating them by recognizing their nature.

To protect ourselves from harmful habits by removing ourselves from their causes is the approach of the Hīnayāna, or individual vehicle. To transform afflictions—negative or self-referent tendencies—into positive and altruistic attitudes based on love and compassion is, for the most part, the Mahāyāna or universal vehicle approach. Simply recognizing the nature of the afflictions and thereby freeing ourselves from them, transmuting them as soon as they arise, is primarily the Vajrayāna or adamantine vehicle method.

The Hīnayāna approach involves maintaining perfect discipline and ceasing to behave in a way that causes harm to oneself and others. This protects the practitioner from obstacles and distractions and allows for single-pointed meditation.

The Mahāyāna approach involves practicing compassion toward all beings as well as meditating on profound emptiness. These two are done simultaneously. On the basis of the altruistic state of mind, or bodhicitta, we practice the six perfections: giving, morality, patience, enthusiastic perseverance, meditation, and wisdom.

The Vajrayāna approach is a way of transmutation that purifies all activities—emotions, impure illusions—and allows us to quickly reach enlightenment through the Generation and Completion Stage meditations.[44]

COMPLEMENTARITY AND PROGRESSION

The Hīnayāna practices are particularly those of outer discipline, or the different vows, whether monastic or lay. Along with the meditative basis, this outer discipline forms the foundations of Dharma. Some people, who have a limited ability to comprehend, do not exceed this level. They are frightened by the Mahāyāna explanations of universal compassion and the meaning of emptiness, covering their ears and expressing strong inner resistance: "No, that isn't for me, it isn't possible, I can't understand that!" If such people hear talk of the Vajrayāna and its various methods, their resistance is even stronger: "Oh, no! It couldn't have been Buddha who taught that! Those are just stories, I don't want to hear about it!"

There are also those who can understand the Mahāyāna but not the Vajrayāna perspective. But in fact, these three vehicles are cumulative approaches from outer, or external, to more internal types of practice. They are three levels that correspond as much to different abilities and mentalities as to progressive stages on the path. Since they are complementary, it is best to be able to practice all three at once.

This complementarity can be demonstrated by the example of building a house. First, you have to have a solid foundation: this corresponds to Hīnayāna discipline. Then, on this strong foundation, the actual infrastructure of the house can be built, which corresponds to the Mahāyāna practice of compassion and emptiness. Then, on that structure, the rest of the building can be finished. This corresponds to the methods of realization unique to the Vajrayāna. The roof of the house requires the building, which has to be built on a solid foundation. The same goes for the progression and complementarity of the three vehicles.

This complementarity is also reflected in the way in which the teachings are presented according to the different types of individuals—those of lesser, middling, and superior capacity—and their aspirations and faculties.

A supermarket contains a huge variety of groceries, all packaged and arranged differently. While the purpose of those products is always to nourish the customers, each shopper chooses what pleases him or her. Similarly, the different Dharma approaches accommodate many different levels among people, but all of them lead toward enlightenment. Whether one is involved with one or another of these vehicles, the most important thing is putting the teachings into practice; that way, one can progress steadily along the path.

The three vehicles are the main Buddhist traditions outside of Tibet, but our presentation is in terms of practice, not in terms of specific systems or schools. In particular, within this classification, the Theravada tradition is not reduced to the level of the Hīnayāna, for that would be inaccurate.[45]

Tibet had the good fortune to receive all the levels of teaching directly from India—Hīnayāna as well as Mahāyāna and Vajrayāna. I am not saying that you are particularly lucky to meet Tibetans per se; they are just like everybody else! But you are very lucky to have met with the Buddhadharma as it was transmitted to Tibet, because it is a perfectly complete and entirely living tradition.

PART TWO

Section Two

The Hīnayāna: Path of Discipline

I

The Path of Discipline

Vigilance is the path of immortal royalty,
Negligence, the path that leads to death.
Those who are vigilant do not die.
Those who are negligent are already dead.

—*Dhammapada*

In order to achieve liberation and leave the cycle of conditioned existence, it is vital[46] to recognize the actual nature of mind. It is our mind that governs our actions and decides what we do: it is neither our body nor our speech. Mind is the primary factor in that it rules body and speech: if we want to go somewhere, mind has the power to direct the body to get going. It also has the power to cause us to say pleasant or harsh words.

All in all, we are made up of body, speech, and mind, and if the most important aspect is mind and realization of its nature, body and speech are also important: by depending on them, spiritual realization can develop. We could say that body and speech are servants of the mind. While it might sometimes seem that they are three distinct factors, they are actually closely related.

From this perspective, the different elements of all Dharma practices refer to these three facets of our being. To travel the path, it is crucial to have correct discipline at the levels of body, speech, and mind. The Hīnayāna or individual vehicle approach is concerned with radically eliminating in ourselves all negative actions and tendencies while developing everything positive at these three levels. This approach is oriented toward individual liberation from suffering and gaining peace and happiness through strict discipline that rests on an understanding of karma, or the sequence of causes and results produced by our positive and negative actions.

THE DISCIPLINE OF VOWS AND MEDITATION

Thus, the Hīnayāna offers different vows for individual liberation which help us to maintain right moral discipline. There is: major monastic ordination, with the vows of a bhikṣu[47] or fully ordained monk; minor monastic ordination of a *śrāmaṇera*[48] or novice monk or nun, with fewer vows; and the *upāsaka*[49] vows, or the layperson's vows. If we do not take the monk's vows, we can take the lay vows, or at least we can take the refuge vow, which involves abandoning the ten negative actions and cultivating the ten positive actions as much as possible.[50]

These vows are important as a way of closing the door on negative tendencies; they greatly facilitate abandoning harmfulness and taking positive actions. In fact, if we are not able to abstain from killing, stealing, or sexual misconduct in the ordinary context, the vows provide the strength to do so, as well as the ability to restrain negative acts of body, speech and mind.

The Hīnayāna approach also involves meditative discipline that cultivates mental stability through states of meditative absorption in which the mind keeps its attention on the object of meditation without deviation or distraction.

To observe discipline and practice meditation in which mind abides single-pointedly absorbed in emptiness is what the Hīnayāna path is about. Its fruits are the spiritual realizations of an arhat and pratyekabuddha.[51]

So we can sum up the Hīnayāna approach as being one of strict observance to discipline as well as to the cultivation of single-pointed meditative absorption.

THE SWEEPER ARHAT

In Buddha Śākyamuni's entourage there was a monk who was not very bright and could not even learn the alphabet. But since he had great faith in Buddha and great aspiration for the Dharma, some of his companions went to Buddha to ask for advice on how to help him. Buddha responded, "He can still attain realization. He should do good deeds, abandon any harmful ones, and be the temple sweeper," and gave specific instructions on how he should sweep the temple, mindfully. The monk did this for years and purified his mind of obscurations. His intelligence grew more acute. Finally, while Buddha was teaching the Four Noble Truths, the sweeper understood the teaching and reached arhat status. He remains known as one of the great arhats of Buddha's followers.

THE DRUNKEN MONK AND THE WIDOW

Another well-known story shows how important it is to maintain our vows. A monk on his alms rounds came upon a house where a widow lived. She asked him in, and once he was inside said to him, "If you want to leave here, either have a drink with me, have sex with me, or kill my goat." With no way out, the monk said to himself, "Well, I'll do the lesser of three evils," and with that he took the drink of alcohol. But then, completely drunk, he succumbed to the woman's seduction, went to bed with her, and finally ended up killing the goat as well....

2

Refuge and the Three Jewels

In essence refuge is unique.
In means it is threefold.

—*Mahāmoksasūtra*

FAITH

Faith is what allows us to progress energetically along the path. It is a state of mind that arises from an understanding of the qualities of the Three Jewels. When we hear about Buddha or enlightenment, the Dharma's qualities, or the benefits of practice, and when we perceive the help we get from the Sangha or community of those who practice and transmit the Dharma, faith and aspiration arise in us.

There are three main forms of faith: admiring faith, or amazement, accompanied by the discovery of the qualities of Buddha and the Three Jewels; aspiring faith, which is based on admiring faith and consists of the aspiration to travel the path; and faith of certainty, which occurs when we gain authentic experience of the truth of the teachings.

So, the path begins based on a kind of faith in the Three Jewels: the possibility of becoming enlightened and realizing their qualities, or spiritual progress itself amazes and inspires us. We wish to advance further and recognize the advantages of doing so. Even though we might not know if the teaching we are hearing is right or not, we still sense its qualities and appreciate its value. That is the first kind of faith: admiring faith, amazement, or inspiration.

This first kind of faith then inspires us to attempt a first step on the path. Opening the door to Dharma, we perceive the truth of some of its aspects, and our certainty grows. Our aspiration to become enlightened gradually deepens, along with enthusiasm toward the teachings, or Dharma, and the Buddha. This is the second kind of faith, or aspiring faith. With it we take enlightenment as the goal and the Dharma as the path to its realization.

Later, as deeper practice gradually increases our awareness, instead of just thinking that the state of buddhahood and the teachings are wonderful and useful, and striving to practice, we taste firsthand that they are correct and authentic; their truth is directly validated. This is the third type of faith, or the faith of certainty.

BUDDHA

The pure nature of mind—emptiness, clarity, and unlimited potential—has been with us forever, although masked by veils obscuring its qualities. Buddhas or great bodhisattvas have purified or unveiled their minds, allowing all the innate qualities of buddha nature[52] to blossom fully; just as when there are no more clouds or haze, the sky is open, bright, and bathed in sunlight.[53] The "rare and sublime Buddha" is the ultimate realization of mind as completely pure and fully bloomed; this is the concrete example we use to refer to Buddha Śākyamuni and all those who have arrived at that state after him.

DHARMA

A buddha is free of all painful conditioning and likely to put into practice whatever is beneficial to beings. That enlightened activity expresses itself in many ways, but primarily through words and teachings on the Buddhadharma. A buddha's speech is endowed with qualities that conventional mind cannot comprehend. It causes a rain of teachings of all the vehicles to fall on beings in a language understandable to every being and suitable to each one's intelligence, faculties, aspirations, potential, and limitations. This harmonious speech is great at the beginning, in the middle, and at the completion of the path. Vast and deep as an ocean, it continuously benefits beings in this world and many other universes, in as many realms as there are beings caught in samsara. Buddha's speech is the "rare and sublime Dharma," of which there are two facets: the Dharma of the scriptures that show us the path toward enlightenment, and the Dharma of realization, which is the practical and genuine experience of the meanings of the written Dharma.

SANGHA

Those who study, practice, and transmit the words and experience of Dharma make up the Sangha—the community of practitioners of Buddhadharma. According to the degree of their realization, we can distinguish between superior Sangha and the Sangha of ordinary beings. The first is made up of realized beings already free from samsara, and the second includes all those who have taken vows for their own personal reasons, whether Hīnayāna vows, bodhisattva vows, or Vajrayāna vows. These two classes together make up the "rare and sublime Sangha."

TAKING REFUGE

Buddha, Dharma, and Sangha together make up the Three Jewels. To take refuge in the Buddha, the Dharma, and those who practice and transmit it—the Sangha—is the first spiritual vow given on the basis of the faith that disposes us toward the Three Jewels and compels us to start our journey on this path.

Taking refuge creates a spiritual connection that, on the one hand, protects us from the fears and anxieties we may have about suffering in samsaric or conditioned existence. It also protects us from obstacles in this life and in death, until we reach enlightenment. On the other hand, it leads and guides us toward enlightenment, showing us the path and guiding us along it. To take refuge until we reach enlightenment on behalf of all beings is to enter on the Buddhist path; it is the basis of Dharma. We take refuge:

- In the Buddha, paying homage to his example, aspiring to realize the state he attained, and requesting his protection and guidance for all beings who remain in the prison of conditioned existence.
- In the Dharma, understanding its value, we exert ourselves with faith in the study and practice of Dharma.
- In the Sangha, by listening with faith and respect to the teachings such persons transmit and practicing to follow their example.

Taking refuge establishes a positive spiritual connection with the Three Jewels. It involves us in Dharma and practice but in no way implies that we reject or renounce faith we might have in other traditions. It is the basis for traveling the path to liberation; it protects us from what might make us turn away from that path, as well as from intentions and actions that would oppose it. When we truly take refuge, no obstacle can make us stumble; we will no longer be reborn in the three lower realms; and finally, because of our refuge vow, transmigration in the cycle of rebirths will eventually come to an end.[54]

THE RELIC DOG TOOTH

An old Tibetan woman who practiced the Dharma had a son who was a merchant and frequently traveled to India for business. One day his mother said to him, "India is the Buddha's country. Please, be so kind as to bring me some relic of Buddha that might inspire my devotion."

The son left but, consumed with worry over his business, forgot his mother's request and returned home empty-handed. Again and again he broke his word, and his elderly mother was desperate to have some relic before she died. So one day she said to him, "If you forget my relic once more when you go to India, I'll kill myself right in front of you when you come back."

But on his next trip to India, the son was again preoccupied with business and forgot. On the way back, he remembered his mother's words. Fearing that she might actually carry out her plans, he wondered what to do. On the side of the road, he saw the skull of a dog, and from it he removed a tooth, which he carefully wrapped in fine cloth. When he arrived home, he said, "Look, Mother, look what I've brought you! A tooth of Buddha Śākyamuni himself!"

His mother believed him and, ecstatic, placed the tooth on her shrine, fervently praying and making offerings. It is said that the tooth made miraculous gems appear and that when the woman died, extraordinary signs manifested.

A dog tooth in itself carries no particular blessing, but because the woman believed it to be Buddha's tooth, the power of her faith caused her to receive the blessings of the Three Jewels. Their blessing is pervasive, but it is our faith that opens us to it.

3
Karma and Outer Discipline

Positive acts bring joy,
Negative acts bring suffering.
Thus virtuous actions, nonvirtuous actions,
and their results are clearly revealed.

—*Smaller Smṛtipratyupasthāna Sūtra*

We penetrate the depths of Buddhadharma when we are sure about the inevitable relationship between the causes and effects of our activities, or what is known as karma. We have already discussed the general workings of karma[55] and how the six classes of beings of the three worlds, with their various kinds of joy and suffering, are actually illusory appearances that manifest by the power of karma.[56]

Karma can be negative, positive, or unmoving. Negative karma is generated by the performance of the ten negative actions, while positive karma results from the ten positive actions; unmoving karma is produced by certain meditative practices.[57] Karma, or, in this case, the results of each of our actions, is the basis of all Dharma discipline, which teaches about misdeeds and the unwholesome attitudes that create negative karma and the benefits of right action that leads to positive karma. Therefore, Dharma discipline is based on an understanding of karma, of abandoning negative actions as much as we can and cultivating positive ones.

NEGATIVE KARMA OF BODY, SPEECH, AND MIND
Negative activity, or bad karma, is made up of acts and their results which harm others and oneself or attitudes of body, speech, and mind produced by self-cherishing tendencies and afflicted behaviors that lead to desire, anger, pride, and so forth. These kinds of activities stimulate and in turn reinforce self-cherishing and afflicted tendencies, contributing to the perpetuation of samsara and the delusions that maintain it. Briefly, negative karma comes from the ten negative actions: three of body, four of speech, and three of mind.

The Different Types of Results of Actions
The different negative or positive acts have four main types of results called dominant or maturation results, results corresponding to the initial act, results corresponding to the initial experience, and governing results.

The dominant or maturation result is the first and strongest result of an

The Negative Tree
After an original drawing by Kyabje Kalu Rinpoche

Discipline based on karma is not morality demanding conformity to religious
commandments or a social code. Karma's perspective is more medicinal; its
prescriptions are like those of a health code preventing "spiritual diseases," which
are the illusions and afflictions and their painful results. The Negative Tree
illustrates the functioning of negative karma. Its roots are ignorance and the
mind's illusions, its trunk is the self-cherishing attitude, its branches are the
afflictive emotions, and its fruit is the painful states of existence.

action; it consists in taking rebirth in a realm corresponding to the nature of the act. So, the maturation result of the act of killing is rebirth in a hell realm.

When this first maturation result is exhausted, the karma will have further results corresponding to the initial act and the initial experience in a subsequent rebirth that could be as a human being. Results corresponding to the initial act consist in a predisposition to commit other similar acts. In the case of killing, it would be the propensity to take pleasure in killing.

Results corresponding to the initial experience consist of a tendency to experience situations in which we are subjected to what our own previous victim experienced. In other words, we ourselves may become the object of similar acts committed by others. In the case of killing, there would be a predisposition to have a short life, to be afflicted by illness, and to see ourselves robbed of life throughout many rebirths.

Environmental results condition the outer environment in which we take birth. Thus, for example, killing creates an outer world of dangerous precipices and abysses.

The Three Negative Acts of Body

KILLING

This is to take life: out of desire or attachment; to acquire riches, meat, bones, musk; to protect ourselves or our kin; out of hatred; to kill rivals or enemies; or just out of stupidity, for example—to sacrifice a live being and see that as a virtuous act.

STEALING

Taking what is not given can be done openly, by force or power; secretly, without being seen or recognized; or by trickery and deceit, for example, cheating with weights and measures.

The maturation result of these actions is birth as a hungry ghost; the result corresponding to the initial act is having a propensity for and taking pleasure in stealing; the result corresponding to the initial experience is to be robbed or to be poor and wanting; and the environmental result is to be born in a place with destructive weather conditions.

SEXUAL MISCONDUCT

This consists of violating domestic relationships, breaking our vows, or violating precepts. This would involve having sexual relations near or in a holy building or close to someone who holds a vow of chastity; or having sex when one has taken temporary vows of chastity or when a woman is pregnant; or having sex many times in a row.

The different consequences of these actions are, respectively, to be reborn as a hungry ghost or, if we are born as a human, to have an unpleasant partner who is like an enemy, to be unhappy with that person, and to always be attracted to other partners. Finally, the last result is to find ourselves in a dirty and dusty environment.

The Four Negative Acts of Speech

LYING

We might lie about our spiritual realization, to harm others, or for an unimportant reason.

The different results of lying are: to be born as an animal or, if one is reborn as a human, to have a tendency to lie, to believe to be true what is not true, and to be in a place where the terrain and climate are extreme.

DIVISIVE SPEECH

This might be done openly, in the presence of two friends whom we want to divide; indirectly and insidiously; or secretly, with one of the two parties involved.

The results of such activity are: to be born in a hell realm or, if we are born as a human, to enjoy sowing discord, to be separated from friends, and to be in a chaotic place.

HARSH SPEECH

Aggressive or harsh words wound and hurt others. They can be thrown at someone who is talking, mixed in with jokes, or spoken straightforwardly, for example, directly mentioning someone's faults to friends.

The different results of this act are: to be reborn immediately in hell; to take pleasure in maligning others; to hear unpleasant words or rumors about ourselves; and to find ourselves in a blazing, dry, and thorny environment.

IDLE CHATTER

This is to chatter or gossip, to talk a lot with no reason, or to explain Dharma to those with no respect for it.

The result of chattering idly is to be born as an animal or, if we are born as a human, to have the propensity to express ourselves in vulgar language, to say things that are unpleasant to others, and to be in a place where the climate is wild or unpredictable.

The Three Negative Mental Acts

COVETOUSNESS

Covetousness can take the form of great attachment to what already belongs to us—family, body, or possessions—or wishing to appropriate the property of others. It is also the desire to possess things that do not belong to anyone in particular.

The results of covetousness are: to be born as a hungry ghost or, in the case of a human rebirth, to be subject to many attachments without being able to attain or realize our wishes, and to be in an infertile area.

ILL WILL

Malevolence or ill will is the desire to harm, which can arise from anger, hatred, jealousy, or a grudge.

Its results are: birth in a hell realm or, if we are born as a human, to have an angry nature, to see ourselves as being treated as an enemy by everyone, with no reason, and to be in an unfriendly environment where living is difficult.

WRONG VIEW

Wrong views are mistaken conceptions that discredit the law of karma, or explanations of Dharma made from the point of view of relative and ultimate reality; they can also relate to the qualities of the Three Jewels.

These result in being reborn as an animal or, if we are born as a human being, to have no inclination to study, to be unintelligent and incapable of understanding anything, and to live in a place where nothing flourishes.

The Ten Particularly Negative Acts

Among the negative acts, it is particularly serious to:

1. Kill one's father, mother, or spiritual master;
2. Steal the property of the Three Jewels;
3. Have sexual relations with someone bound by vows not to;
4. Disparage a buddha or deceive our lamas with lies;
5. Create discord between members of the Sangha or between fellow students of Dharma;
6. Speak harshly to our parents or to a spiritually superior being;
7. Distract by meaningless chatter those who wish to practice Dharma;
8. Covet things intended for the Three Jewels;
9. Be so malevolent as to be able to commit the five heinous acts with immediate results, these being: to kill one's father, mother, or an arhat (on up); to create a schism in the Sangha; and to cause blood to flow from a tathāgata; and
10. Have sectarian views that lead to quarrels and conflicts.

The Positive Tree

The tree that grants all wishes
Takes root in a mind that turns away from samsara
And aspires only to liberation.
Faith and compassion form its trunk.
Abandoning harm and the practice of virtue are its branches,
While all the virtues are its leaves.
Its flowers are the realization of the qualities essential to meditation.
From these arise its fruit, the perfect state of buddhahood.

—Kyabje Kalu Rinpoche

POSITIVE KARMA OF BODY, SPEECH, AND MIND

Unlike negative karma, positive karma or beneficial acts proceed from the transcendence of self-cherishing attitudes and are based on feelings of love, compassion, goodness, and so forth. They direct us toward enlightenment and the attainment of buddhahood. The ten positive actions are the opposite of the ten negative ones already described.

The Three Positive Actions of Body

Protecting life and refraining from killing has as its maturation result birth in a divine or human realm. The result corresponding to the initial act is a disgust for killing and an inclination to protect and preserve life. The result corresponding to the initial experience is to have a long, happy, healthy life, endowed with various riches; the environmental result is to live in pleasant surroundings.

Refraining from stealing and being generous results in wealth and power, becoming a leader or influential person, and, within an ordinary human rebirth, a love of generosity, possession of wonderful treasures, and a luxurious environment.

Abandoning sexual misconduct and following proper sexual conduct results in birth in a divine realm or, if born as a human, having beautiful and gracious friends with whom we have a good relationship and with whom we are always satisfied, and being in a pleasing environment.

The Four Positive Acts of Speech

Not telling lies and telling the truth results in rebirth in the divine or human realm, enjoying speaking truthfully, seeing others understand our words as true, and living in a harmonious environment.

Not sowing discord and favoring consensus and harmony results in birth in a divine or human realm, always appreciating harmony, having everyone consider our words as true and pleasing, and living in an affluent environment where bad weather is infrequent.

Refraining from harsh speech and speaking kindly results in being born in a divine or human realm, hearing pleasant things about oneself, having a respectful entourage who praise us, and living in a place with a pleasant and temperate climate.

Refraining from idle chatter and speaking meaningfully result in being reborn in a divine or human realm, preferring to speak little, saying things that raise morale and please others, and living in an agreeable environment with moderate climate and pleasant terrain.

The Three Positive Mental Acts

Abandoning covetousness, being content, and knowing how to be satisfied with what we have results in rebirth in a divine or human realm, satisfaction with what we have, the happiness of having our wishes fulfilled, and living in a pleasing environment.

Abandoning ill will or the wish to harm, wishing others well, or being kind result in a divine or human rebirth, enjoying exerting ourselves in study, being respected for our intelligence and wisdom, and living in a fertile place with abundant delicious fruits.

The better we understand the nature of mind, the more deeply we can penetrate the inevitable chain of cause and effect which is karma. This understanding forms the basis of the practice of Buddha's teachings. It helps us on the one hand to avoid or minimize negative acts that cause suffering by harming others and ourselves, and on the other hand to cultivate and increase positive actions whose results are beneficial. In the context of real practice, negative karma decreases and positive karma increases; this way, we accumulate merit, followed by wisdom, and gradually we progress toward buddhahood.

BLACK AND WHITE PEBBLES

There once was a man by the name of Drakhen who had great faith in Dharma and who wanted to change his behavior and truly practice. Upon requesting his lama's advice, he was told to pay close attention to what he was doing: when he noticed that he had a negative attitude, he was to abandon it and place a black pebble in a cup, and when he observed himself doing something good, he was to place a white pebble in another cup.

At first, he had a cup full of black pebbles and very few white pebbles. Then, gradually, through his perseverance in paying close attention to abandoning negative attitudes and cultivating positive attitudes, the two cups had equal numbers of black and white pebbles. Finally, he had virtually all white pebbles.

With mindful vigilance and attention, we can change our behavior.

4

The Components and Results of Actions

The varieties of karma create the diversity of beings

—*Karmaśatākasūtra*

We have already commented on the relationship between afflictions and samsaric states of consciousness[58] and the ideas of collective and individual karma, as well as propelling karma that leads to a particular rebirth and the completing karma for that birth.[59] In the preceding chapters, we touched on the different types of karmic results: maturation results, results corresponding to the initial act and initial experience, and environmental results. Now we will go into the makeup of karma as it manifests in the specificity and intensity of results.

QUALITATIVE AND QUANTITATIVE DIFFERENCES

First of all, if indeed each of the six root mental afflictions produces specific karma corresponding to birth in one of samsara's realms, the overall intensity of the karma also determines this rebirth. While a karma that is mostly negative and powerful—the result of an accumulation of many harmful acts—leads to a hell realm, a karma that is negative overall but of medium intensity leads to a hungry ghost realm, and a generally negative karma that is committed with even less intensity leads to rebirth as an animal. On the other hand, if a karma is mostly positive, we will be reborn in one of the three higher realms because of the power of that positive karma.

The power of a specific act, wholesome or unwholesome, and that of the resulting happiness or unhappiness, depend also upon the quality of the being toward whom the act is done or intended. Moreover, with the act itself, the presence and absence of several factors intervene. So, the strength of a karma depends on the intention to do it, the action itself, its completion, and the feeling it causes afterward.

For example, the karmic power and the results of the action of killing would be strongest with several factors coming together: the spiritual quality of the victim,[60] the intention of committing the action, the premeditation of the murder, the attempt to murder, the actual killing, the resulting death, the satisfaction that it was accomplished, and the contentment of having killed. The presence of all of these elements gives the karma maximum power; when one, two, or three of these elements are missing, the karma's intensity and consequences are diminished correspondingly.

Similarly, for a positive act like giving, the quality and power depend on the quality of the being to whom one is giving; the intention and the benevolent motivation with which the gift is given; the gift itself (its appropriateness); the manner in which it is given (respectfully and properly); the result (the manner in which it is received); how it will benefit the recipient; and finally the resulting attitude of the giver (satisfaction without attachment to what has been given nor regret at having given).

There are also different ways of producing karma. We can do it actively, in a positive or negative manner; but one can also develop karma without acting physically, for example, rejoicing at the positive or negative actions of others.

THE KING AND THE BEGGAR

A great king had invited Buddha Śākyamuni and his entourage to his palace and presented them each day with many sumptuous offerings. Every evening, Buddha would utter a special dedication, mentioning the king's good deeds, of which the king was very proud.

One day a very poor old woman from a neighboring village arrived in the audience. In light of the king's generosity, she regretted having nothing to offer Buddha Śākyamuni and thought this was surely the result of previous lives, in which she must have been greedy and stingy, while the king must have been very generous to be able now to make all those offerings. She found the king's good deeds magnificent and, truly delighted with him, rejoiced sincerely in his activities.

That evening, at the time of the dedication, instead of mentioning the king's name as usual, Buddha Śākyamuni mentioned the old woman's name. Surprised, the king inquired after her.

Of course, Buddha Śākyamuni, knowing the king's mind as well as the old woman's, declared: "You have given great offerings to my disciples and me. This is a wonderful accumulation of merit,[61] but the fact is, this old beggar woman has collected even more merit, by her sincere joy in seeing you make these offerings."

The king was annoyed because the old woman had outdone him. So, a cunning minister devised a scheme to please his sovereign. He would attract the beggars with sumptuous food offerings, and then he would beat them. The old woman would then get angry at the king and would thereby collect very bad karma; that day, Buddha would not mention her name at the time of the dedication.

This story shows that a good deed depends more upon motivation and mental attitude than on the act itself.

The production of karma depends on the intention as well as on the action. A bad motivation can accompany a generally positive action, as in the case of an offering made in order to become famous. Inversely, a good motivation can accompany an act usually considered negative: this is the case if we spank or speak firmly to a child in order to assist him or her. In any case, motivation is the determinant.

WHEN BUDDHA WAS A CAPTAIN

In one of his previous lives, Buddha was captain of a ship. One day, as the ship was transporting five hundred merchants, a pirate came on board, intending to kill everyone in order to seize their riches. Overcome by great compassion for the pirate and for the merchants, and thinking that if the pirate actually followed through on his plan he would have to suffer for innumerable eons in hell, the captain decided, with an altruistic and compassionate motivation, to kill the pirate, thus saving the lives of the five hundred merchants. While he himself committed a murder, his sincerely altruistic and detached motivation was the source of enormous positive karma, because the action was beneficial.

A lie can also be positive in certain cases; for example, to save a life. If a murderer is looking for someone who he wants to kill and asks where that person is, to give him the wrong directions in order to save the person's life is good.

THE COMPONENTS AND RESULTS

The different constituents of our karma combine to produce results which are all our experiences. When the results of a karma are exhausted, the corresponding karma occurs; the first might be positive and the second negative, or the inverse.

For example, the combination of karmas already mentioned, such as having protected life in our own previous lives, results in the tendency to have a long life in the present. But if we were also violent and treated others badly, we might be sick frequently.

If, during a previous life, we were generous while wishing others harm, we might be rich in this life but also have many enemies. If, in a previous life, we abandoned sexual misconduct while still sowing discord, we might have the perfect partner but argue a lot and not get along.

If, in the past, we avoided using harsh words while coveting others' things, we might be treated well by all but be poor.

If we were generous in the past and made offerings while coveting the goods of others, we might be born rich but become poor in the same lifetime.

If we have practiced generosity only a little, we will subsequently be born poor, but if we have respected, honored, and protected our father, mother, and elders, we will still be powerful, praised, and respected by everyone.

If we have been generous but judged the Dharma displeasing, we will later be wealthy but misunderstand the teachings.

If we have previously done extremely powerful good deeds but also, under the sway of afflictions such as jealousy, made malevolent wishes, we might have a lot of wealth and power but use them to perform large-scale negative activities.

It is because of positive karma created in the past that we now have a precious human life with all the necessary qualities to be able to practice Dharma.[62]

5

The Karma of Meditation

The limitless and formless meditative states
cause one to experience Brahma's bliss and other divine states.

—Nāgārjuna, *Ratnāvalī*

The karma of this third main category[63] is not created by physical, verbal, or mental acts but by different states of mind in meditation.[64]

The karma produced in meditation is called unmoving karma; it proceeds from first having abandoned negative activities and practiced positive ones, which should have become habits. The causes of unmoving karma are different practices of mental stabilization, or *dhyāna* in Sanskrit; their results are rebirths in states of absorption corresponding to those of the mind. These meditation levels or mental absorptions make up the divine realms in the subtle-form and formless realms.

The cause of the karma of immobility, then, is a virtuous mind abiding in absorption on a single object. Its causes and results develop in eight stages, each of which has a preliminary, a practice, and a resulting state.

The first of these levels or stages of meditative absorption is characterized by an experience in which conception, evaluation, pleasure, and happiness are still present in the mind. Meditation at this stage establishes the mind in the first degree of absorption. When conception and evaluation no longer remain in one's practice, but pleasure and happiness still do, one has arrived at the second degree of absorption. When the experience of pleasure no longer remains, and there is nothing but happiness, one is established in the third degree of absorption. Finally, the state in which all conception, all evaluation, and any notion of pleasure or happiness are transcended, corresponds to the fourth degree of absorption. Realization of these four degrees of meditative absorption corresponds to birth in the four divine levels of the subtle-form realm.

Afterward, the subtle attachments of these first four degrees of absorption are transcended, and birth can occur in the formless realm, in one of four domains named for the formless-realm experiences that occur there. So, we can take birth in the realm of limitless space; then, transcending any attachment to this experience, we enter the domain of unlimited awareness, then the realm of nothingness, followed finally by the realm where there is no conception nor nonconception.

By recognizing the unsatisfactory nature and alienation of each level, we can eliminate our attachment to it and proceed through the next. Each successive level has fewer and fewer fixations. Although these eight absorptions are lofty meditative states, they still occur within samsara and therefore are conditioned by its illusions and subject to transmigration.[65]

Everything that exists within samsara is brought about by the three types of karma: negative, positive, and unmoving. All three are said to be contaminated because they imply a distinction between a subject, an object, and an action, and they condition all dualistic experiences.[66]

PART TWO

Section Three

The Mahāyāna:
Path of Opening and Compassion

Introduction

From *Hīnayāna* to *Mahāyāna*

On the Hīnayāna path, an altruistic motivation develops toward the benefit and happiness of all beings. When the mind of enlightenment, or bodhicitta, arises, the Hīnayāna path becomes the Mahāyāna path.

In the context of this compassionate motivation, the universal vehicle is the understanding and then the experience of all things as fundamentally illusory; their actual nature is emptiness. At the same time, because of this understanding, immense compassion springs forth spontaneously toward all sentient beings who suffer as prisoners of their illusions, deceived by their own projections. The understanding of emptiness and universal compassion are the two pillars of Mahāyāna Dharma.

I

Bodhicitta and the Bodhisattva Vow

When we have attained the limits of space,
When sentient beings are all enlightened,
When karma and the afflictions have all been exhausted,
Thus emptied, my vow will have come to an end.

—*Bhadracaryāpraṇidhāna*

Bodhicitta literally means "mind of enlightenment." It is a mental attitude of benefiting others, based on love and compassion. By becoming aware of the suffering of all sentient beings, we begin to feel genuine love and compassion for them.

This realization develops as we recognize the suffering of one person close to us toward whom we can easily feel compassion and good will. Wishing to rescue or help one single being and feeling love and compassion for that person is bodhicitta's point of departure, but the point is to feel more and more love and compassion for *all* beings—human and nonhuman, friends or enemies.

To awaken the mind of enlightenment, or bodhicitta, allows for rapid progress toward the state of buddhahood. In fact, practicing bodhicitta accumulates enormous positive karma. And, if being loving, compassionate, and benevolent toward one single being is extremely beneficial, then extending those attitudes to all sentient beings is infinitely more so! Buddha Śākyamuni taught that if the positive karma of practicing bodhicitta were visible, it would be so vast that all of space could not contain it. Thanks to the power of cultivating bodhicitta, it is possible to realize buddhahood in a single lifetime.

This benevolent and altruistic attitude of love and compassion is often called the philosopher's stone. Just as this stone transforms ordinary metals into gold, bodhicitta transforms all activities of ordinary life, whatever they may be, into activities that lead to enlightenment.

THE DIFFERENT ASPECTS OF BODHICITTA

Bodhicitta, the mind of enlightenment, has two levels: ultimate and relative. The realization of the fundamentally empty nature of all things is ultimate bodhicitta; the attitude of loving-kindness and compassion toward all sentient beings is relative bodhicitta.

At the ultimate level, bodhicitta is the experience of the pure nature of mind; it is the realization of selflessness, or emptiness. At the relative level, bodhicitta has two aspects: wishing bodhicitta and engaged bodhicitta.

Wishing bodhicitta is the wish to reach enlightenment for the benefit of all beings. On the basis of this motivation, it is necessary to proceed to actual practice. The aspiration to help others is not enough, just as it is not enough to want to go to a place in order to get there: it is necessary to travel the path. Engaged bodhicitta consists of practicing the six perfections or transcendent virtues.[67]

Buddha Pulling a Chariot in Hell

In one of his previous lives, Buddha was born in a hell realm, hitched to a chariot that he had to pull with another unfortunate companion. They tried with all their might but could not make it go forward. The guards had got nowhere flogging and stabbing them with their burning weapons. The task was beyond their ability.

The future Buddha had a profound feeling of compassion for his partner. He thought that, since they couldn't make the chariot move, it was useless for the two of them to suffer, and he told the guards, "Please free my companion, I shall pull the chariot myself." The guards became irritated, saying, "How can you possibly do the work alone when the two of you together can't do it?" Angry, they whipped him until he died. By the power of the karma of his good intention, he left the hell realms and was reborn in a celestial realm.

The Bodhisattva Vow

Bodhicitta is closely related to the bodhisattva vow. The activity of the bodhisattva is to develop bodhicitta. The person who does that is a bodhisattva, or one who has the courage to live bodhicitta.

Unique to the Mahāyāna, this activity of developing bodhicitta doesn't deal merely with a rule of conduct, as in the Hīnayāna, but with a state of mind, a motivation, an inner attitude. The essence of the bodhisattva vow is to renounce self-cherishing attitudes in order to engage in an attitude that is firmly directed toward others. This is compassion.

To embark upon the bodhisattva path is to be involved in exchanging oneself for others, or putting others before oneself, regarding them as just as important as and, ultimately, more important than oneself.

The Sacrifice of the Messenger

Once upon a time, seven people—six monks and one messenger—boarded a boat to cross a great river. When they arrived at the strongest current, the ferryman declared, "We are too heavy. If we don't do something, we'll sink! If anyone here knows how to swim, he should jump in the water; if not, I myself will have to jump and one of you will have to take the oars."

But no one knew how to swim, and no one was able to guide the boat at all. So the messenger said, "Rather than all of us die, it would be better if only one of us was sacrificed," and so he plunged into the water. At that moment, a rainbow appeared in the sky, along with a showering of flowers, and, although he didn't know how to swim, the messenger miraculously reached the other riverbank. This miracle occurred because of his extremely pure intention.

Reference is often made to three types of bodhisattvas who behave, respectively, like a king, a shepherd, and a ferryman.

One is like a king who leads all beings to enlightenment by going first, showing the way, as a chief or boss would.

One is like a ferryman who brings them and himself to the other shore together.

One is like a shepherd who drives the herd, letting all beings go before him.

These three attitudes correspond to the growing power of bodhicitta motivation, with the attitude of the shepherd being the most profound.

Because of its nature, the bodhisattva vow differs from the vows of outer discipline. The bodhisattva vow is like a golden pot, the others like earthen pots. When an ordinary commitment or earthen pot is broken, it has no more value; however, the bodhisattva vow, like a golden pot, can be remodeled and refashioned—its material remains precious.

2

Compassion

Just as the earth and the other elements abundantly and perpetually
provide for the needs of beings in myriad ways,
May I too, in as many ways possible,
Provide for the beings that fill space
until all of them have attained nirvana.

—Śāntideva, *Bodhicaryāvatāra*

Compassion, kindness, and love together form the essential Mahāyāna attitude. Their foundation is a non-self-cherishing frame of mind oriented toward others, aspiring to the well-being and happiness of all other beings, whether human or nonhuman, friends or enemies.

THREE LEVELS OF COMPASSION

There are three kinds of compassion: compassion with reference to beings; compassion with reference to reality; and compassion without reference. They occur consecutively.

Compassion with reference to beings arises when we perceive the suffering of others. It is the first kind of compassion to arise and causes us to strive deeply to do everything we can to help all those who suffer. It emerges when we perceive the pain and suffering of others. This form of compassion is marked by no longer being able to remain unmoved by the suffering of beings and by aspiring to do everything possible to help alleviate their suffering.

Compassion with reference to reality arises when we have a genuine experience of the power of ignorance, when we actually perceive how beings create their own suffering. This compassion occurs when we really see how others strive to be happy and avoid suffering but how, not understanding the causes of happiness nor the means of avoiding suffering, they produce more causes of suffering and have no idea how to cultivate the causes of happiness. They are blinded by their ignorance; their motivations and actions contradict one another. Through understanding the illusory nature of reality, genuine perception of this situation brings forth this second type of compassion, which is more intense and profound than the first kind.

Compassion without reference retains no notion of subject, object, or intention; it is the ultimate form of a buddha's or great bodhisattva's compassion and depends upon the realization of emptiness. There is no longer any reference to a "me" or "other." This compassion opens naturally and sponta-neously. It is important to be familiar with these three types of compassion, to understand their order, and to begin to work at the first level, which is the most accessible to us.

TONGLEN

We have transmigrated in cyclic existence an incalculable number of times, to the point where all beings have already been our father or mother. Buddha taught that they have been our parents an infinite number of times. To count the grains of sand on the earth is in the realm of possibility, but it is impossible to count how many times all beings have been our own parents.

In order to cultivate kindness and compassion toward all these beings, we first think about the love we have received from our own parents in this life, the manner in which they have raised, educated, helped, and protected us, and everything they have done for us. We then imagine how we would feel if the person most dear to us—usually our own mother—were in a state of intense suffering right in front of us. We couldn't remain unmoved; we would immediately do something to help her. That is how we discover a capacity for love and compassion, which is being receptive to others and wishing the best for them. With this attitude, we do the practice of *tonglen,* literally, "giving and taking," over and over, which trains us to mentally give all our virtues and happiness to another and to accept in exchange all their pain and suffer-ing. Initially, we practice this with the person closest to us, and little by little we extend our meditation to all beings, including even our enemies. Then, we consider that all beings in the universe, which have been from beginningless time our own parents, have felt this very same kindness toward us, this same love, and this same devotion.

If we can sincerely view them this way and realize that they are now in the ocean of samsara's suffering, then love, compassion, and the sincere wish to help them arise spontaneously.

MAITRI-YOGI AND THE DOG

There was once a great Kadam lama, Maitri-yogi, one of Atīśa's masters, who had a profound realization of bodhicitta. One day while he was giving teach-ings to his disciples, they heard a dog cry out, and then it suddenly stopped crying. At that very moment, Maitri-yogi gave a cry of pain, shrinking almost to the point of fainting.

Astonished, everybody questioned him. He revealed a large bruise on his back. Then he explained that someone had thrown a rock at the dog, whose suffering he had taken upon himself in order to spare the dog. His realization of bodhicitta was such that he had the capacity to literally take upon himself the suffering of others.

Compassion and kindness allow us to truly help others. When we can do something concrete to help someone, we do it easily; when we cannot, we become aware of our present inability to help in a meaningful way. We make the wish to progress toward enlightenment, to develop the qualities that would allow us to help in a real and profound way. In meditating like this again and again, we develop the aspiration to liberate all beings from their suffering and to establish them in a state of true happiness. It is in this way that bodhicitta develops.

UNIVERSAL LOVE

Buddha Śākyamuni, in his transcendent wisdom, taught about the six classes of beings and the suffering specific to each.

The agonies of extreme heat and cold rage in the hell realms; the hungry ghosts are tormented by hunger and thirst; in the animal realm, the suffering comes from stupidity and servility. With humans there is the suffering of birth, illness, aging, and death. The jealous gods suffer from their constant quarrels, and the gods from having to transmigrate and descend again to lower realms. All of samsara's beings deserve our love and compassion. Clear understanding extends our radiance toward all, without distinction, while incomplete understanding limits us to those touched by misery. In fact, we easily have compassion for the poor, but we think the rich, the powerful, and those who appear happy need not be objects of compassion.

Right compassion is directed toward all beings, including the rich and powerful. Like all beings, they have been our mothers and fathers in past lives; each has his or her suffering. Their present situation, their wealth or power, results from previous positive karma, but they are no less marked by a strong sense of ego and by many afflictions. It has been said by Buddha Śākyamuni:

> Desire is wealth's companion.
> Harmful actions are the companions of the powerful.

Desire and harmful actions lead them to lower realms and consequent suffering, so these people should be special objects of our compassion.

At first, we try through meditation to engender compassion and cultivate the wish to help a person toward whom it is easy to feel this way. Afterward, we expand this attitude of loving-kindness to others, to everyone we meet in our daily life, then, little by little, to all humans and nonhumans, and finally even toward those for whom it is most difficult, our enemies and those who hate us, without exception.

The Meeting of Asaṅga and Maitreya

Asaṅga was on retreat practicing meditations on Buddha Maitreya. After six years of intensive meditation, he had not had the least bit of success. Discouraged, he gave up his retreat and departed. On the way, he encountered a man who was rubbing an iron rod with a cloth. "What are you doing?" Asaṅga asked him. The man responded, "I am rubbing this iron bar so I can sharpen it, because I need a needle." Stupefied by this man's energy and perseverance, he thought, "So much diligence for something so trivial. How can I give up the most meaningful practice?" So he returned to his retreat and began again to meditate on Maitreya for three years, still with no success whatsoever. Again discouraged, he left his retreat and, while on the road this time, he met a man who was rubbing a huge rock with a great feather. "What are you doing?" Asaṅga asked him. "This rock casts a shadow on my house, so I am rubbing it to wear it down and make it disappear."

Once again Asaṅga said to himself, "How could anyone waste so much energy on something so absurd?" And he felt he was a failure, he who was practicing in order to reach enlightenment...so again he went into retreat. Three years later, still with not the least sign of success in his practice, utterly discouraged, he departed. Making his way along the road, he came across a very old, sick dog whose body was covered with oozing sores infested with maggots that she was desperately trying to get rid of. Overwhelmed by intense compassion for this old dog, Asaṅga wanted to help her but realized that by removing the maggots with his fingers, he was crushing them. Feeling equally great compassion for the maggots, he decided he could spare them as well if he removed them with his tongue. Overcoming his revulsion, he closed his eyes and leaned over to lick them off. But instead of finding wounds, his tongue touched the sun. He opened his eyes and saw Buddha Maitreya encircled in a halo of light. Stunned, Asaṅga said, "For twelve years I have been meditating on you, desperate to meet you, and only now you appear?" Maitreya explained that he had been at his side from the beginning, but that the many obscurations darkening his mind until now had prevented Asaṅga from seeing him, and that it was not until today, with the great compassion he'd felt for the old dog, that the darkness had lifted. Maitreya added, "If you have any doubts, take me on your shoulders, and let's go to the village." Asaṅga took Maitreya on his shoulders, and, as he met up with villagers, he asked them gleefully: "Do you see who's on my shoulder?" But no one saw anything. There was only one old woman whose karma was particularly good, who saw an old sick dog with oozing sores!

Asaṅga became a great Mahāyāna master, and Maitreya transmitted to him the sequence of teachings known as *Maitreya's Five Teachings*.

THE EIGHT ASPIRATIONS OF A GREAT BEING
Text composed by Kyabje Kalu Rinpoche

1
By the power of the truth and goodness of the supreme refuges,
And by virtuous actions and a pure motivation,
May I, with all my heart, exert myself in removing
The myriad sufferings of beings filling space.

2
By the excellence of virtuous activities
Of this world and beyond,
May I, according to the needs of each,
Satisfy the hopes and aspirations of all beings.

3
May my body, flesh, and blood,
Everything I am made of,
Contribute in the most appropriate way
To the welfare of all sentient beings.

4
May the suffering of all beings,
My previous mothers,
Dissolve in me,
And may they have my joys and virtues.

5
However long this world lasts,
May I never have,
Even for a single instant,
A malevolent thought toward another.

6
May I always strive with energy
For the welfare of beings,
Without relaxing my efforts
In times of sadness, exhaustion, or other obstacles.

7

For those who are hungry or thirsty,
For the poor and needy,
May I naturally lavish on them
The abundance they wish for.

8

May I bear the heavy load
Of the terrible suffering of beings
Of the hells and other realms,
And may they all be free.

3
Emptiness, Heart of Compassion

Scriptures say that both wisdom lacking means
and means lacking wisdom are bondage.
Therefore do not abandon either.

—Atiśa, *Bodhipathapradīpa*

Whoever has received bodhisattva vows gradually learns relative bodhicitta—love and compassion—and ultimate bodhicitta—the experience of emptiness. Finally, he or she practices the union of emptiness and compassion.

FROM COMPASSION TO EMPTINESS

The inner attitude of compassion begins, as we have already discussed,[68] when we become aware of the suffering of those near and dear to us. It then gradually extends to universal love. The bodhisattva who practices this way gradually eliminates every self-cherishing attitude and cultivates a state of mind truly oriented toward others. This is relative bodhicitta; it is the introduction for going beyond ego or self to nonself, or selflessness, which is emptiness.

EMPTINESS: TWOFOLD SELFLESSNESS

By practicing as described in scriptures and meditation instructions,[69] we can arrive at the absolutely certain conclusion of no-self.[70] This understanding begins with the subject's own experience of the self's nonexistence: the self or "me" has no inherent existence.

What we generally call "our mind"—me, the subject—has no characteristics in terms of forms, colors, or anything else. It is not an autonomous *thing*, nor can it actually be identified; it is indeterminate and undefinable. This lack of existence as an independent and definable thing is what we call its emptiness. But it is not that mind is empty because it is nothing at all, since it is knower of all things and creator or producer of the various thoughts and emotions. By investigating and examining through direct experience, we can gradually develop a sure understanding of the nature of mind and the absence of a self-subject.

Moreover, objects in the outer world—everything that manifests to us as forms, tastes, objects of touch, or objects of knowledge—are projections of this mind, which is emptiness. All its experiences are by nature similar to an illusion or dream. They involve the interaction of interdependent factors and lack inherent existence. Meditation gives rise to the unquestionable conclusion that all objects of knowledge lack an autonomous entity or a "self-object."

The lack of an autonomous entity, a self, in objects in the outer world as well as in the subject, is the twofold selflessness. To abide absorbed in that experience is to meditate on the perfection of wisdom, or ultimate bodhicitta.

FROM EMPTINESS TO COMPASSION

All beings who have not realized the meaning of this twofold selflessness have been our parents, our dear ones, our children; they have watched over and helped us. Blinded by their ignorance, not recognizing the nature of reality or the two kinds of selflessness, they are deluded by the basic propensity that causes them to cling to an "I" where none actually exists, and to take as "other" that which is not.

This subject-object, me-other dichotomy gives rise to all mental afflictions, which cause beings to continue to behave in harmful ways, thus prolonging the cycles of lives, and to experience the endless suffering of the six realms. No one wants to suffer, yet beings perform harmful actions, which are the very causes of suffering. Although everyone strives to be happy, they are incapable of achieving happiness, since they don't know that its source is the practice of virtues! A profound understanding and experience of this paradoxical and painful situation fills us with compassion for them. This example shows how an initial understanding of emptiness can grow into profound compassion.[71]

The bodhisattva meditates this way on the union of emptiness and compassion and, finally, on emptiness which has compassion at its heart. This is the foundation of Mahāyāna practice, the flawless path that leads to buddhahood.

MILAREPA ATTACKED BY DEMONS

One day, upon returning to his hermitage while on retreat, Milarepa found himself face to face with a horde of terrifying demons with eyes as big as saucers. The demons made a display of their powers, causing the sun to tremble and creating all sorts of horrifying manifestations. Milarepa attempted to drive them away in various ways: he prayed to his lama Marpa, meditated on his protective deity, threatened the demons, and tried all kinds of strategies. The demons mocked him, saying, "Judging from his attitude, it seems he's lost his equanimity and we've rattled him."

So Milarepa said to himself, "Marpa Lodrupa taught me that all appearances are projections of the mind and that the nature of these projections is empty and clear; to look upon these demons as 'out there' and to wish to drive them away is illusion." Realizing that the nature of mind cannot in any way be affected by its manifestations, and that mind abides unchanged even when faced with the worst, most petrifying demons, he understood them instead to be the expression of his own fixations and dualistic thinking. So, overcoming his fears, he accepted their visitation and generated authentic compassion for them.

Milarepa then said to himself, "If these demons want my body, I'll offer it to them. Life is fleeting; it's a good thing I can make such a great offering right now."

This attitude of profound compassion and understanding of emptiness appeased the demons, and finally their leader said to Milarepa, "Thinking you were afraid of us, we thought we could harm you, but if the thought 'demons' never arises in your mind, you have nothing to fear." After that, they vanished.

4

The Two Accumulations

The accumulations of merit and wisdom
are the perfect causes of enlightenment.

—Atiśa, *Bodhipathapradīpa*

All Dharma practices can be categorized as purification and accumulation, that is, the purification of the veils[72] that obscure the mind and the practice of the two accumulations of merit and wisdom. This process can be illustrated with the following image. Veiled or obscured, mind is like a sky darkened by clouds that cover its infinite vastness and brightness. The two accumulations are like the wind that dissipates these clouds, revealing the immensity and clarity of pure mind.

THE ACCUMULATION OF MERIT

The accumulation of merit includes all benevolent and beneficial activities done for others as well as ourselves. These are actions that generate positive karma. What we call good deeds include all positive actions of body, speech, and mind: generosity, discipline, all Dharma activities, and so forth. For the accumulation of merit, the act itself is important, but the underlying motivation is even more important; any act motivated by love and compassion is therefore a source of great benefit.

If we continually perform positive activities with the right motivation, we become happy and create what actually produces happiness: the accumulation of merit.

MOTHER AND DAUGHTER DROWN

A mother and her daughter were crossing a river, holding each other by the hand. Suddenly, the strong current carried them away. They stayed together, clutching each other, but there they were, just about to drown. The mother thought, "It doesn't matter if I die, but at least let my daughter be saved!" And the daughter said to herself, "Please let my mother live, even if I have to die!"

Finally, they both drowned, but by the power of their positive and altruistic motivations, they were both reborn in a heavenly realm.

THE ACCUMULATION OF WISDOM

The second accumulation is the accumulation of wisdom, which develops on the basis of an accumulation of merit, just as a seed grows in fertile soil.

Wisdom is direct experience of reality beyond dualistic illusions. These two accumulations—positive deeds, or merit, and wisdom—are complementary and give rise to each other sequentially; the first being right action, or beneficial activities, and the second, the nondual experience of pristine awareness, which develops in meditation practice.

Practically speaking, these two accumulations can also be practiced simultaneously. For example, if you give money to a beggar, your generosity is a good deed that serves as an antidote to any stinginess or attachment you might have. If, however, you give with the understanding that giver, gift, and recipient all lack inherent existence, and so during the "giving" no distinction is made, this action strengthens wisdom as well.

If the right activity of the accumulation of merit is obvious enough to be applied and practiced by everybody, the accumulation of wisdom is more delicate. It is a subtle practice that demands as much skill from the student as from the teacher.

So at first it is useful to concentrate our energies on the accumulation of merit and thereby prepare the ground for wisdom, which develops later with meditative experience.

Meditation is fundamental to Dharma practice, but it should always be done together with the accumulation of merit. One of the accumulations without the other leads to errors and impasses. The two are indispensable: good activities without wisdom cannot lead to perfect enlightenment. Practiced together, the two accumulations facilitate each other, and doing them in conjunction leads to enlightenment. The accumulation of merit is like a traveler's legs, the accumulation of wisdom like eyesight: they are complementary, and both are absolutely necessary to reach buddhahood.

5

The Six Perfections

Subāhu, in order to attain perfect enlightenment quickly,
a bodhisattva mahāsattva should always
and continuously practice the six perfections.
What are they?
Generosity, discipline, patience, energy, meditation, and wisdom.

—*Subāhuparipṛcchāsūtra*

Bodhisattva practices, or "bodhicitta in action" based on bodhicitta motivation, involves exercising the six transcendent virtues or perfections, which are: generosity, discipline, patience, energy, meditation, and wisdom.[73]

GENEROSITY

The practice of giving, or generosity, is the first perfection. A distinction is made between offerings made to the Three Jewels and gifts intended for all beings.

Offerings

Knowing and calling to mind the qualities of the Three Jewels, we can make different kinds of offerings with great faith. Traditionally, we make symbolic offerings: pure water, flowers, incense, light (butter lamps, candles, and so forth), perfumed water, delicious and aromatic foods, and beautiful sounds and melodies. We can also offer the Sangha food, clothes, lodging, other material goods or necessities, or different ornaments for temples.

A second category of offerings, those produced by the mind, can include everything that has existed forever, divine or human lands with earth, mountains, rivers, oceans, all bodies of water, meadows, prairies, forests, fruits, fertile fields, homes, foods, clothing, silk, brocade, jewels, all goods or possessions, young men and women, domestic animals, deer, pets, birds, and wild animals.

In fact, we can make mental offerings by imagining magnificent objects, beautiful sounds, exquisite fragrances, delicious flavors, gentle touches, every object of knowledge pleasing to the mind, as well as the various actual or symbolic offerings such as the eight auspicious symbols, the seven royal attributes of temporal power, the eight auspicious substances, and so on. Imagining that all these offerings extend throughout space, we present them to the Three Jewels and the Three Roots.[74]

What is the purpose of these offerings? The lamas, buddhas, and bodhisattvas to whom we offer them have completed the two accumulations of merit and wisdom and therefore have realized the actual nature of all things. Having actualized supreme understanding, they have mastered and freed their minds and are utterly devoid of dualistic grasping or attachment to offerings. Nevertheless, because they are sublime, they happily accept offerings so the positive karma of those who have faith in them can increase. Because they have this love and these abilities, if we make offerings to them with faith and respect, we can complete our own accumulation of merit and achieve the accumulation of wisdom. Making offerings allows us to increase the two accumulations.

The seed of a tree carries the potential for fruit through the interactions of various interdependent factors like earth, water, sunlight, and air. Similarly, the sublime nature of those to whom we make offerings, their benevolent acceptance, the excellence of the offerings, and the fervent devotion that motivates us to make offerings together form a group of beneficial agents and causes. By practicing these together our whole lives, we complete the two accumulations, which in turn yield the fruit: the three bodies of the Buddha.[75]

Giving

Giving is inspired by compassion toward all beings tossed about by the waves of illusory appearances. There are four main kinds of giving:

1. Giving material things: giving food to the hungry, drink to the thirsty, clothes to those who have none, and things to the poor and needy.
2. Giving protection: offering a refuge to those who are frightened, medicine to the sick, and so forth.
3. Giving love: comforting the unhappy. With great love we can give away our things and even our body.
4. Giving Dharma: whispering into the ears of sentient beings the names of Buddha, holy syllables, and mantras, or giving Dharma teachings and instructions to those who desire them, and so on.

The objects of giving are beings, the cause is great compassion, and the activity is the four types of giving. Practicing generosity ensures the completion of the two accumulations. Its result is twofold: gaining the dharmakāya ourselves and the two form bodies that manifest to help beings.[76]

GESHE BEN AWAITS HIS PATRONS

There once was a Geshe Ben, who, while waiting for some important patrons to arrive for a visit, started to clean up his place, arranging lovely offerings on his altar to impress his guests and have them think well of him. When he had finished, he realized that his motivation had not been right at all, and so he threw some dirt from the ground on his offerings. When they arrived, his benefactors were disconcerted, but grateful for Geshe Ben's honesty. It is said he could not have made a better offering.

When making any offering, we should check our motivation.

DISCIPLINE

Through the different vows—refuge, layperson's, minor and major monastic, bodhisattva, and Vajrayāna—we abandon negative behaviors or any actions that cause harm and lead, directly or indirectly, to disturbance for ourselves and others. We avoid transgressing these vows and maintain discipline continuously. This is the foundation for the happiness and well-being of others. Maintaining discipline is calming and causes us to take mindful precaution, so that afflictions are weakened while faith, energy, and wisdom increase. Discipline facilitates the achievement of the two accumulations.

PATIENCE

Patience is the ability to endure, through faith, compassion, or understanding emptiness, all the suffering and misfortunes we might encounter, whatever their cause. These might be inflicted on us directly or indirectly, by beings who err because of dualistic illusory appearances, by ignorant beings bound by the notion of ego, by our own minds overpowered by afflictions, or by interruptions or obstacles opposing our Dharma practice.

EFFORT

When we practice Dharma on the path to liberation, whether listening to teachings, reflecting, or meditating on them, great effort is required to overcome cold, hunger, thirst, and various other difficulties and to abandon all desire for comfort, all distraction, and all suffering.

KHARAK GOMCHUNG'S BUSH

There was once a meditator named Kharak Gomchung who practiced in an isolated area. At the entrance to his retreat hut, there was a spiny bush that caught his clothes each time he walked by.

"One day," he said to himself, "I'll have to cut this bush down," but, always keeping impermanence in mind, he quickly returned to his practice.

For years he meditated with energy and without distraction. When he left his retreat, the bush was still there, but Kharak Gomchung had become a realized master.

MEDITATION

Meditation practice, according to the literal meaning of the Tibetan term, is "mental stabilization." In order to develop a stable mind, it is necessary to begin by abandoning attachment to sense objects and distracting activities. To do this, we enter into retreat, restraining our desires and learning to be satisfied with what we have. We sit down in the meditation posture and observe perfect silence; this way the mind can learn to abide in single-pointed concentration, whether on lucid emptiness, absence of fixation, the coming and going of the breath, contemplation of an aspect of Buddha, seed syllables, points of light, or other objects of meditation.

To let the mind abide in single-pointed concentration is the practice of meditation. At first, mind has neither focus nor discipline, and it cannot remain fixed on one thing for even an instant; various thoughts constantly distract it. By keeping the attention on one thing, mind acquires power over itself, which is the purpose of the practice. This is the training on mental tranquility, or *samatha* in Sanskrit.[77]

There are numerous levels of mental stabilization: the four main ones are characterized by the presence or absence of conception, discrimination, joy, and happiness.[78]

Through stabilizing the mind in meditation, bliss develops in the body and mind while habitual faults are erased and many qualities manifest.

Finally, we gain clarity about ultimate reality, or self-knowing pristine awareness. Here we gain the first bodhisattva ground, then the next, and so on; the qualities that blossom are as vast as the ocean.[79]

TRANSCENDENT WISDOM

As we've already seen,[80] all objects of knowledge are illusory appearances of relative truth. They are emptiness, that is, they have no autonomous reality. But they are also lucidity, because, though empty, they appear in their myriad aspects. Their manifestation is similar to the following eight examples of illusion: they have the fleeting nature of what is impermanent and changeable and are like an illusion, a dream, a moon reflected in water, a rainbow, a shadow, a mirage, a reflection in a mirror, and an echo. If we recognize this, we transcend our fixation on them as real and are no longer attached to them.

In ultimate reality, the knower itself, the one who projects all these appearances has neither beginning, end, nor locality. It is not an object of knowledge that can be characterized in terms of its form, color, and so forth. It cannot be determined as one or many, existent or nonexistent, created or uncreated, appearance or nonappearance. Its essential nature is emptiness, which is like celestial space.[81]

Recognizing the deceptive nature of appearances and the knowing mind that projects them is the perfection of transcendent wisdom. It is crucial to have a direct experience of this, and this realization must also be stable, with the mind resting single-pointedly in it, because merely understanding it intellectually has no liberating power whatsoever.

A fledgling practitioner does not have, at birth, the power to fly to the firmament of enlightenment. In order to get there, he must protect himself from dangers through disciplined conduct, build up his strength through generosity, remain in the nest of meditation, and maintain continuous and enthusiastic effort. It is only after having practiced transcendent wisdom that he can finally take flight. Similarly, with the help of the other five virtues to cultivate transcendent wisdom, we will have a stable realization of it and will attain buddhahood.

Without the realization of the meaning of perfection of wisdom, we are like a bird without wings. We may have all the strength, or the first five perfections, necessary to reach higher realms, but we won't be able to reach nirvana, or buddhahood.

Without authentic transcendent wisdom—that is, without an understanding of profound emptiness—generosity, discipline, patience, effort, and meditation cannot really, in the strictest sense, be called perfections or transcendent virtues, because they alone cannot cause us to transcend samsara's illusions.

In fact, it is only with transcendent wisdom—the realization of the illusory nature of subject, object, and action—that the other virtues become transcendent, or perfections, and thus causes of attaining buddhahood.

What is called perfection occurs when what needs to be eliminated has been, and there is nothing else to look for; having shifted from illusion to perfection, the whole practice is accomplished.

THE CRIMES AND TESTS OF MILAREPA

Milarepa's father, a wealthy man from Ngari, died when Milarepa was very young, leaving him alone with his mother and sister. Milarepa's greedy uncle took over the entire inheritance and left them in a state of abject poverty.

So, Milarepa's mother begged him to take revenge on the uncle, exhorting him to learn magic. He learned to cast spells and curses, to make hail, and finally, when his uncle and aunt had a feast, he used his magic to make their house collapse, killing thirty-five guests, including the uncle's son and daughter-in-law. He also took revenge on the people of the country who had mistreated him, by bringing on hailstorms that devastated crops and animals.

After committing these wrongs, he realized that their karmic consequences would come and, overcome with regret, decided to exert himself in Dharma practice. Initially, he met a lama who taught dzogchen, the "great perfection," and received from him the teachings in which it is said, "If you meditate all day, you are Buddha all day. If you meditate at night, you are Buddha at night." Milarepa thought, "I had success with magic right away, and now I receive teachings that allow me to become a buddha instantly. I must have really good karma!"

He relaxed and practiced nothing. After a few days, the lama said to him, "You told me when you came here that you had done many bad things; it is true, and I have taught you in vain. I will no longer guide you, but go and see Marpa the Translator. You have a connection with him."

Merely upon hearing the name Marpa, Milarepa quivered with joy and left to find him.

At this time, Marpa and his wife were having dreams that Milarepa would come. While waiting for him, Marpa went to plow his field. When Milarepa arrived, he didn't know whom he was supposed to deal with, so he asked a laborer where Marpa the Translator lived. Marpa replied, "I'll tell you, but first finish plowing this field."

He gave Milarepa a pitcher of beer and left. Milarepa drank all the beer and plowed the field. When he had finished, Marpa returned and introduced himself. Milarepa prostrated before him and confessed all his crimes, saying, "I offer you my body, speech, and mind; please accept me and teach me."

Marpa said to him, "I can't help you if you've done a lot of bad things. You can't have it all. Either I give you food and clothing and you go elsewhere for teachings, or I give you teachings and you provide for your own needs."

Milarepa said, "Fine, since I came for Dharma, I'll find food and clothing somewhere else."

Some time later he went begging in the area and received a lot of barley, which he used to buy a copper pot with four handles, and returned to offer it all to Marpa. Upon arriving before Marpa and putting down his heavy load, Milarepa made the house tremble. Marpa arose, furious, "Do you intend to kill us by destroying this house? Get that barley out of here!" Then Milarepa offered him the empty copper pot.

At another time, Marpa said to him, "Some of my disciples who come here from central Tibet have been attacked and robbed on their way here. Send hail to all those who have attacked and robbed them. Do this for me and I'll give you the instructions."

Milarepa did as he was told and returned, requesting the instructions.

"Do you think I'm going to give you the precious teaching that I went to great lengths to bring back from India, for a few hailstorms you've brought down?" Marpa asked. "If you want instructions, cast a spell on those who have beaten my disciples and disrespected me. Then I will give you the teachings of Nāropa that bring enlightenment in this lifetime."

Once again, Milarepa used his magic. When signs of success manifested, he returned, again requesting teachings.

"Don't think I'm going to give you my teachings for having gone and done such evil deeds! If you want the teachings, first give the farmers back all those crops you destroyed with hail and revive all the animals you killed. Then I'll give you the instructions. If not, get out of here!"

Desperate, Milarepa broke down in tears. The following day, Marpa came looking for him, saying, "I got a bit excited last night. Since you certainly know how to work, build a house for my son Darmadode, and then I'll give you the teachings."

Milarepa, uncomfortable about the results of all his past wrongs, asked him: "But what if I die first?"

Marpa assured him that this would not occur and that if he practiced his instructions, he could attain enlightenment within his lifetime. So Milarepa went and built the house, a round one facing east, which he was ordered to destroy when it was half done, then he built one in the shape of a half-moon facing west, which he was also instructed to demolish when it was near completion, and finally a rectangular one facing north. Each time they were halfway built, Marpa came, scolding Milarepa, claiming that it wasn't what he had told him to do, that he had been mistaken or drunk when he had heard the orders. So he made Milarepa demolish the houses and replace each stone exactly where he had found it. From his labors, an enormous wound opened on Milarepa's back, but he didn't dare show it, fearing that he would again bring down Marpa's wrath.

Damema, Marpa's wife, interceded on his behalf, and Marpa invited Milarepa for lunch. He then gave him refuge and told him about the life and tests of his master Nāropa, saying, "If you want these teachings, you should do as he did." Milarepa felt a devotion so intense it made him weep.

A short time later, Marpa pointed out a place to the southeast and told Milarepa, "Go build a house there with nine floors and a roof. I promise this one won't be demolished, and afterward I'll give you the teachings."

Milarepa began. One day as he was working, some old students of Marpa's came and, to amuse themselves, made a huge boulder roll down, which they then inserted at the base of the wall. Even though Milarepa had already finished two levels of the house, Marpa came over and asked, "Where did that huge rock come from?" Milarepa told him what had happened. "My great disciples are not there to serve you," Marpa replied, "so lift that rock and return it to its place." Milarepa had to demolish what he had done in order to extract the rock, after which Marpa asked him to reinsert it into the building. When he had finished the seventh story, he had a large sore at his waist. Marpa told him to stop work on that building and to build a house with a temple in front of it. Milarepa carried out the instructions, but he soon broke out in new sores.

At this time, some of Marpa's disciples arrived to request the initiation of two important meditational buddhas, Cakrasamvara and Guhyasamāja. Milarepa thought that all this work entitled him to participate in the initiation, and he took his place in the assembly. Furious, Marpa chased him out with blows.

Milarepa's back was still covered with sores, but again he took up his work, making sure to carry the stones in a different way. Some time later, another disciple came to Marpa to request the Hevajra initiation.

Damema had given Milarepa a turquoise that belonged to her to use as an offering in order to receive the initiation, so he presented himself to Marpa yet again. But again Marpa beat him and chased him away.

Totally desperate, thinking he would never receive any teachings, Milarepa left. He was then hired by a family to give a reading of the *Prajñāpāramitā* texts, in which he read the story of Taktungu, a master who, to please and obey his lama, exerted himself with extraordinary diligence. The story made him reflect, and he returned to Marpa, who received him even more harshly. Feeling sorry for Milarepa, Damema sent him, without Marpa's knowing, to one of his teaching disciples, but not having Marpa's approval, her action was fruitless. Moreover, after learning what had happened, Marpa ordered him to return and scolded both Milarepa and Damema.

Seeing that in addition to his own misfortune he had now created some for Damema, in total despair Milarepa said to himself, "Since I do nothing but one bad thing after another without ever receiving the teachings, it's better if I disappear." As he was about to take his own life, Marpa's disciple, who had given him teachings, talked him out of it just in time. Learning this, Marpa was brought to tears to see Milarepa in such desperation. He gave him teachings and initiations, calling him from then on Mila Chepa Dorje. Afterward, Milarepa practiced the teachings with extraordinary energy, living alone in caves and eating only nettles. He attained ultimate realization and became Tibet's best-known yogi, a model for all practitioners of great devotion and effort.

6

Śamatha-Vipaśyanā

The state of nondistraction
Is the body of meditation; teach yourself thus.
The essence of every thought that arises is pristine awareness.
In the meditator who abides in uncontrived simplicity,
Inspire a meditation free from intellection!

—Pengar Jamphel Sangpo, *Short Invocation of Vajradhara*

MEDITATION

Meditation is the tool that allows us to recognize the nature of mind, its thoughts and afflictions, and to attain peace, happiness, and freedom.

We are prisoners and suffer, ultimately, because we are not aware of what is really happening when mind thinks or feels. Not understanding the emptiness of mind and its productions, we find ourselves exposed to emotional problems and subject to their painful conditioning.

In the West in particular, the main source of suffering is of a mental sort. Westerners are tormented by many afflictions, agitated, and often joyless. To alleviate this, several things can be done. Buddha Śākyamuni once said that working with the passions is like handling thorns. If the whole world were covered with burrs and we wanted to walk, we would have two choices: to lift the burrs off our path, which would be rather bothersome, or to wear a pair of thick-soled shoes. Likewise, confronted by our own afflictions, we can use a similar method: deal with each situation at a superficial level, or understand the nature of the mind and the mental afflictions, which provides protection and freedom, allowing us to deal with all situations without any problem.

ANALYTICAL AND CONTEMPLATIVE MEDITATION[82]

There are two main important and useful types of meditation. The first is an intellectual, analytical approach, the second an intuitive, contemplative approach.

In the first approach, we receive instructions from a teacher, then we study and practice them by reflecting on what has been taught and comparing it with our personal experience in order to validate it or not. We examine and analyze at a conceptual level what we have been told in order to determine its correctness. This is very beneficial, but it does not yield an authentic experience of the nature of mind.

Thus, there is a need for a second, intuitive, immediate approach, which entails perceiving the nature of mind without searching intellectually. Unlike the analytical approach, which has an objectifying nature—mind searching itself—this second approach consists of abiding in the state of "bare awareness" in which the basic nature of mind reveals itself "from itself to itself."

Rather than consciously searching for what mind is, we open ourselves to the immediate revelation of its nature. There is no one who searches and nothing to search; there is no subject or object, only a state of awareness in which mind's nature is revealed. At this level, we no longer observe mind as in analytical meditation, but instead we see it without looking and understand it without thinking.

Śamatha, Vipaśyanā, and Mahāmudrā

In the usual approach to meditation, first comes the practice known as calm abiding, or *śamatha* in Sanskrit and *shi-ne* in Tibetan. In it we learn to remain tranquil, to leave the mind in a state in which thoughts and afflictions are pacified. Śamatha allows the mind to rest without distraction, peaceful and calm.

Next comes insight meditation,[83] which leads the mind to recognize its own nature, to understand its emptiness, lucidity, and unobstructedness by direct experience. Mind recognizes itself by itself and finally reaches the experience of mahāmudrā.

There are, in fact, different approaches to śamatha and vipaśyanā: the ordinary level and the unique level of mahāmudrā, which is the ultimate form of vipaśyanā.

Let's take an example. Early on, śamatha practice stabilizes the mind, which is habitually agitated by its thoughts and emotions. Mind here is like the ocean during a storm; thoughts and emotions are its waves. Śamatha cuts short the energy sustaining the agitation, which in this example is like the wind. When the wind stops, the ocean settles. In the absence of stimulation, the previously agitated mind calms down. Mental agitation is the source of our illusions and painful conditioning, and we must learn to let it settle. Progress in śamatha introduces mind to a state of clarity, rest, and peace, which is also a blissful state.

The practice of vipaśyanā later allows us to recognize the very nature of mind. The mind at rest is like the ocean, and the perception of its nature is like the reflection of the moon in its waters. An ocean agitated by waves cannot clearly reflect the moon, but if the ocean is still, the moon will be reflected precisely. When mind reaches a state of complete stillness, its profound nature can be revealed. Stillness of mind corresponds to śamatha, and the experience of mind's nature to vipaśyanā.

Another example illustrating the complementarity of śamatha and vipaśyanā compares the ocean of mind to troubled waters made opaque by the agitation of thoughts and emotions, which are like sludge. Śamatha practice stops the mental agitation, and, just as waters settle and become limpid, mind becomes clear and transparent. This transparency of mind allows us to see its depths, just as it is possible to see into the depths of an ocean with clear waters. This profound vision is like vipaśyanā practice. The practice of śamatha is therefore a necessary preliminary to the practice of vipaśyanā.

Silent meditation without form or object is the essential aspect of śamatha; the experience of pure attention without object develops tranquillity and stability of mind as the first experience of mind's nature. But it is at the vipaśyanā level—clear seeing or insight—that mind's emptiness is actually realized, in a completely nonconceptual experience free of all reference and mental fabrication. Beyond mental constructs, it is simply the direct experience of the intangibility of mind. This is not something we can experience at the start, because in the beginning our practice is inevitably blended with mental fabrications. But vipaśyanā gradually leads the mind toward the experience of emptiness and intangibility, free of all conceptions. When the practice of śamatha-vipaśyanā becomes stable, it introduces us to the experience of mahāmudrā.[84] To understand what this entails, we have to discover it through experience, then slowly stabilize that experience through practice.

THE PRACTICE OF ŚAMATHA

The Tibetan word for śamatha is *shi-ne*. It is formed from two syllables: *shi*, which means "tranquil" and *ne*, which means "to remain" or "to abide." So shi-ne or śamatha is literally "tranquil abiding." The meaning of the word explains the meaning of this practice, which is to teach the mind to remain at rest, leaving alone the thoughts and emotions that agitate and disturb it.

There are several types of śamatha: with or without an object. Śamatha without an object is the practice of pure attention or vigilance. Śamatha with an object can use different objects. One of the best objects with the most advantages is the breath.[85]

Mental tranquillity alone is not proper śamatha practice. In fact, the quality of the mind at rest can vary a lot. It can be quite coarse, somewhat less coarse, or fine. The coarse level is like the animal state. Think of marmots—in the winter they hibernate, lethargic in their holes. They don't eat, urinate, move, or need anything. Their bodies can remain like this, without mental or emotional problems, for about six months. This is obviously not the state of tranquillity we're aspiring to! In śamatha meditation, tranquillity is a state in which mind is not in conflict with its thoughts; it is undisturbed and remains very clear and lucid. If the mind lacks clarity, it goes into a state of dullness, torpor, even sleep, and correct meditation is lost. The mind should be neither too tense, because then it is agitated, nor too lax, because then there is the risk of falling asleep.

MEDITATING LIKE THE STRING OF A VINA

Ānanda, Buddha Śākyamuni's well-known cousin disciple, was teaching meditation to a player of the vina (a kind of mandolin), but the musician was always either too tense and agitated or too relaxed and sleepy.

One day, he discussed it with Buddha Śākyamuni, who said, "You are a great vina player. Tell me how the strings of your vina should be in order to make the right sound."

"For the strings to vibrate harmoniously, they must have the right tension."

"Well, the same is true of your mind," Buddha replied. "To practice with the correct attentiveness, it should not be too tight, nor too relaxed."

As śamatha meditation deepens, experiences of bliss, clarity, or the absence of thoughts occur. These are indications that the practice is developing well, but it is vital not to fixate on these experiences. If they arise naturally, we should not become attached to them or try to reproduce them. If mind clings to the happiness that arises in śamatha meditation, it will be led toward higher states of consciousness called the divine states of the desire realm. If mind becomes attached to states of lucid clarity, we will be reborn in the divine states of the subtle-form realm. And finally, if it becomes attached to thought- and conception-free states, mind eventually enters into the divine formless realms.

All these meditative absorptions, though extremely lofty and subtle, do not lead to actual liberation, and it is important to be very careful not to become attached to these states, which are all samsaric.[86] True liberation cannot be gained except by the highest form of śamatha, which is related to the vipaśyanā experience: mind calmly abiding in the experience of its lucid, empty nature.

INSIGHT PRACTICE

We can meditate whenever we have time. Morning is a good time because the mind is not yet agitated by all the activities of the day, and the body is rested. But this is relatively unimportant and we can, in fact, meditate at any time. For the practice to be fruitful, it is crucial that we practice as diligently and steadily as possible.

The body provides important assistance to the practice of meditation in general and śamatha in particular, because mind and body are clearly related and interdependent. The posture facilitates meditation, although it is not absolutely indispensable. Ultimately, we can meditate in any position, but posture is important when we are starting out. Good physical posture fosters correct positioning of the mind. The body has different subtle channels within which the winds or subtle energies circulate. These animate our thoughts and states of consciousness.[87] With a straight posture, the channels are also straight and the winds can circulate freely, causing the mind to come naturally to a state of equilibrium and rest.

To begin, we hold ourselves straight and relaxed. Tibetans use vajrāsana posture, with the legs crossed like Buddha Śākyamuni's. Because Westerners have access to chairs, they can afford the luxury of sitting in the posture of Maitreya, the future Buddha.

We then let our minds remain at rest, open and without strain, fidgeting, or distraction, and we abide attentive to the mind as it is. Some people will have no problem letting the mind remain at rest, but it may be in an inert state, heavy and nearly sleeping. This state of stupor is not at all the correct śamatha state. It is essential for the mind to remain lucid, attentive, and vigilant, in a state of rest that develops spontaneously—in other words, without strain or fabrication.[88] This practice might appear ridiculously easy, but because we are not used to it, and because our mind always has the tendency to follow its thoughts, it is actually rather difficult. It is therefore important to familiarize ourselves with it and gradually find the proper state of abiding.

As we said already, in the practice of śamatha, we can use different objects to stabilize the mind. Among them, the most frequently used is the breath. We place our attention on the breath and breathe normally through the nostrils, aware that we are breathing, fully attentive and mindful of what is taking place, but without saying to ourselves, "I am breathing softly," "I am breathing forcefully," or "My respiration is short, or long…." We are simply present and attentive to our breath; we allow our mind to be absorbed in it without distraction. The main thing is not to tell ourselves that we are inhaling and exhaling, but to do nothing except breathe, without letting our attention wander. Each time our mind wanders and we stop paying attention to the breath, we are distracted and must return immediately to the awareness of the breath. The ability to return to the breath, and thereby to remember the meditation, is called recollection. Attention and recollection are two essential elements of śamatha practice. When we practice this way, thoughts gradually and naturally diminish, while different signs appear indicating progress in the successive stages.

Those among you who have the opportunity to meditate can discuss these with a competent guide, or lama.

Practically speaking, there are nine levels of tranquil abiding, nine stages that the progressively stabilized mind passes through. They are illustrated here in the traditional drawing called The Path of Śamatha.

The Path of Śamatha

THE PATH OF ŚAMATHA

This illustration is a reproduction of a Tibetan original that represents nine scenes, the nine stages of the śamatha path.

There are two characters: the man, or the meditating subject, the observer; and the elephant, which represents his mind. To develop śamatha, the mind uses two tools: attention and recollection. The sharp hatchet represents the acuity of vigilant attention, and the rope with a hook is recollection of the practice. Since many distractions interrupt his vigilant alertness, the meditator must return to it through constant reminders. Vigilance is the acuity at the base of meditation, and recollection assures its continuity. The state of śamatha has two main obstacles: the first is the agitation or scattering created by fixating on passing thoughts and emotions; the second is torpor or sluggishness, mental dullness. Torpor is represented by the black color of the elephant and agitation by the monkey. The fire that decreases along the path represents the energy of the meditation. As we advance, the practice requires less and less effort. The six curves or bends in the path mark off six plateaus successively mastered by the six strengths of practice, which are: listening to instructions, assimilating them, remembering them, vigilance, perseverance, and perfect habit. At the side of the road there are different objects: a scarf, some fruit, a conch filled with perfumed water, small cymbals, and a mirror, representing the objects of the senses: tangible objects, tastes, smells, sounds, and visual forms that distract the meditator, who strays from the path of śamatha by following after them.

(1) At the bottom of the illustration, at the first stage, there is a fairly great distance between the meditator and his mind. The elephant of mind is guided by the monkey, or its agitation. The large fire shows that the meditation requires a lot of energy. Obstacles are at their worst; everything is black.

(2) At the second stage, the meditator gets closer to the elephant because of his attention. The monkey—agitation—still leads the mind, but the rhythm slows down. Dullness and agitation decrease; some white filters into the black of the elephant and the monkey.

(3) At the third stage, the meditator no longer chases after his mind: they are now face to face. The monkey is still in front, but he no longer leads the elephant. Contact between the meditator and the mind is established by the cord of recollection. A subtle form of dullness occurs, represented by the little rabbit. The darkness of dullness and agitation decreases.

(4) At the fourth stage, progress becomes clearer, and the meditator gets even closer to the elephant. The whiteness of the monkey, the elephant, and the rabbit increases. The scene becomes more calm.

(5) At the fifth stage, the situation becomes reversed. The meditator now

leads the elephant of mind with continuous attention and recollection. The monkey no longer leads at all, but the rabbit is still there. The scene takes on still more clarity. In a nearby tree, a white monkey picks white fruit. This represents the mind's activity of engaging in positive actions. Even though such actions should normally be cultivated, they are nonetheless distractions in the context of śamatha practice; that is why the tree is black and off the path.

(6) At the sixth stage, progress is more definite. The meditator leads, and recollection is constant; he no longer has to place his attention on the mind. The rabbit is gone, and the situation becomes increasingly clear.

(7) At the seventh stage, the scene has become very peaceful. The walk no longer requires direction. The scene has become almost completely transparent. A few patches of black indicate trouble spots.

(8) At the eighth stage, the elephant walks tamely with the meditator. There is virtually no more black, and the flame of effort has disappeared. Meditation has become natural and continuous.

(9) At the ninth stage, mind and the meditator are both completely at rest. They are like old friends used to being together calmly. Obstacles have disappeared and śamatha is perfect. The next scenes, borne by the ray of light emanating from the meditator's heart, represent the evolution of practice at the heart of this stage of śamatha. Realization of śamatha is characterized by the experience of joy and radiance, illustrated by the meditator flying or riding on the elephant's back.

The last scene refers to the joined practices of śamatha and vipaśyanā. The direction is reversed. Mind and meditation are united; the meditator sits astride the mind. The fire reveals a new energy, that of wisdom, represented by the flaming sword of transcendent wisdom, which slices the two dark rays of mental afflictions and duality.

THE PRACTICE OF VIPAŚYANĀ

When mind abides in its natural state, its profound nature can gradually reveal itself, and all its qualities are uncovered. This is vipaśyanā practice.

Vipaśyanā, or "clear seeing," is called *lhag-thong* in Tibetan. *Lhag* means "clear" or "superior" and *thong* means "to see." *Lhag-thong* is to see clearly, to have insight into mind's nature and clear vision of its basic state.

In the practice of vipaśyanā, first we receive instructions, then we meditate and bring our experience to a lama. He confirms or not the correctness of our experience and helps us to recognize, little by little, mind's actual nature.[89]

There are differences in the approaches of śamatha and vipaśyanā. Śamatha meditation uses an object or reference, although a subtle one, upon which the mind meditates; a dualistic relationship is established between the mind and its object. In vipaśyanā, however, mind and the object are essentially one, not two, and remain this way.

In śamatha, attention remains apart from thoughts in a certain sense, and the practice is difficult. We are like a beginner learning how to drive a car; we have to pay close attention when turning right, left, and so on. In vipaśyanā, many thoughts go through the mind, but they are neither suppressed nor followed. They arise and pass away without our having to interfere. If we allow them to arise, pass, and disappear this way, there won't be any problem. Mind is clear and transparent; thoughts appear on its surface and disappear like waves on the surface of water. They come from the water and return to the water. When we are familiar with vipaśyanā meditation, which consists of letting go of thoughts, letting them be pacified and liberated by themselves, meditation is easy, like riding with a chauffeur who's mastered the art of driving.

Śamatha practice initially requires a retreat—a certain distancing from disturbing distractions. Progress in meditation requires this detachment, which can be gained through sitting meditation. But later, with vipaśyanā practice, direct presence and attention arises, an immediate experience of things. Having reached this stage, we can meditate in any and all situations.

If we do śamatha-vipaśyanā meditation without having received adequate instructions, the practice may go astray. Mind should remain clear and lucid; if it becomes heavy and still, the meditation can become marmot practice! Some people who are lazy continue to meditate without doing anything at all, and their mind is dull and closed. This is a form of stupidity. Remaining like this for a moment, the mind can seem to be without thoughts, and even happy in a way. People who practice this way might think they have become quite good at meditation and even think they no longer need to cultivate good karma and abandon harmful activities. But this kind of meditation is neither correct nor useful. It is actually a form of laziness that leads to mental dullness or stupidity. This is in no way śamatha-vipaśyanā and is good only for being reborn in a particularly stupid animal state, like the marmot's. This is why, when we meditate, we must keep the mind transparent, lucid, and clear.

Milarepa, while teaching one of his disciples, sang:

Meditate on the unborn nature of mind:
Like space, no center, no limit;
Like the sun and moon, bright and clear;
Like a mountain, unmoving, unshakable;
Like the ocean, deep, unfathomable.

This woman practiced for some time, after which she returned to see Milarepa, singing:

> I am happy to meditate like space,
> But distracted by clouds and haze that appear there.
>
> I am happy to meditate like the sun and moon,
> But distracted by the stars and planets that arise with them.
>
> I am happy to meditate like the ocean,
> But distracted by waves and backwash that arise.
>
> I am happy to meditate like a mountain,
> But distracted by the plants and flowers that grow.
>
> I am happy to meditate on the unborn nature of mind,
> But distracted by thoughts and images that emerge in it.
>
> Master, please teach me about these!

Milarepa said that she had had a good experience in meditation and responded with another song:

> In meditation like space,
> Clouds and haze are its pleasures:
> Remain in its vastness without center or limit.
>
> In meditation like the sun and moon,
> Stars and planets are its jewelry:
> Remain in their space, bright and clear.
>
> In meditation like a mountain,
> Plants and flowers are its finery;
> Remain in their sphere unmoving, undisturbed.
>
> In meditation like an ocean,
> Waves and backwash are its movements:
> Remain in their sphere deep and unfathomable.

In meditation on the unborn,
Thoughts and images are its manifestations:
Remain in their immensity, vast and lucid.

If we know how to let go of thoughts and allow them to subside by themselves, meditation is easy, because mind is open and lucid.

When we have some experience of the mind's emptiness, clarity, and infinite awareness, we experience its contents as manifestations of this empty,
clear, and unimpeded nature. Thoughts and emotions habitually restrict us
because we believe them to be solid and real. This subjects us to their control,
so they determine and dictate our actions. But if we don't grasp on to our
thoughts and emotions, we will not attribute any reality to them, and they
will remain void manifestations of a void mind. If we understand all
thoughts, emotions, and mental activities as experiences of mind which are
not independent things in themselves, then, when a passion or affliction arises,
we can perceive it for what it is—merely an expression of the clear, empty
nature of mind.[90] Recognizing and realizing them as such yields freedom.[91]

7

The Stages of Realization

The person who turns toward enlightenment,
and practices diligently
the different disciplines,
traverses the stages of a bodhisattva
that lead to enlightenment.

—Gampopa, *The Jewel Ornament of Liberation*

THE FIVE PATHS

The stages on the spiritual path are outlined in what are known as the five paths of realization. Dharma practice begins with taking refuge in the Three Jewels and practicing according to an understanding of karmic causality—avoiding harmful actions and performing positive ones. Based on these, we gradually cultivate compassion, meditation, devotion, deity yoga, and so forth. Directing our energies toward the practice of the six perfections, we gradually deepen those practices to a lesser, middling, or greater degree and gather an accumulation of merit that establishes us on one or another of these three levels on the Path of Accumulation.

Later, as positive qualities increase, perfect wisdom develops. At this point we enter the Path of Preparation, whose name reflects that it is an intermediate stage relying on a direct experience of the essential nature of mind. The Path of Preparation itself has three degrees—lower, middling, and superior—corresponding to the degree to which one has gathered the accumulation of wisdom.

When we actually perceive emptiness—the nature of mind—directly, we are at the threshold of the Path of Insight. Mind's actual nature is authentically recognized, like an old friend. At this point, we attain the first bodhisattva ground, called Sublime Joy. The first actual realization of the nature of mind is what leads to the first bodhisattva ground; this occurs at the same time as the development of extraordinary qualities, such as the ability to produce one hundred emanations at once. The first-level bodhisattva also possesses twelve groups of qualities multiplied by a hundred. The Path of Insight also includes three levels: lower, middling, and superior, based on the extent of the recognition of emptiness. When the empty, clear, and infinite nature of mind is fully and definitely recognized directly, with no doubt whatsoever, this is the superior level of the Path of Insight.

Next comes the Path of Meditation. By completing the two accumulations of merit and wisdom, mind becomes accustomed to a stabilized experience of emptiness. The bodhisattva gradually advances through the bodhisattva bhūmis or levels; first through the relatively "impure" seven levels, then the three pure levels. This progression up to the tenth stage, called the Cloud of Dharma, is the Path of Meditation.

Finally, the Path of No More Learning is attained when the ultimate antidote, which is the state of adamantine absorption, overcomes the very subtle remaining obscurations that form the subtlest veil obscuring awareness. This is enlightenment: "purification"—*sang* in Tibetan—of everything to be abandoned and "fully blossomed"—*gye* in Tibetan—in primordial wisdom, whose result is buddhahood. These stages are basically the same whether the approach is Hīnayāna, Mahāyāna, or Vajrayāna. The three yānas vary in their methods but not in their objectives. They are different vehicles that serve one path, traverse the same stages, and arrive at the same place.

NARO BÖNCHUNG CHALLENGES MILAREPA

Once Milarepa went to the shore of a very large lake, where a Bönpo master by the name of Naro Bönchung resided. They met and the Bönpo challenged Milarepa.

"Let's have a contest to see who has the greatest powers. Loser converts, along with all his disciples, to the tradition of the other!" Milarepa accepted the challenge.

This lake shore was so vast that it took several days to travel around it. The Bönpo began the contest by manifesting a huge body. He put one foot down on one side of the lake and the other on the other side.

Milarepa said, "Those are your powers? My turn!" So he sat on the lake, but, incredibly, though the lake was not reduced in size, nor did Milarepa's body get larger, he covered the entire lake, exactly like the lid on a jar. It may be hard to imagine, if the lake didn't get smaller and his body didn't get bigger, how the two could be exactly the same size. But that's just what happened, and this is recorded in Milarepa's biography.

The Bönpo said, "You've won the first match, but I demand a rematch. Way over there is a mountain. Let's see who can get closest to it just by stretching his arms."

The Bönpo raised his arm and reached about halfway to the mountain, which was very far away. But Milarepa barely budged his arm and instantly he made an imprint of his hand on the side of the mountain!

The Bönpo said, "You won for today, but we'll take this up again tomorrow. See that summit way over there? The first one to get there wins!"

With those words, Milarepa retired for the evening, while the Bönpo took advantage of the evening to begin his climb. Riding horseback, he beat his drum to make the horse go faster. At the crack of dawn, he had almost arrived at the mountain's summit. Milarepa's disciples, Rechungpa and a few others who were there, quickly awakened him, saying, "Master! Naro Bönchung has practically arrived at the summit!"

Milarepa smiled. "No hurry. He isn't there yet, right?" At that moment, the mountain leaned over and placed its summit just in front of Milarepa, who got up to sit on top of it, and then whoops! the mountain straightened itself. The Bönpo was rather disappointed. "I think I've lost. You won all the contests, but if you don't mind, please let me just go home now." Milarepa agreed.

This Bönpo definitely had ordinary siddhis or powers, but Milarepa had the supreme accomplishment: complete realization of the nature of mind.

When things are beyond our comprehension, we have a tendency to think they are just myths. Yet, just as the nature of phenomena escapes our awareness, events can escape our understanding!

8

Enlightenment
and the Three Bodies of the Buddha

Buddhahood is not existent because
it has as a characteristic non-existence of the self and phenomena.
Neither is it nonexistent
because it exists as suchness.

—Asaṅga, *Mahāyānasūtrālaṅkāra*

At the start of their spiritual journey, future buddhas first generate bodhicitta, or the mind of enlightenment. Then, for three immeasurable eons, they practice the accumulations and purification, gathering the two accumulations and purifying their minds of obscurations, and performing an infinite number of bodhisattva activities through the different perfections. In perfecting these activities, bodhisattvas advance through the five paths of realization and the ten bodhisattva grounds.[92] This is how they become perfectly accomplished buddhas.

THE BUDDHAS' ENLIGHTENMENT

The enlightenment of the buddhas has three aspects:

By nature, they completely lack mental obscurations. They are free of the veils of ignorance, the basic propensity, the passions, and karma.[93] This is called the great cessation.

Their primordial wisdom can see every object of knowledge directly, clearly, and without confusion. This is called the great realization.

Finally, with inconceivable compassion, they work spontaneously, always, and everywhere for the benefit of all beings. This is called their great courageous spirit.

THE QUALITIES OF A BUDDHA'S BODY, SPEECH, AND MIND

A buddha's mind is endowed with incomparable qualities: there is no object of knowledge of samsara, nirvana, or the path that leads from one to the other that they do not know or perceive directly and immediately through their primordial wisdom. They perceive everything as though it were in the palm of their hand and they know authentically, exactly, and without confusion all past, present, and future karmas, their causes, and their results. This direct and instantaneous awareness is clear and stripped of all obscuration. It is called the omniscience of their primordial wisdom.

Buddhas have immense and equal love for all beings, watching over them with compassion no matter who or where they are, with no partiality or attachment whatsoever. This is called their loving-kindness.

Buddhas' enlightened activities emanate endlessly and uninterruptedly, helping beings in appropriate ways and working for their welfare regardless of whether the beings' attitude toward the buddhas is positive or negative. So, through various aspects, this activity opens the door to the three classes of higher-realm beings and finally to liberation. It manifests perpetually as long as samsara has not been emptied of beings, and it is called their engaged enlightened activity.

By the power of the blessing of this enlightened activity, faith, devotion, loving-kindness, and compassion grow in the minds of beings who finally recognize the emptiness of all phenomena, whether object or subject. They therefore realize the illusory nature of all things and cease to grasp at an inherent existence. Practicing diligently in letting the mind rest in śamatha, and recognizing its actual nature in vipaśyanā,[94] they advance by means of the six and then the ten perfections,[95] the ten bodhisattva grounds, and the five paths of realization, thereby attaining buddhahood. Through their enlightened activity, buddhas' ability to give refuge to beings confronted by suffering in the cycle of samsara and to establish them in the state of buddhahood is called their power of refuge.

In addition to these qualities, a buddha's body has thirty-two major marks and eighty minor marks of accomplishment. Their speech possesses characteristic qualities, and their mind includes ten powers, four fearlessnesses, and eighteen unique qualities; in all, they have ten million qualities arising from their minds' freedom from all obscurations and conceptual grasping, as well as the maturation of their positive karma.

THE THREE BODIES OF THE BUDDHA[96]

Upon the attainment of buddhahood, enlightenment manifests at three levels known as the three bodies of the Buddha. They are: the Absolute or Truth Body, or dharmakāya; the Enjoyment Body, or sambhogakāya; and the Emanation Body, or nirmānakāya.

There is a correspondence between these three enlightened spheres and the three ordinary planes of mind, speech, and body. The enlightened mind is dharmakāya, purified speech is sambhogakāya, and pure body is nirmānakāya. From another angle, the three aspects of the pure nature of mind which we discussed before as emptiness, clarity, and unobstructedness also correspond to these three bodies of the Buddha: the empty aspect is the dharmakāya, the clear aspect the saṃbhogakāya, and the unobstructed aspect the nirmānakāya.

There is also a correspondence between the five root mental afflictions (anger, pride, desire, jealousy, and ignorance) and, at the level of a buddha, the five primordial wisdoms, five expressions of enlightened wisdom which are the ordinary five afflictions transmuted respectively into mirrorlike wisdom, wisdom of equanimity, discriminating wisdom, all-accomplishing wisdom, and emptiness wisdom.

The two accumulations of merit and wisdom generated by a bodhisattva practicing the six perfections result in the three bodies of the Buddha. The dharmakāya is formless and specifically issues from the accumulation of wisdom. The saṃbhogakāya and nirmānakāya are both form bodies and are associated particularly with the accumulation of merit. These latter two emanate jointly from the emergence of the dharmakāya's potentialities and from wishes made in the past by buddhas.

The dharmakāya is obtained by a buddha "for his own good," while the other two form bodies, the saṃbhogakāya and the nirmānakāya, manifest for the benefit of beings. The dharmakāya reveals itself when the veil "which covers what is to be known" dissolves; the saṃbhogakāya, when the veil of the afflictions is dissolved; and the nirmānakāya, when the veil of karma is purified.

The dharmakāya is the indeterminate aspect of buddha nature. It abides in the omnipresent palace of the infinite realm of the dharmadhātu, encompassing and pervading everything, samsara as well as nirvana, and transcends all mentally produced categories. It is without beginning or end, without appearance, destruction, or location.

In this infinite domain, beyond samsara's three realms, the saṃbhogakāya manifests with form to tenth-level bodhisattvas. Resulting from the conjunction of two factors—the appearance and qualities innate in the dharmakāya, and the positive karma of bodhisattvas who perceive it, it is called the saṃbhogakāya resulting from the conjunction of the two factors that each make up a half.

The nirmānakāya is the body by which a buddha manifests in the ordinary world. It can be perceived by ordinary beings in three forms. The first are emanations that educate beings through traditional activity in this world, or those that manifest as artisans and craftspeople. There are also emanations that are born to educate beings by taking on various forms: humans for helping humans, animals for animals, and so on. Finally, the supreme emanations, such as Buddha Śākyamuni, work for the welfare of beings through twelve activities: leaving Tuṣita heaven, entering a womb, being born, studying the traditional arts and sciences, getting married, renouncing the world, practicing asceticism, sitting beneath the bodhi tree, overcoming Māra's armies, attaining enlightenment, turning the Wheel of Dharma, and departing in parinirvāṇa.

PART TWO

Section Four

The Vajrayāna: Path of Transmutation

The Path of Transmutation

In the Mantra approach, with its many methods and few austerities,
a person of sharp faculties and high intelligence
may gather the two accumulations during all activities
and never do even a trace of anything meaningless.

—Jamgön Kongtrul Lodrö Thaye, *The Outline of Essential Points*

What we have seen in terms of the Hīnayāna and Mahāyāna up to this point applies to all schools of Buddhism; it is the fundamental Dharma.

UNIQUENESS OF VAJRAYĀNA

The Vajrayāna rests on the same foundation as the Mahāyāna, of which it is a branch. It is, however, distinguished from the usual Mahāyāna teachings by the many skillful means it uses. The usual Mahāyāna teachings rest on the sūtras, while those of the Vajrayāna are based on texts called tantras. The goals of their teaching are identical, but their perspective, methods, and efficiency differ. We have already discussed the complementarity of the three vehicles.[97] Now we will see that each vehicle has its own unique approach.

Within the various approaches, there are differences in motivation: Hīnayāna followers think of samsara as an ocean of suffering to be crossed in order to gain the freedom of nirvana, and they seek to free themselves from samsara mainly for their own welfare. Mahāyāna followers aspire to attain enlightenment for the purpose of helping all beings. Thinking that each of those beings, at some time throughout the course of countless lives, has been their own parent, recalling their kindness, and, feeling a sense of universal compassion, Mahāyāna followers wish to free all sentient beings. So, Hīnayāna practitioners have been compared to kings who use their powers to further their own interests, while Mahāyāna practitioners are like those same kings using those same powers for everyone's benefit.

Perspectives also differ with regard to illusions and their results. The Hīnayāna path teaches renunciation of impurities, which is difficult and takes a long time to realize but is easier to teach than the Mahāyāna and Vajrayāna approaches. The Mahāyāna approach proposes to change those "contaminated" qualities into their opposites, which is more difficult to understand than the Hīnayāna approach but easier to practice once assimilated. The Vajrayāna involves transcending perceptions of pure and impure, which is very difficult to understand and teach but, once mastered, the quickest and easiest method for attaining enlightenment.

The three vehicles use all kinds of more or less radical methods that can be compared to the three ways of cutting down the tree of ignorance, suffering, and negativity: Hīnayāna gets rid of the leaves, Mahāyāna cuts the branches, and Vajrayāna eliminates the tree from its roots. All suffering occurs in mind. Directly realizing mind's nature and removing the afflictions generated in mind is the Vajrayāna approach.

To take another example, we could compare enlightenment to an image of a buddha. In order to obtain that image, we could paint it on a piece of cloth, first drawing the outline and then painstakingly applying paint, paying close attention to every detail. We would certainly achieve the desired result, but it would take a long time. This is a bit like the sūtra path. The other method would be to get hold of a good traditional painting and take a photograph of it. That way you get an immediate result. This is the tantric approach, the Vajrayāna way.

The three vehicles do not differ so much in goal—which is actually the same for each—as in the methods for getting there. If enlightenment is a faraway country like India, the Hīnayāna approach would be like walking there on foot; the Mahāyāna, like going by horse or car; and the Vajrayāna, like taking a plane or a rocket. They may have the same destination, but the three vehicles' speed and efficiency are entirely different.

Hīnayāna and Mahāyāna paths are practiced over many, many lives. Vajrayāna is quicker, allowing us to realize enlightenment either in this very life, at the moment of death, or within a period of seven to sixteen lives at the very most.

It is indeed a quick path, but at the same time, it can be dangerous if you don't have great faith in your guide.

THE SECRET TEACHING

In general, buddhas teach the Dharma according to disciples' minds. They transmit many teachings that serve as antidotes to the 84,000 kinds of afflictions that can arise in the minds of sentient beings. Not all buddhas teach the Vajrayāna, but the buddha of our era, Śākyamuni, out of extraordinary compassion, gave particularly profound instructions that are quick and efficient.

The Vajrayāna is the quintessence of Buddha's teaching. For that reason, it is extremely precious, and we are inconceivably fortunate to have encountered it, but it is easy to misunderstand, and this can cause us to make grave mistakes that produce miserable lives in hell or animal realms. It is therefore quite dangerous. This is why Vajrayāna is called a secret teaching. Its essential practices are only transmitted orally, and at the proper time, from master to disciple.

The Vajrayāna path leaves nothing out, no matter what. Nothing can be rejected; we simply transmute our mind and its experiences by recognizing their actual nature. It is a path of transmutation from what is impure to what is pure. This is what makes it fast and easy.

Vajrayāna involves no great difficulties, nor any particular austerities, so it would be possible for a person with sharp faculties and great intelligence to practice and attain genuine realization even in his or her usual context. To this end, Vajrayāna practitioners use "sacred vision" with which they recognize that this world is already fundamentally pure; it is already a pure land, a realm where all buddhas and bodhisattvas are visible and the Dharma is understood.

Likewise, they consider that all beings are fundamentally buddhas and that there is no real distinction between samsara and nirvana, which are merely appearances. In the practice of this sacred vision, the world is meditated on as a pure land and beings as aspects of Buddha; all forms are enlightened aspects, all sounds are mantra, and mind is pure mind.

The correct understanding of sacred vision and its practice is delicate. It is crucial at the outset of involvement in Vajrayāna not to give rise to false views, to have faith, and not to reject Vajrayāna. Certainly we are all very different: some are very bright and intelligent and others are less receptive; some already have a good knowledge of Dharma, while others have studied little. To teach Vajrayāna methods to a person who is not ready to receive them, who is not properly prepared because he or she lacks sufficiently mature knowledge or experience of Dharma, would be to risk giving rise to false views or, even worse, rejection of the teaching. This is why the Vajrayāna cannot be approached directly unless we have a solid foundation produced by an understanding and practice of both the Hīnayāna and Mahāyāna paths.

That said, in this "path of means" which is the Vajrayāna, there are many levels of teaching and understanding, so revealing just a few aspects of the first levels of practice presents no real danger and may even be quite helpful.

THE STORY OF SUKHASIDDHI

The woman who became known as Sukhasiddhi[98] was born in Kashmir in the same area as Niguma. Born into a very poor family, she lived very modestly with her husband, three sons, and three daughters. One year, when a famine ravaged the land and there remained in the house but a bowl of rice, the entire family went in search of food: the three daughters went north, the three sons went west, and the father went south. Only the mother remained at home. While she was alone in the house, a mahāsiddha came along who, through his clairvoyance, knew she had a little food hidden away. He told her that he hadn't eaten in a very long time and begged her to give him a bit of rice. Moved by his pleas and his virtue, she agreed. She cooked the rice, offered it to him, and had a little bit herself.

When the rest of the family returned from their search empty-handed and starved, and asked her to go ahead and cook up the last of the food, she had to confess the whole story, explaining that she had been sure they would bring back something to eat. Furious, they threw her out.

On the advice of neighbors, she headed west and reached the land of Oḍḍiyāna, a marvelous, prosperous place with generous people. Arriving during the harvest, she begged and received a huge quantity of rice. She used it to make beer, which she then sold. The money she earned allowed her to buy whatever she needed and to set up a beer business and eventually to open up a restaurant. Among her daily regulars was a young woman who always bought beer and meat, although she never consumed anything. One day, the lady asked about her, and the young woman replied that not far up the mountain lived the mahāsiddha Virūpa, whom she supplied with food every day. The woman said to her, "In that case, take this beer as an offering for him," and she proceeded to tell her the whole story of her misadventure. After that, every day she would offer Virūpa a large amount of her best beer. Some time later, Virūpa asked his young attendant how she could bring so much beer without ever having to pay for it. The young woman explained that the beer came from a woman who had great devotion for him. Virūpa then said, "This woman must have excellent karma; if I meet her, I can guide her to full enlightenment."

The story got back to the woman, who was very enthusiastic and went to visit Virūpa, bringing generous offerings of beer and meat. He conferred on her an initiation that immediately led her to manifest as a primordial wisdom ḍākinī in mind and body. Although she was already sixty-one, she took on the form of a sixteen-year-old girl and became known as Sukhasiddhi. She had the same realizations as Niguma and also received transmissions directly from Vajradhara. Since then, for more than a thousand years, beings who are qualified can still meet with her in her unchanged, youthful aspect.

She was one of Khyungpo Neljor's main teachers; he encountered her in a charnel ground where she appeared to him in a bright white luminous body, her hands in the "gesture of the uncreated," surrounded by a group of ḍākinīs and clouds of light. Sukhasiddhi transmitted the teachings to him and prophesied that he would be their principal holder. These, known as the teachings of Sukhasiddhi, have been transmitted up until the present day.

2

The Guide and Spiritual Direction

No sūtra, tantra, or śastra speaks of any being ever attaining
perfect buddhahood without having followed a spiritual teacher.
We can see for ourselves that nobody has ever developed
all the accomplishments of the stages and paths
by relying on their own efforts and abilities alone.

—Patrul Rinpoche, *The Way of Great Perfection*

We need someone who can guide us on the path, teach us, direct us, help us, and show us the dangers and the right way.

THE LAMA: SPIRITUAL FATHER-MOTHER

This guide is not a director in the ordinary sense, or a person who controls us. A lama is someone whose role is somewhat difficult to describe but, to use a worldly example, could be considered a bit like parents, both father and mother at the same time. A lama is someone who helps and guides us at the spiritual level, in the same way that our parents have educated us in worldly matters. They taught us what was dangerous and what was right to do. Similarly, a lama teaches us what is wholesome or unwholesome, positive or negative, on the spiritual level. He can guide and lead us to spiritual maturity. In following our parents' counsel, we learned about the world and we grew up. Likewise, by listening to the counsel of our own lama, our spiritual father-mother, we can gradually cultivate what is positive, abandon what is negative, deepen our inner maturity, and open our mind to realization. Just as we appreciate our parents' kindness and acknowledge our indebtedness to them, it is important to appreciate our lama's kindness and have similar gratitude.

There are, however, differences in level: while our parents have educated us, given us things, and taught us what is good for this life for now, our spiritual father-mother teaches us what is meaningful both now and for future lives until we reach enlightenment. We should therefore recognize this added dimension as we extend to our lama the gratitude that we have for our parents.

Another difference in these relationships has to do with the extent of the motivation of a parent's love and a lama's. Parents love their children, but this love is usually restricted to their sons and daughters, while a lama has an attitude of love and compassion toward all beings.

Still another important difference is blessing or spiritual inspiration: our parents have helped us and done everything for our benefit, but their benevolence is without any spiritual influence. On the other hand, the lama who helps us is the source of a blessing connected by an uninterrupted lineage to enlightenment and Buddha Vajradhara, the ultimate realization. The lama is the expression of the teaching and of realization. He transmits to us what is useful for our mind; thanks to him, we can receive blessings from all the buddhas.

Another fundamental difference is in the realization of accomplishments. With what we have learned from our parents, we can function in the world; we can have social standing, earn money, be rich, and have a successful worldly position. Through our relationship with our lama, we can accomplish something incomparably more profound because this relationship can awaken us to spiritual realization, to buddhahood, which is invaluable as much for this life as for all lives, and not only for ourselves but for all beings. Therefore, a lama's activities are endowed with unique abilities and accomplishments. He is the channel through which these abilities and realizations can be conveyed, can reach us, and help us attain the most profound level.

LEVELS OF RELATIONSHIP WITH THE GUIDE

In general, there are progressive levels in a relationship with a lama, which are frequently described in relation to the three yānas.

At the Hīnayāna level, we respect the teacher and have immense gratitude for his kindness in giving us Dharma; he is called a *loppön,* "professor," or *khenpo,* a master of the teachings. He is an instructor, gives the precepts, or administers a monastery.

In the Mahāyāna, the relationship with the spiritual guide acquires a more important dimension. He becomes a "spiritual friend," a counselor at the inner level.

The Vajrayāna places even more importance on the spiritual guide. At this level, he is a lama. The "root lama," or the lama who personally guides a Vajrayāna practitioner, is regarded as Buddha Vajradhara, the essence and union of all the buddhas of the three times and the ten directions. He is the essence of their body, speech, and mind, their virtues, their special qualities, and their activity. For the Vajrayāna practitioner, the lama is exceedingly important. He is Buddha's equal in his qualities, and even more esteemed than any other aspect of Buddha because of his kindness in transmitting the teachings to us. It is this essential relationship that allows the transmission of the blessing and provides spiritual direction at the deepest level, the Vajrayāna level.

GAMPOPA MEETS MILAREPA

Gampopa was in the habit of circumambulating a stupa every day. One day, while a famine ravaged the area, he was circumambulating when he overheard the conversation of three starving beggars. One said, "I sure would like to be the king and have all his gold, so I could have myself a feast."

Another one said, "If only I could have some tea and a good bowl of soup, that would be just wonderful. "

The third one said, "What I would like best would be to meet the great yogi Milarepa, the one who lives alone in the mountains and needs no food other than samādhi."

The name Milarepa resonated in Gampopa, awakening emotion from the depths of his being. Suddenly he wanted to know more and went after the beggar, asking, "Who is this Milarepa? What does he do?"

"Milarepa is a hermit yogi, an amazingly accomplished being who lives in the mountains."

At Gampopa's request, the beggar explained where and how to find Milarepa.

At that very moment, Milarepa was giving teachings in the mountains, surrounded by a number of disciples. He said to them, "In a few days, an excellent monk who is a real bodhisattva is going to come from the south to meet me. If a few of you could help him, it would be very good and greatly help your progress toward enlightenment. "

Soon after that, Gampopa arrived in the region where Milarepa lived. He met one of his disciples who had heard the prediction and said to her, "I have come from the south looking for Milarepa the yogi. Would you know where he is?"

And the woman said, "You come from the south, you are a monk...you must be the great bodhisattva who Milarepa said would come. I will help you meet him. He wanted us to."

Gampopa thought, "I must be very special for the great Milarepa to make such a prediction." He swelled with pride. When the woman led him to Milarepa, the yogi could see his state of mind because of his extraordinary knowledge, and he wouldn't give Gampopa an audience for a fortnight, even though he was a noble monk. The waiting deflated Gampopa, and, finally, seated in his hermitage, Milarepa called him. As he entered, Gampopa respectfully prostrated three times. Then Milarepa invited him to sit down.

"Welcome! Here, drink!" he said, offering him a skull full of alcohol.

Disconcerted, Gampopa hesitated. On the one hand, he couldn't refuse what was offered him by the person he came to receive teachings from. But on the other hand, a good monk cannot drink alcohol. What a terrible dilemma. Milarepa insisted.

"Don't hesitate! Drink!"

So, stopping all thought, Gampopa drank in one gulp the entire skull of alcohol.

"Excellent! What a great sign of your capacity to assimilate all the teachings of the lineage!"

Gampopa remained for a very long time with Milarepa. He received the teachings, practiced them, developed deep understanding, and arrived at enlightenment.

The Marpa-Kagyu Patriarchs

3

Transmission and Blessing

First you followed a supreme Master and obeyed him;
Then you practised, undertaking great hardships;
Finally, your mind and your teacher's became one,
And you inherited the lineage.
Peerless teacher, at your feet I bow.

—Patrul Rinpoche, *The Way of Great Perfection*

CONTINUITY OF THE LINEAGE

The Vajrayāna has been transmitted since Buddha Vajradhara through the channel of an uninterrupted lineage, from master to disciple. This lineage conveys the word and mind of the teachings with a blessing transmitted through empowerments or initiations *(abhiṣeka* in Sanskrit), scriptural transmissions, and instructions.[99]

To clarify the idea of transmission and lineage, and the reason it should be uninterrupted, let's take the example of a light bulb. Electricity comes from a central source, which transmits it along a wire. The generator, the source of the electricity, is like buddhahood; the wire that carries the electricity is like the transmission lineage; and the electrical current is like the blessing whose energy clarifies our practice and enlightens our mind. If the wire is cut, the current cannot pass through it, and the bulb cannot produce light.

We are extremely lucky, because the Vajrayāna tradition remains completely intact and alive. All its instructions have been passed down to the present, undamaged and undiminished. From Buddha Vajradhara to the present day, an uninterrupted lineage of realized beings has transmitted them, and their blessing is still directly accessible to us through their initiations and other transmissions.

This blessing and inspiration is not something physical; it has no form, color, aspect, or anything else we could grasp with the ordinary senses. It functions by way of tendrel—interconnections or interactions.[100]

This blessing is accorded particular importance in the Vajrayāna and mahāmudrā approaches; the inspiration of the lama and the lineage is what allows for a much faster recognition of the nature of mind than occurs on other paths. One ancient and well-known Kagyu master said:

If the sun of the disciple's faith and devotion do not strike the snowy mountain of the lama's blessing, the waves of inspiration that purify impurities won't flow down.

Great faith in our lama and deep devotion[101] allow us to receive his blessing and, through that, to quickly purify negative tendencies and cultivate positive ones.

THE ROLE OF THE ROOT LAMA

The lama whom we choose to be our personal guide and with whom we establish a spiritual relationship is our root lama. It doesn't matter which qualified lama we choose; it could be one we meet in a Dharma center or elsewhere, as long as we have an affinity and connection with him or her through a Vajrayāna initiation.

At a vital level, the root lama is the one who causes us to recognize the nature of our mind; he is the source of the blessings that introduce us to mahāmudrā, the ultimate nature of mind; he shows us how to recognize our mind as the dharmakāya. He directly gives us appropriate teachings that we then examine and practice. After that, we discuss our experiences with him and he guides us further. Recognizing the nature of mind is delicate: if it had a form or color, the lama could show it to us and say, "Look here," but that is not the case, and he can only give us subtle suggestions to guide our personal examinations in meditation. We also report our experiences back to him regularly. He helps us to process these and gives us new instructions, so we can continue this exchange in the right way, until we arrive at an experience beyond all doubt, and actual realization.

Certain criteria can help a disciple in choosing a root lama. First of all, the lama should have an authentic traditional connection, guaranteeing the correctness of the transmission; his understanding of Dharma should be profound and his realization genuine. His words and actions should accord with one another, and he should be detached, that is, not motivated by material interest or personal satisfaction. His motivation for helping disciples and all beings should be sincere, based on bodhicitta, deep love, and compassion. Moreover, lama and disciple should be able to communicate with each other well, with complete trust. The person who has those qualities and qualifications can be our root lama. If we sincerely commit ourselves to him as a disciple, he becomes the transmitter of the lineage of all buddhas and the source of their blessings.

As for the disciple, he or she should have great faith and should exert effort to put the lama's teachings into practice completely.

The benefits derived from this relationship basically depend upon two elements: on the one hand, realization and the lama's compassion and love for his disciples, his students, and all those who surround him; and on the other, his disciples' faith in him. To use a traditional image, the lama's compassion is like a hook and the disciple's faith like a ring: when they come together, they make a strong connection that liberates the disciple from samsara.

Many lamas have sublime qualities, but even if they do not, if their connection, motivation, and desire to help beings are right, a relationship with them can be beneficial and lead us to enlightenment.

In any case, if we have established a relationship with a lama on the Vajrayāna level through receiving an initiation from him, it is vital that our relationship with him be positive; whatever his behavior, it is crucial that we maintain sacred vision. We must consider his actions as skillful means for helping us. If we can develop that attitude, it will open us to authentic blessing and carry us toward enlightenment. We can receive exactly the same help as we would get from someone who was perfectly pure. Even if the lama himself is not completely enlightened, he can still advise and help us. For example, someone who is familiar with a region can give us directions whether or not he or she is a great person. We cannot always judge by their actions who is a great lama or adept and who merely claims to be one. At a certain level, great adepts often act in an odd or even outrageous manner, for example, drinking a lot of wine or being involved with many women. On the other hand, someone who pretended unjustifiably to be an adept would find himself in a hell realm where he would become some monstrous creature. The disciple, however, can be helped by any authentic lama in whom he has faith.

NĀROPA MEETS TILOPA

The great pandit Nāropa was the best-known master of the great Indian university of Vikramaśīla. One day, while he was studying a scholarly treatise, an emanation of his meditational buddha, the yidam Vajrayoginī, appeared to him in the guise of a hideous old woman.

"Do you understand what you're reading?" she asked.

"Yes, of course," he replied.

"Do you understand the words or the meaning?"

"The words," he said.

The old woman, delighted, began to laugh and dance. Thinking it would make her even happier, he added, "I understand the meaning, too."

The old woman was upset and started to cry. Nāropa asked her, "Why are you happy if I tell you I understand the words and sad if I tell you I also understand the meaning?"

"You are a great scholar, and I was happy that you told me the truth, that you understand the words; but it really disturbs me that you say you understand the meaning when you understand none of it," she replied.

Realizing his inadequacies, he asked her what he needed to do to understand the real meaning, and she advised him to seek out and commit himself to Tilopa, a great adept who lived in the east, who was to become his lama and could teach him. She then vanished in a rainbow in the sky. Nāropa left the university and went in search of Tilopa.

He traveled east for quite a while, but no one knew Tilopa the great adept. After he had searched a long time, someone said to him, "There's no Tilopa the great adept around here, but we know a beggar named Tilopa."

Nāropa told himself that great adepts sometimes have an unlikely appearance and that this could very well be him. So he went to find him and came upon a man cooking fish on a grill over an open fire and swallowing them while snapping his fingers. Shocked, Nāropa thought this couldn't be Tilopa and reproached the man, saying how harmful it was to kill these fish. Tilopa replied, "Oh, then I'd better stop." He snapped his fingers, and the cooked fish revived and jumped back into the bucket. At that, Nāropa prostrated before him and asked to become his disciple.

"I am just a beggar!" replied Tilopa.

After Nāropa insisted, Tilopa agreed to give him a few instructions, but he taught only four lines and disappeared. This was the start of Nāropa's apprenticeship. Moreover, he discovered later that Tilopa didn't kill the fish because he was motivated by hunger or any other personal desire; it was because by eating them he had the power to free them from their negative karma and send them to Buddha's pure land.

Nāropa had to endure many tests as Tilopa's disciple, mainly those known as the twelve great tests. Nāropa followed Tilopa everywhere, but for a long time Tilopa would not give him any instruction.

One day they found themselves at the top of a very high tower. Tilopa said, "If I had a disciple, he would jump into the void from the top of this tower."

Since they were alone, Nāropa felt this was intended for him, so he leapt off the tower and crashed to the ground. Tilopa started down the stairs. "What's wrong?" he asked. Nāropa expressed his agony, but Tilopa urged him to watch his mind, healed him, and gave him a teaching.

Another time, when they were near a huge fire, Tilopa said, "To obey the master's orders, one must learn to jump into the fire."

In the same state of mind as before, Nāropa jumped in and burned himself, and Tilopa again asked, "What's wrong?"

Again he told Nāropa to watch his mind, cured him, and gave him another teaching.

Another time, they were watching a marriage procession go by. Greatly impressed by the beauty of the bride, Tilopa expressed his wish to have her as a consort and sent Nāropa to pick her up. Nāropa was beaten nearly to death by the furious guests, and when he finally returned to Tilopa, he was scolded for being gone so long.

On another occasion, Tilopa sent Nāropa to beg for food, which he did. Very satisfied, Tilopa sent him away to get some more, but the people who had given the food didn't want to give him any more. However, having seen his master so happy with what he had brought him, Nāropa proceeded to steal a bit more, and he was caught, beaten up, and left practically dead. Tilopa came over, asked what was wrong and told him yet again to watch his mind, and again cured him.

At another point, they had to cross a stream full of leeches. Tilopa asked Nāropa to make a bridge with his body so he wouldn't get wet, but he was so heavy that Nāropa slipped and Tilopa was splashed with water.

"You wanted to make me fall!" cried Tilopa. He beat Nāropa hard, and on top of that Nāropa was completely drained of blood by the leeches.

Nāropa was subjected to twelve major tests and twelve minor ones. After these, one day Tilopa asked him to fetch some water. When Nāropa returned, Tilopa took him by the nape of the neck, picked up one of his sandals, and hit him hard with it on his forehead. Nāropa passed out, and when he came to he had attained perfect realization of mahāmudrā. None of Nāropa's tests were usual Dharma activities, but, by following his teacher's instructions, he cleared away the obscurations in his mind, received his blessing, and thereby reached ultimate realization.

In the relationship with a lama, it is important to watch and examine our own mind, because as long as mind is not disciplined, it has the tendency to see only the faults in others. In that relationship, we must consider that what we see as wrong with the lama is merely a projection of our own mind, our own negativity. As ordinary beings, we are propelled by many afflictions. We always tend to perceive others' faults. If we have dirt on our face and look into a mirror, we will see our own dirt. When we are involved with a lama, we often perceive faults in him, but if we know how to examine our mind, we will see that these perceived flaws are actually expressions of our own negativity. If we cannot do that, it is best simply to accept the situation, thinking, "What he does is his problem. As for me, may I practice and understand the Dharma well." However, even when faced with an insurmountable problem, it is not at all appropriate to take an attitude of negativity and rejection. As a last resort, it is acceptable simply to leave the relationship and let it be, without a negative attitude.

THE MISADVENTURE OF SĀDHUJYOTI

Sādhujyoti the monk had served Buddha Śākyamuni for twenty-four years. He knew the teachings by heart but saw deception in Buddha's every activity. One day, he said to Buddha Śākyamuni, "I've been your attendant for twenty-four years, and I don't see the slightest extraordinary quality in you, aside from the aura that encircles your body—in every way you're just like me. From now on I will no longer serve you."

Ānanda, who became Buddha's new attendant, asked him what would happen to Sādhujyoti.

"He will die within a week and be reborn as a hungry ghost," replied Buddha.

Ānanda warned Sādhujyoti, who said to himself, "It's another one of his deceptions, but you never know, sometimes he's right." For a week he was on his guard, and fasted. On the evening of the seventh day, starved and thirsty, he ate, drank, died drunk, and was instantaneously reborn as a hungry ghost.

One well-known quote from a previous Karmapa, the great master of the Kagyu lineage, says:

> Of those who have seen me, none will go to lower realms.
> But those who live with me will never reach the higher realms.

Why? Because those who meet the Karmapa with faith, deep aspiration, and a positive state of mind establish a spiritual relationship that frees them, while those who live with him in the vicissitudes of day-to-day life tend to have a negative attitude toward him that is the source of extremely bad karma. A lama is like a fire whose presence and blessing heats and clarifies. If we are too far from the fire, we receive neither its light nor its warmth; on the other hand, if we are too close, we can get burned.

Most important is to properly understand the meaning of the teachings and truly apply them through the relationship we establish with our lama. We do not have to be disturbed by whatever doubts and hesitations we might have. Since our mind is in a confused state, of course we will have doubts about what is true, false, real, unreal, correct, mistaken, and so on. On the other hand, it is important for us to accept our doubts and hesitations and work with them in our relationship with our lama, discussing them with him honestly and using his responses to help clarify and eliminate them. It is in right relationship with the lama that we gradually open to authentic devotion for him; faith and aspiration allow us to receive his blessing, which leads us to realization.

4

The Three Roots

Crowned with the Three Jewels of the outer refuge,
You have truly realized the Three Roots, the inner refuge;
You have made manifest the three kayas, the ultimate refuge.
Peerless teacher, at your feet I bow.

—Patrul Rinpoche, *The Way of Great Perfection*

The Hīnayāna and Mahāyāna refuges are the Three Jewels; in addition to those, the Vajrayāna refuge includes the Three Roots or Three Sources: the lama, the yidam, and the protector, or dharmapala. The term "root" or "source" refers to the fact that the lama is the source of blessings, the yidam the source of attainments, and the dharmapala the source of awakened activity.

LAMA

The lama is the one who guides us and gradually transmits the essential points of the Vajrayāna teachings. He is the lineage holder and possesses the blessings of these practices,[102] and he grants empowerments or initiations—*abhiṣeka* in Sanskrit—which ripen our karma and the various currents of our consciousness, as well as the scriptural transmissions and oral instructions relating to them.

Scriptural transmissions support the teachings, and the instructions reveal the meanings of the initiations. The lama is therefore the source of the different facets of the transmission and the source of blessings.

YIDAM

The meditational deity—*yidam* in Tibetan—is an aspect of Buddha possessing the three bodies of the Buddha and the five primordial wisdoms.[103] Out of compassion, Buddha manifests as different aspects or yidams, each of which literally is, according to the meaning of that term, "the divinity or deity to which we devote ourselves." It is so called because a practitioner has one as his personal, chosen deity and devotes himself to that deity's practice, which consists of the two meditation stages called Generation Stage and Completion Stage.[104] Their practice results in the realization of the nature of mind and all the attainments.[105]

DHARMAPĀLA

The Dharma protector—*dharmapāla* in Sanskrit—is also the manifestation of enlightened aspects of mind, appearing in order to assist practitioners in attaining the four types of enlightened activities: pacification, increase, power, and destruction. They are the source or root of enlightened activity beyond karmic causes and effects.

OUTER, INNER, AND ABSOLUTE REFUGES

The Three Roots make up the inner refuge, and their significance is extremely profound. It isn't possible for us to completely understand it at first, but with study and practice it gradually becomes more clear.

We might ask ourselves, if we are intrinsically a buddha, why do we have to have a refuge that appears to be outside of ourselves? Can there be an outer refuge?

Take the example of the prime minister of a country. A priori he seems like an ordinary person, and we might wonder how he came by the qualities that allow him to govern. The answer lies in his knowledge and experience. If we woke up one day and decided we wanted to be the leader of a country, we would not know how to do it or where to begin; however, if we received the necessary instruction, we would be perfectly capable of doing the job. If a boss put us in charge and made us go through all the necessary training, we could eventually become his equal. Similarly, while we already possess the buddha nature, we are still ignorant, and so Buddha's qualities are not manifest in us. In order to realize these qualities and lift the veils that obscure them, we must turn toward Buddha, who has already reached that state, so that he can guide and assist us. At first when we turn toward Buddha, he seems to be outside of us. It seems the same when we receive teachings from our lama. As long as we are blinded by the delusion of "me" and "other," it is necessary and useful to take refuge. However, we must not forget that the mind of all beings and that of Buddha are not fundamentally different. Right now, our mind is like a student to whom his teacher hasn't yet imparted his knowledge. Once our mind is awakened to wisdom, it will be identical with Buddha's. The teachings can help to awaken us because we already have buddha nature. If we didn't have it, then trying to purify our mind would be like trying to wipe off a piece of charcoal: no matter how much we scrubbed, it would still remain black. On the other hand, purifying mind is like cleaning an object: once the dirt is gone, its nature can reveal itself. The diamond-like buddha nature has always been there, but covered over, and therefore imperceptible. The gold of enlightenment is in the ground of our own mind, but if we don't dig for it, we won't find it.

At the beginning, when you meditate on the Three Roots in general, or on your yidam in particular, you can perceive them as outer. In this way, the obscurations will begin to disappear. Holes in the screen of these obscurations will allow some light to filter through; the blessing of the yidam will bring even more clarity, and you will eventually realize that the yidam and your mind are not different.[106] You will thereby attain the three bodies of the buddha mind which are the absolute refuge.

5

Progression in Vajrayāna

One single torch can dissipate the
accumulated darkness of a thousand eons.
Likewise, one single instant of clear light in mind
eliminates the ignorance and obscurations accumulated over kalpas.

—Tilopa, *Mahāmudrā of the Ganges*

SLOW PATH, INSTANT PATH

The Dharma in general and the Vajrayāna in particular offer many methods for eliminating obscurations and letting the clear light of mind emerge.

These veils, like haze or clouds, are initially so thick they let nothing show through. But when the fog lifts, when the thick low clouds and then the light veil of high wispy clouds disappear, space is gradually revealed, and the sun shines in all its splendor. Similarly, the two accumulations of merit and wisdom are like the wind that blows away the haze and clouds of the mind, making them all disappear and revealing the bright space of clear light. This is the image of the gradual path.

However, there is also an immediate, instantaneous path. Let's say a room has been completely dark for centuries. Flipping an electric switch is enough to illuminate it, and the darkness is gone in an instant. Likewise, if a disciple who has faith, diligence, and spiritual intelligence meets a master possessing the profound Dharma, and if this master opens him to the understanding of mahāmudrā or dzogchen, all the veils of ignorance will disappear in an instant, just as flipping a switch can instantly light up a room.

The Vajrayāna teachings combine the two paths, and it's mostly the disciples' particular inclinations that steer them to one approach or another. These methods of realization are adapted to different practitioners' different needs, faculties, and abilities—superior, middling, or inferior.

STAGES OF PROGRESS

For practitioners of middling or inferior abilities, Dharma practice in general and Vajrayāna in particular involve, first of all, gathering the two accumulations of merit and wisdom by various means. Practitioners adopt the discipline of the Hīnayāna[107] and meditate on the common preliminaries, which are to develop an acute awareness of: the value of the precious human rebirth and its significance; impermanence and death; karma; and the problems and suffering inherent in all conditioned samsaric existence.[108] They practice the six perfections of generosity, discipline, patience, effort, meditation, and transcendent wisdom.[109] They learn how to pacify and stabilize the mind through śamatha or calm-abiding practice and to understand its nature through vipaśyanā or insight meditation.[110] Then, they generate the altruistic attitude of compassion through lojong, or mental training, and practice taking and giving meditation, or tonglen.[111] After that, they prepare themselves with the Vajrayāna foundations, or *ngöndro*. These Vajrayāna preliminaries consist of four practices of 100,000 repetitions each of: special refuge and bodhicitta practice accompanied by prostrations; Vajrasattva purification with mantra recitation; the practice of the two accumulations through offering the maṇḍala; and guru yoga.[112] After these preparations, they practice deity yoga, through reciting the yidam's mantra until signs of success appear.[113]

Finally, they can do the subsequent practices, with Niguma's or Nāropa's six spiritual yogas—the yogas of *tummo*, illusory body, dream state, clear light, bardo, and ejection of consciousness—and gradually realize the bliss-void, which is the essence of mahāmudrā.[114] Practicing in this way, they gradually advance through the bodhisattva bhūmis, or paths of realization, and eventually reach buddhahood.

Practitioners with sublime faculties[115] are those for whom merely encountering the Dharma awakens in their hearts renunciation of samsara, aspiration for enlightenment, compassion for all beings, and trust in the lama and the Three Jewels.

The meaning of emptiness, the practice of mahāmudrā or of dzogchen, fills them with great joy and great aspiration. Their body, speech, and mind have matured through the transmission of initiations, and they recognize in a flash the meaning of mahāmudrā or dzogchen practice. They know how to meditate in the realm of nonmeditation, nongrasping, and nondistraction, and, therefore, there is no doubt that they will attain buddhahood in this life or at the beginning of the bardo.[116]

THE ENLIGHTENMENT OF MIPHAM GONPO

At one time in Tibet, there was a man by the name of Mipham Gonpo who had great respect for the Dharma but had spent his whole life doing business and occupying himself with all kinds of worldly matters—so much so that he had never taken the time to practice. Eventually, when he reached the age of ninety-nine, he could no longer move and had to remain lying down all day long. He was extremely depressed and said to himself, "I spent my whole life in business without practicing Dharma, and now I'm going to die and who knows what will happen."

At this same time, there was a very well known lama called Vairocana, and the old man thought, "If only I could meet Vairocana and request a teaching from him."

Vairocana perceived the old man's wish and came to see him one day. He entered and the old man said, "Who are you?"

"I am Vairocana."

Overjoyed, Mipham Gonpo explained that he was going to die soon and very much wanted to receive a teaching.

"I will give you a teaching, but you must sit up; when the body is lying down, the mind isn't too clear."

It was painful for him to sit, and since he couldn't stay seated for long, he used a meditation girdle and a meditation cane with a chin rest on top and a base resting on the ground. This allowed him to sit up almost completely straight. Vairocana then gave him mahāmudrā instructions and opened him to the nature of mind. The old man was able to meditate, and within a few days he realized mahāmudrā. This is an example of a person of superior ability.

In the following chapters, we will briefly discuss this progression: first, the common preliminaries, or the four ideas that reverse our thinking; then the ngöndro, or the unique preliminaries to the mahāmudrā transmission; then deity yoga; the subsequent practices of Niguma and Nāropa; and finally the practice of mahāmudrā.

6

The Common Preliminary Practices

If our mind has not assimilated the four ideas reversing thought,
Were we to meditate for years,
We would most likely just become more rigid and more attached.
In this way they are indispensable as a basis for practice.

—Kyabje Kalu Rinpoche, *The Essential Bindu*

Through reflection and meditation, the common preliminary practices aim to make us aware of four realities that stimulate our motivation and urge us to practice. These meditations rest on four ideas: the precious human rebirth, impermanence and death, the faults of samsara, and karmic causality. They are known as the common preliminaries insofar as they are not specific to Vajrayāna but are part of the progression in all the yānas.

When we wish to do Dharma practice, we must first become conscious of the difficulty of attaining this precious human existence endowed with all the conditions favorable for reaching enlightenment. This gives us the resolve to enter the path. Meditating on the impermanence of all things, and especially of our own life, will help us to overcome any laziness and impel us to practice with energy. Then, if we recognize that suffering pervades cyclic existence, we will develop an aversion to it, and all our efforts will be directed toward attaining liberation. Finally, if we are convinced of the truth of karma, the relationship between causes and results, we will reject all harmful activities and instead practice what is positive, and thus proceed correctly.

THE PRECIOUS HUMAN REBIRTH

The first thing to meditate on
Is our precious human life, free and endowed,
Hard to come by and easily destroyed.
I will now give it meaning.
—The Ninth Karmapa, *Ngöndro Text*

If we had never encountered the Dharma, we could easily imagine that this world in which we live is all there is. We might take for granted that we were born human. But the fact is, among all of samsara's existences, human life is a remote possibility. Moreover, among humans, only a minute number have a "precious human rebirth," or the "free and endowed human life," that is, the human condition endowed with the freedoms and qualifications necessary to practice Dharma. On the one hand, we must be free from circumstances that allow no leisure for practice; on the other hand, we must have all the personal qualifications and necessary environmental factors that allow for adequate Dharma practice. Buddha Śākyamuni illustrated the difficulty of obtaining such a life in three ways.

The rarity of the precious human rebirth is described in the following way: If a blind turtle swimming in the vast ocean surfaced only once every hundred years, the chances of her slipping her head through a floating wooden yoke tossed about by the wind on the surface of the water is greater than the chances that a consciousness transmigrating in the collection of possible lives will obtain this precious human rebirth!

Now consider all the possible existences in terms of quantities. The number of beings in the hell realms is like the number of grains of sand on the earth; the number of hungry ghosts, like the grains of sand in the river Ganges; the number of animals, like the snowflakes that fall in one year in Tibet. The number of beings in the three realms of existence exceeds the number of stars in the night sky. Therefore, those who have a precious human rebirth are as rare as a star in the daytime. Finally, consider this rarity by meditating on its karmic cause: perfect discipline. In fact, the cause of obtaining this human life is previous positive actions—not one or two here or there, but many and frequent. Rare are those who can do it. We can awaken to the rarity of this precious human existence by contemplating all these points of view.

We also meditate in a number of ways[117] to actually perceive the qualities and possibilities of human life. This impels us to take advantage of it as much as possible, which we will accomplish at an essential level only by using the precious human rebirth as a point of departure for traveling the path to enlightenment.

IMPERMANENCE AND DEATH[118]

It is vital to become aware of impermanence and to develop the habit of perceiving it in all things, because the idea that things are stable and lasting is an illusion, the source of fixation and suffering. Meditating on impermanence has the power to reduce our attachments to this life and to encourage us to practice what is beneficial.

This life is not so important in and of itself, yet we are constantly obsessed with it. It would be better to think about the moment we will leave this world for the unknown one of the bardo. At that time, we will be alone, at an unimaginable distance from the people and things that were familiar to us. This body is a hotel whose guest is consciousness. Soon, this traveler going from country to country will take off for new destinations, leaving behind the hotel that hosted him. [119]

Our life is fleeting. It will soon end. Nothing is more important than Dharma practice to prepare for this departure, because nothing else can really help us at that moment. We should always be ready to die and prepare ourselves as though we were going this very night. If it does not happen, that's fine—the preparation is never wasted.

Impermanence is a universal reality. This world, which looks solid and stable to us, will nonetheless be destroyed slowly by fire, water, and air at the end of the cosmic cycle. Impermanence can be seen in the constant transitions of the world, in the passage of time and the change of seasons. In spring, the reddish-brown earth becomes soft; trees and plants bud. When summer comes, the green-blue ground is moist, and leaves and flowers bloom. Then the force of autumn hardens the now ochre earth; crops ripen; and finally, when winter comes, the earth freezes and becomes grayish; trees and plants dry up and become brittle.

Nothing is permanent; the sun and the moon rise and fall; the clear, transparent day follows the deep, dark night. Everything changes, hour by hour, minute by minute, second by second, like the coursing of a waterfall, which, though it always looks the same, never is; the water is always being replaced.

> The nature of impermanence is such that:
> All accumulated things and wealth are ultimately exhausted;
> Everything erected ultimately collapses.
> All those who have met must ultimately separate.
> Everything that is born ultimately dies.
>
> What goes up must come down;
> What is low becomes high.
> The rich become poor;
> The poor become rich.
> The enemy becomes friend;
> The friend becomes enemy.
>
> There is no thing whose nature is not impermanent.
> To take as permanent what is fleeting
> Is like the delusion of a fool.

Meditation on the impermanence of all things, and especially our own lives, helps us to overcome laziness and practice Dharma energetically. [120]

When we have meditated on impermanence and understood the fleeting nature of all composed things, our attachment to this life and the strength of the six afflictions will decrease while our faith in Dharma increases. We will be able to practice vigorously without any difficulty) and finally gain the supreme realization of mahāmudrā, knowing mind to be beyond birth and death.

DAWA DRAKPA'S FATHER

If we don't keep impermanence in mind, we risk being like Dawa Drakpa's father, a poor man who one day found an enormous sack of barley. Thrilled at having found it, he tied the sack to the ceiling above his bed in order to protect it, then lay down and dreamt that he could sell the barley and make a lot of money, which would allow him to find a wife and have a family. He told himself that he would surely have a son and wondered what to name him. At that moment, a ray of moonlight entered his room and he thought, "I'll name him Dawa Drakpa." While he was caught up in these fantasies, some mice bit through the cord that held the sack of barley, which fell on the man and killed him.

FAULTS OF SAMSARA

> Places, friends, pleasures, possessions,
> And other samsaric things are always ruined
> by the three kinds of suffering.
> Regarding them as the spectacle of an executioner
> leading me to my death,
> Free of attachment,
> I will exert myself to gain enlightenment.
> —The Ninth Karmapa, *Ngöndro Text*

In order to understand what is going on around us, we must keep in mind the reality of suffering.[121] If we are really conscious of samsara's suffering,[122] we will have no fascination for its attractions and we can be detached, thinking of them as a party given in honor of our own execution.

NANDA'S MOTIVATION

Nanda, Buddha Śākyamuni's brother, had a beautiful wife he was very attached to. Despite his brother's example, he did not want to renounce worldly life.

Finally, Buddha Śākyamuni convinced him to become a monk, but Nanda was worried that he wouldn't be able to keep his vows. His attachment persisted, and he wanted to run away.

By his miraculous powers, Buddha Śākyamuni led him to a mountain where there lived a decrepit old woman. "Who is more beautiful, this old woman or your wife?" he asked him.

"My wife, of course! There's no comparison!"

Then Buddha led him to the celestial realms, where he saw sumptuous palaces and beautiful gods and goddesses. In one palace, there were magnificent goddesses but no gods. Nanda asked why and was told that a monk named Nanda, a member of Buddha's family, would take rebirth here by the power of the good deeds he would actually accomplish. Nanda was delighted; he turned to Buddha Śākyamuni, who asked him, "Who is lovelier, these goddesses or your wife?"

"The goddesses are infinitely more beautiful, although my wife was prettier than that decrepit old woman."

Nanda returned to the human realm and, inspired by this adventure, became very diligent in his monastic discipline. But Buddha Śākyamuni said to the monks, "Nanda is keeping discipline in order to be reborn in a celestial realm near young goddesses, while you are keeping discipline to transcend all suffering. His motivation is not right. Do not associate with him." Nanda was extremely upset and asked Buddha what to do.

Buddha suggested that they pay a visit to the hell realms. He led Nanda to a place where torturers were bustling around a boiling pot. Nanda asked what they were doing and they answered, "Buddha has a brother, a monk called Nanda, who practices discipline so he can be reborn in the divine realms, but he'll be reborn here as soon as that divine karma runs out."

Nanda changed his mind upon returning from their visit to the hell realms. He practiced to be delivered from samsara's suffering and became an excellent monk.

We do not think enough about the fact that we depend on one another. On the basic material level, we are all interdependent for our daily needs, and for that reason we are in debt to all beings. By becoming deeply aware that all beings want happiness but end up suffering in many ways, we can cultivate authentic bodhicitta.

As we become conscious of beings' pervasive suffering, our love and compassion will grow, and we will strive to move as quickly as possible toward buddhahood, so that we may develop the qualities that will allow us to help all beings in a meaningful way.

KARMIC CAUSALITY

Death doesn't free us:
Our karma owns us,
So, I will abandon negative actions
and devote myself continuously to positive actions.
Thinking this way, I check my mind daily.

—The Ninth Karmapa, *Ngöndro Text*

Everything we consider as "I," in both its inner and outer aspects, is a result of our previous activities. The actions of this "I" then become causes that generate their own results; this is how karma works.[123] The mind's births and transmigrations are produced by karma and will not stop until the karma is exhausted. This will happen only when illusions are exhausted. Karmic causality is the basis of Dharma discipline.[124] All our actions of body, speech, and mind are like seeds whose fruits and flowers will ripen throughout the series of our lives; the bad seeds yield bad fruit and the good seeds, good fruit. We harvest painful results if we act negatively and happy results when we act positively. Attached to the pleasures of the present, we continue to act non-virtuously, generating negative effects. We strive to be happy but fumble in the darkness of ignorance, as if shooting arrows at night at an invisible target.

If we create a lot of negative karma, we will experience the lower realms, and what we experience there will depend upon that karma.[125] Throughout the course of transmigrations, we are not free. Karma determines our birth and the happy or painful experiences we create. There is no judge who says, "You have been bad, you deserve to suffer." Our misfortunes as well as our good fortune result from karma that we ourselves have created. It is because of their karma that Westerners think they have to work so hard for material comfort and security and that they spend all their time working and have no time to study and practice Dharma. It isn't God or any other external agent that created this world in its complexity; it is the karma of the beings living here. Because karma is so profound, we cannot completely understand it. It is an extremely subtle reality that cannot be perceived unless we have attained enlightenment. But even though we do not understand it completely, we can still understand aspects of it and at least begin to refrain from committing harmful actions and try at every moment to cultivate positive ones. This way we will avoid miserable rebirths and progress through more fortunate lives until we reach enlightenment, at which point we will be able to understand karma completely.

These four common preliminary practices, or "basic ideas," are extremely important, and we should reflect on them until they pervade our thoughts, our words, and our actions. If we act in accordance with these ideas, we can apply ourselves to Dharma practice without any problem, and no obstacle will trip us up. If we assimilate them well, we will strive toward enlightenment and have the energy necessary to proceed along the path.

7

The Ngöndro

Don't rush into mahāmudrā meditation;
First prepare the ground with the preliminaries
By planting positive qualities.

—Jamgön Kongtrul Lodrö Thaye, *The Torch of Certainty*

The ngöndro practices are special preparations for Vajrayāna practice in general and mahāmudrā or dzogchen in particular. Let's say that enlightenment is America and we are in India—or the other way around. The practice of mahāmudrā or dzogchen is the plane that gets us there.

We really want to make the journey but need the money for the airline ticket. In order to take this mahāmudrā or dzogchen plane, we need to gather together enough wisdom and merit. This is the objective of doing ngöndro, or the special preliminaries to the transmission of mahāmudrā or dzogchen.

It is not possible to use these extraordinary methods—mahāmudrā or dzogchen—correctly without having done at least one of the preliminaries. Those who can benefit from their transmission without at least one of the preliminaries are extremely rare. These preliminaries prepare the field of our mind. When the ground is well prepared—when pebbles and weeds have been removed and the soil has been fertilized—the seeds we plant can grow with no problem. Similarly, the preliminaries prepare us for transmission by eliminating obscurations and gathering the accumulations of merit and wisdom. Receiving mahāmudrā or dzogchen transmission exposes us to the dangers of not really understanding the teachings and of being reborn in the divine formless realms or, worse, in the form of a stupid animal.

Tackling such instructions without the necessary preliminaries and without sufficient connection prevents any real or profound practice because we are unprepared. Then, having had no success, we risk thinking that the teachings have no power or that the lama has no spiritual influence. This gives rise to extremely serious misconceptions. Therefore, it is crucial to approach these teachings with the necessary maturity and preparation.

You could say that the preliminaries build the road we travel upon. To drive a car, you need a road! Moreover, it is much better to drive on a road free of rocks and potholes than on one that is so rough that even a good car cannot get very far. So the function of the preliminaries is to prepare for the path.

Depending upon how you count them, there are four or five preliminaries.

They are often referred to as the Hundred Thousand, because each one consists of 100,000 repetitions of the practice. They are: the practice of special refuge along with prostrations; Vajrasattva purification accompanied by recitation of the hundred-syllable mantra; gathering the two accumulations by offering maṇḍalas; and finally guru yoga done with a prayer.[126]

REFUGE AND PROSTRATIONS[127]

This is a special refuge practice[128] that creates a very strong connection with enlightenment and the lineage. For this connection to be established effectively, there are two necessary elements: on the one hand, faith and aspiration, which we have already compared to a ring, and, on the other hand, the blessings and compassion of the buddhas, which are like a hook. The hook is always there, but to get caught by it, we need the ring of our own faith. This faith joins us to the object of refuge and removes obstacles, while at the same time creating favorable conditions for us. This is why this special practice of taking refuge is the first of the four preliminaries.

In the presence of the field of refuge which we visualize in front of us, we and all beings go for refuge to the Three Jewels and the Three Roots. The Three Jewels are the outer refuge, and the Three Roots are the inner refuge. These six are united in the person of the lama, forming the secret refuge; the enlightenment of the three bodies of the Buddha being the suchness, or absolute refuge.[129] Thus, taking refuge is a very powerful practice that we do with our whole being: body, speech, and mind. With our mind, we imagine the presence of the field of refuge and generate deep faith and aspiration; we recite the refuge prayer with our speech; and we prostrate with our body.[130]

VAJRASATTVA PURIFICATION

Although we may not be aware of it, we have accumulated in our mindstreams an inconceivable amount of negative karma and obscurations since beginningless time. Our mind is completely steeped in them, and unless we eliminate and purify them, it is impossible to progress toward enlightenment. Our mind is like a piece of dirty linen, which, in order to be dyed—to receive transmission—must first be washed. A piece of dirty linen won't take dye, while clean white linen will take on any color.

Vajrasattva practice, done undistractedly and with great sincerity, effects this purification, this cleansing. Vajrasattva is an aspect of Buddha representing the fundamental purity of enlightenment and activates a purifying power. There is also great blessing associated with this practice.

When we have dirty clothes to wash, we need water, soap, and our hands for scrubbing. Similarly, to effect purification through this practice, we need several elements at once: Vajrasattva's blessing, the power of his mantra, and the strength of our practice. This approach might seem similar to the Christian idea of washing away sins, but the difference is that Christians believe the cloth and water come from God who created them, while Dharma does not regard Vajrasattva in this way.

Our mind is by nature empty; it has neither form, nor color, nor any other characteristic. Negative imprints, the mind's thoughts and emotions, are equally empty, invisible, formless, and colorless, yet they are present and have the capacity to harm us. They exist as a multiplicity of interdependent factors that delude and confuse our mind. In order to purify them, Vajrasattva practice uses other interdependent factors, which are the elements of the meditation we have just described. Through practice, purification takes place by means of the four forces: the regret of previous negative actions; the support of the different vows we have taken; the visualization and recitation of the meditation itself; and the resolve not to repeat negative actions. Practiced together, these allow complete purification no matter what we may have done.

In the West, many people admit that meditation is a good thing but find mantra recitation a bit odd. If the mind is indeed most important, there is no reason to think that way, because we are made up of the totality of body, speech, and mind, so it is vital to include all of these when we practice Dharma: we meditate with our mind, recite the mantra with our speech, and hold the correct posture with our body. Reciting the mantra without distraction is important because it has a particular impact on the mind. In fact, the mantra is tendrel,[131] or interdependent factors, itself empty of sound.

In addition, the veils and negative imprints that are to be purified are themselves dependently arisen; they are empty. This is why it is possible to purify them. The interaction of the two sets of dependently arisen factors, of mantra and negative imprints, dissolves the latter and brings about purification. This is how the practice can have a truly purifying effect. To actually understand dependent arising and emptiness is to be close to enlightenment; it is in failing to understand these that we err in samsara. In any case, the most important thing is that the mind be completely present during recitation.

OFFERING THE MANDALA

After Vajrasattva purification, which undoes negativity, it is important to cultivate positive factors, that is, to practice the two accumulations of merit and wisdom. This is the function of the third preliminary practice, or offering the mandala.

In this practice, we make offerings to the Three Jewels and Three Roots. These are aspects of primordial wisdom, completely free of attachment to whatever we may offer them, but we still dedicate all the goods and wealth in the universe to them. Why? Because we are so utterly subject to grasping at an "I," and always think in terms of "me," that we have the feeling of actually existing separate and apart, and because of this self-grasping, we attribute different things to ourselves; we think, "my possessions, my wealth, my house, my family, my friends, my body," and so on. In order to loosen this grasping and attachment to things as our own, we offer it all to the field of refuge on the one hand, and we practice generosity[132] toward ordinary beings on the other; thus, offering the maṇḍala includes both enlightened and ordinary beings. Offering maṇḍalas is an all-encompassing gift in which we direct everything we have to the Three Jewels—our whole world, everything in the universe that is beautiful, every delightful thing we can imagine—in the form of a maṇḍala of the universe.

Maṇḍala is a Sanskrit term which is translated into Tibetan as *kyilkhor*. *Kyil* means "center" and *khor* means "limit" or "periphery." A maṇḍala is a structure consisting of a center and a circumference. In the case of the maṇḍala of the universe, the center is the central mountain, and its circumference is a group of continents. Above and below these are the different planes of existence, the higher and lower human realms. This is an extremely profound representation which includes not only the visible world but all the realms of existence in the universe. We offer infinite numbers of this maṇḍala of the universe, imagining that there are as many maṇḍalas as there are atoms in the world, and we dedicate all of them to enlightenment.

The benefits of this practice are proportionate to the size of our offering, and we pray that by this immense offering all beings may attain enlightenment. Thus, there is a significant bodhicitta dimension to the practice of offering the maṇḍala. Through the accumulation of merit that this unlimited offering generates, we approach the ability to accumulate wisdom.

GURU YOGA

Lama or guru yoga is, according to the literal meaning of the word "yoga," the practice of union with the lama. It is the last of the four preliminaries and the most important, because it is especially through this practice that we receive the lama's blessing, the lineage's blessing, and, ultimately, enlightenment. Through this blessing, transmission and transformation can operate deeply.[133] It is like the sun, while our mind is like a flower that grows and blooms beneath its rays. Guru yoga cultivates devotion, *mögü* in Tibetan, which literally means "respect and aspiration" or "admiration."

In this practice, the lama is the main refuge; arranged within him are all refuges, which include the Three Jewels. The lama's mind is the Buddha; his speech is the Dharma, and his body is the Sangha. He also incorporates the Three Roots: the lama's mind is the yidam, or meditational deity; his speech is the dharmapala, the Dharma protector; and his body is the lama. Thus the lama is the union of all the refuges, and he is considered as Buddha Vajradhara himself, the personification of the Absolute Body, or dharmakāya, and thus it is possible to open oneself to his blessing. It is said that:

> To see the lama as Buddha
> Yields the blessing of Buddha.
> To see the lama as a bodhisattva
> Yields the blessing of a bodhisattva.
> To see the lama as a good spiritual friend
> Yields a corresponding blessing.
> To see the lama as an ordinary being
> Yields no blessing.

Meditating this way, we pray to our lama intensely and sincerely. It is through our own devotion that we can receive his blessing.[134]

One traditional image compares the lama to a magnifying glass that concentrates the rays of the sun—the buddhas' blessings. This concentration is so intense that it can ignite the tinder of our mind's delusions.

Because they had complete faith in their lamas, all the great lineage masters—Nāropa, Marpa, Milarepa, and others—were able to attain enlightenment within their lifetimes.

Chenrezig, the Buddha of Compassion

8

Deity Yoga

The basis of purification is the eternal,
non-composite realm of reality
that fully permeates all beings as the buddha nature.
Sentient beings thus also possess the qualities of the Body of Reality,
such as the marks and signs,
that exist as an integral aspect of awareness:
this is the basis for purification.

—Jamgön Kongtrul Lodrö Thaye, *Outline of Essential Points*

The Vajrayāna path, which includes many methods for advancing, is called the path of means or skillful means.

After completing the four special preliminary practices, the next step is to practice deity yoga, or meditation with a yidam or meditational deity. This method is used to transform mind and facilitate mahāmudrā realization. After the preliminaries, we generally engage in the practice of a yidam along with the recitation of that deity's mantra.

Basically, all yidams[135] are of the same nature; there are no essential differences between them. However, some deity yoga practices, such as Vajrayoginī or Cakrasaṃvara, require particular conditions; we must go into strict retreat and carefully follow the rules of practice. In the course of ordinary activities, this is not easy. By contrast, there is a yidam practice—Chenrezig, or the buddha of compassion—that is not as restrictive and can be done easily in daily life.

In general, I think it is the best practice because it is both easy and very beneficial; this is why I have taught it in centers all over the world. In any case, it is an excellent introduction to Vajrayāna practice.

RELATIVE DEITY, ULTIMATE DEITY

The form of Chenrezig used in the sādhana or meditation practice represents the Buddha's compassion. Beyond his form, Chenrezig's ultimate aspect is independent of our meditation; it is the pure nature of mind. A yidam or deity exists at two levels. The ultimate level of the yidam is beyond form; it is the ultimate wisdom aspect. The goal of the practice is to reveal this wisdom aspect through the intermediary of the form aspect, or the relative deity.[136] During the first phase of the sādhana, we meditate on the relative deity, which ensures a bond with the ultimate deity, the aspect that is beyond form, inaccessible to conceptual mind. The relative or relational aspect allows for the realization of the ultimate wisdom aspect.

THE TWO STAGES OF DEITY YOGA

In order to understand a bit about the skillful means used in the Vajrayāna, we must return to our mind, which ordinarily thinks, "I exist, I am," and identifies strongly with a "me" experienced as our body, speech, and mind. These fixed identifications are the source of suffering and errors in samsara; they are the primary obstacle to the realization of mahāmudrā, and it is very difficult to abandon them. The Vajrayāna, therefore, teaches us first to exchange these fixations for other, more subtle and less solid ones: fixations on the body, speech, and mind of the yidam. After this, it is easier to let go of all fixation and to move on to a meditation completely devoid of forms and objects, which, when realized, is the actual mahāmudrā meditation. These phases of substituting identifications and then abandoning all fixation correspond with the two phases of all deity yoga. We will clarify them, using as an example the Chenrezig sādhana practice.

We are all habitually fixated on our body, and when we experience "me," we cling to the image of our body. To go beyond this fixation, the Chenrezig meditation substitutes for our usual experience of our body that of Chenrezig's body. The practice is not to imagine ourselves in Chenrezig's form as if it were a physical, substantial body like a statue—this would be of no benefit—but to *be* Chenrezig as an empty form, like a rainbow, a reflection of the moon on water, or a dream. Our body is Chenrezig's body, visible yet empty, a conjunction of emptiness and appearance, or what is called an empty appearance.

Sounds are transformed in a similar way. In fact, if everything we said was something solid, all of space would not be enough to contain all our speech. Unfortunately, we do not recognize the empty nature of our words, and we fixate on them as though they were real. This is why pleasant words make us happy and unpleasant ones upset us. These reactions show that we believe in the reality of words; we grasp at them as real. To transcend these fixations, in the sādhana we transform these sounds and ordinary words into the sound of Chenrezig's mantra, whose nature is empty sound, like the void resonance of an echo.

Finally, there is our mind with its contents, which is itself also fundamentally empty. We have studied a lot in school, in college, and have a lot of knowledge in our memory. If everything we have learned had a solid form, it could never fit in our heads, or in this room, or even in all of space! Fortunately for us, mind is empty and its contents have no tangible form.

Most likely, we have a lot of disturbing emotions. If there were a room where we could stockpile anger, another for desire, jealousy, and so on, they would quickly be packed full. The fact that this is not possible is a sign of their emptiness, but here too, even though thoughts and emotions are empty, we do not recognize them as such and create lots of problems for ourselves by fixating on them. To alleviate that, during the sādhana, we substitute our ordinary thoughts with Chenrezig's presence and meditate on our mind and its contents as having Chenrezig's nature, in which thoughts and emotions are transparent. He has wisdom but it is empty; he has wisdom and emptiness, void wisdom.

Through these substitutions, practicing Chenrezig's sādhana effects a transformation[137] of the impure aspects of our body, speech, and mind, whose natures are empty form, sound, and wisdom, respectively.

This phase of substitution, during which we visualize the yidam and recite its mantra, is the first phase of deity yoga, or the Generation Stage (*utpattikrama* in Sanskrit). Our fixation on the reality of appearance, sounds, and thoughts is the illness that deludes us and causes us suffering. In the Generation Stage, the remedy is threefold. At the level of forms, we meditate on all of them as being inseparable from emptiness; all have a nature of the void appearance of Chenrezig's body. Sounds are also inseparable from emptiness and meditated on as having the nature of the empty sound of Chenrezig's mantra. All mental phenomena—thoughts and cognitions—are meditated on as the union of wisdom and emptiness, as Chenrezig's mind, which is mahāmudrā. In the Generation Stage, there is no reason to eliminate thoughts or interfere with their energy; only their aspect changes. Ordinary thoughts are substituted with thoughts of Chenrezig's presence, and this versatility of mind is thus integrated and transformed in practice.

The second phase of deity yoga is the Completion Stage, which is silent and formless. The visualization and representations of the Generation Stage dissolve, blending with a light that is reabsorbed into Chenrezig, which we are, and finally disappears completely. There is no more reference point, and mind remains in its natural state, open and detached, lucid and watchful, uncontrived and free of distraction. When realized, this meditation becomes mahāmudrā practice. The practice of deity yoga, through the joint practices of Generation and Completion Stages, is a very quick method for attaining realization of mind, or mahāmudrā.

The Tree of the Five Golden Teachings

These Five Golden Teachings are usually presented using an image of a tree whose roots are the six yogas of Niguma. The trunk is the mahāmudrā reliquary, the branches are the three methods of integration, the flowers are the white and red ḍākinis, and the fruit is faultless immortality.

9

The Subsequent Practices

Ripened by the four initiations,
Those endowed with faith and energy,
If they first understand impermanence, renunciation,
And the unsatisfactory nature of conditioned existence,
And exert effort in this supreme path,
Whoever they may be,
Within six months, a year, or this life,
They will attain enlightenment.

—Niguma, *Diamond Verses*

For a glimpse of the progressive path that can be followed after practicing deity yoga, we will look at examples from the practices of the Shangpa lineage, which presents this progression as the Five Golden Teachings.

THE FIVE GOLDEN TEACHINGS

The Five Golden Teachings are a complete approach to enlightenment which goes back to the great adept Khyungpo Neljor, a master and contemporary of Marpa the Translator. In his youth, he studied Bön and later the dzogchen teachings. Dissatisfied, he decided to seek teaching in India. He had 150 masters, of whom the most important were two women, the primordial wisdom dākinis Niguma and Sukhasiddhi. Since Khyungpo Neljor had practiced the purification and the accumulations and had excellent karma from previous lives, he had at his disposal an enormous amount of gold that he brought with him to India on his search for teachings. Each time he requested teachings, he would offer hundreds of ounces of gold. He thereby acquired the reputation of being generous with gold, and his teachings were subsequently known as the Golden Teachings.

THE STORY OF NIGUMA

Niguma was born in Kashmir, in the country called Land of Great Magic, which was also the birthplace of several mahāsiddhas, including Nāropa, who was her brother. She had chosen to take rebirth as a woman to be able to help beings. In previous lives, she had attained an extraordinarily advanced level of realization.

In her manifestation as Niguma, she was a primordial wisdom dākini who had reached the tenth bodhisattva ground, or perfect enlightenment. Her body, a rainbow body, completely transcended the ordinary level. She received teachings directly from Vajradhara and had Khyungpo Neljor as her principal disciple.

After Khyungpo Neljor had received teachings from the greatest masters, they told him that someone of his caliber should go and seek teachings from the great bodhisattva Niguma, inseparable from Vajradhara. He asked them where he could find her, and they replied that ordinary beings could not find her because she no longer had a physical body but only a rainbow body. Still, her presence could manifest anywhere to beings with a high level of realization, and from time to time she visited the larger charnel grounds, accompanied by a band of dākinis, and presided over enormous vajra feasts. Hearing about Niguma, Khyungpo Neljor was overcome with emotion and wept streams of tears. He departed immediately to search the great Sossaling charnel ground, hoping and praying intensely that he would find her.

When he arrived, he saw high in the sky a deity with brown skin who was holding a trident and a kapāla and decked with bone ornaments. While contemplating her, he saw at first just one dākini and then many; some of them were seated in meditation and others in different dance postures. Certain that it was Niguma with her entourage, he paid homage to her and requested teaching. At first the apparition mocked him, warning him, "I am an ogress dākini, and my entourage are as well, so save yourself before we devour you!"

But Niguma's words did not discourage Khyungpo Neljor, who reiterated his request. Niguma told him that if he really wanted to receive the teaching, he should offer gold. Khyungpo Neljor immediately offered all of his gold powder. Niguma took it and tossed it into the air, scattering it over the forest. Khyungpo Neljor was shocked. Then Niguma told him that she had no need of any gold because, for her, the three spheres of the universe were already gold. This confirmed Khyungpo Neljor's faith in her, as a real ogress would definitely have been attached to the gold.

Khyungpo Neljor received from her transmission of the six yogas of Niguma, mahāmudrā, and the Five Golden Teachings. He recorded these teachings on a piece of parchment he kept rolled up in a reliquary around his neck. This is how the mahāmudrā reliquary tradition got its name.

After transmitting all the teachings to him, Niguma told Khyungpo Neljor that only she and the mahāsiddha Lawapa had received them, that they should be kept secret for seven generations, that they were to be transmitted to only one lineage holder, and that only after seven generations could they be publicly transmitted.[138] She also predicted that not only he but all his successors would have the chance of meeting her in the future.

The first Golden Teaching—represented by the roots of the tree, or the foundation—consists of the six yogas of Niguma,[139] called tummo, illusory body, dream, clear light, transference of consciousness, and bardo.

In *tummo* or *inner heat yoga*, practitioners apply themselves in mastering a four-part respiration—inhalation, retention, release, and exhalation, called vase respiration—along with exercises on the channels and main points—*bindu* in Sanskrit, and *thigle* in Tibetan—of the subtle body. Through mastery of the descent, retention, and ascension and diffusion of the "white substance," heat and ecstasy are produced. This bliss progressively leads to the union of great bliss and emptiness, which is the very experience of mahāmudrā.

The *yoga of the illusory body* allows us to realize the illusory nature of our experiences, letting attachment and aversion free themselves. This yoga facilitates the recognition of all things as an illusion or magical creation, very much like movies or television shows!

Dream yoga allows illusions to be purified by themselves. There are several stages: making dreams lucid or "seizing the dream," then, during the dream itself, there is training, multiplication, projection, transmutation, and, finally, understanding appearances.

Clear light yoga spontaneously eliminates ignorance or mental dullness, allowing us to have deep and lucid sleep at night and to experience the clear light during sleep.

Transference or *ejection of consciousness* allows for the attainment of enlightenment without meditation, and especially at the moment of death.[140]

The *yoga of the bardo* yields recognition of the nature of the bardos[141] and through them, the three bodies of the Buddha.

THE TREE OF THE FIVE GOLDEN TEACHINGS

These Five Golden Teachings are usually presented using an image of a tree whose roots are the six yogas of Niguma. The trunk is the mahāmudrā reliquary, the branches are the three methods of integration, the flowers are the white and red dākinis, and the fruit is faultless immortality.

The practice of these six yogas is done on the basis of a particular initiation and requires that certain samaya, or sacred bonds, be kept. Practicing them together leads to realization of mahāmudrā, but the practice of a single yoga, such as tummo, the illusory body, or the clear light, can lead to realization by itself.

The second Golden Teaching—the trunk of the tree—is the mahāmudrā reliquary, the mahāmudrā tradition that Khyungpo Neljor received from the primordial wisdom dākini Niguma. Its preliminaries are called the three natural methods—*rangbab* in Tibetan—of body, speech, and mind. Later comes spontaneous liberation from the four obstacles that prevent recognition of mahāmudrā: mahāmudrā is too close to be recognized, too profound to be grasped, too simple to believe, and too marvelous to be understood conceptually. Freedom from these four obstacles reveals the spontaneous presence of the three bodies of the Buddha.[142]

The third Golden Teaching—the branches—consists in three methods of integration that help us to cultivate the continuous experience of mahāmudrā in all circumstances. They are related with the lama, the yidam, and the experience of the illusoriness of all things.

The fourth Golden Teaching—the flowers—consists of two practices involving the white and red dākinis. If we keep our vows or samaya perfectly pure, these practices allow the practitioner to go to the dākini realms without even leaving the body.

The fifth Golden Teaching—the fruit—is faultless immortality. At the moment of ultimate enlightenment, mind is realized beyond deaths and births; this is what the allusion to immortality refers to.

These different practices are generally to be done in retreat,[143] especially in the three-year retreat. Retreat is not mandatory in order to do them, but it is difficult to be able to practice them intensely enough to succeed outside of the retreat context.

THE YOUNG PRINCE AND THE MAGICIAN

There was once a young prince of a royal family in India. His mother did not wish to see him ascend the throne and hoped instead that he would practice Dharma. His father, the king, however, wanted his son to succeed him and cared little whether the prince practiced Dharma. The king ruled in the family, and so the mother wondered what to do. At that time in India, there were many expert magicians, so she went to see one and asked if he couldn't use his magic to make her son renounce worldly activities and pursue Dharma.

The magician acquiesced. "It can be done, but you must tell me what your son loves most."

"He loves horses," she said.

"Fine," said the magician. "Come back tomorrow with your son." And they arranged a meeting.

The following day, the queen organized a ride with the king and their son to the agreed-upon place. The magician was there with a fantastic horse that he had created magically, a magnificent stallion like those the prince dreamt of. Captivated, and unaware that the man he was talking to was a magician, the prince said, "May I buy this horse?"

The magician replied, "If you want, why not?"

"I'd like to try him first."

"But of course, go right ahead!"

The prince mounted the horse and departed at a great gallop; he couldn't stop it. He went very, very far away, to an unfamiliar country. When he finally stopped, he didn't know where he was or which way to go. Just then, a short way off in the distance, he noticed some smoke and decided to investigate. He discovered a house; at the threshold stood a woman with her daughter, a ravishing young woman.

"I'm lost," he said. "May I stay here?"

"If you like. We live near the sea and you are most welcome."

So he remained, because he no longer knew where his own country was, and these people had never heard of it. Since the young woman was so pretty, he married her; they had many children and were a very happy family. His father-in-law, who also lived with them, was ill and couldn't walk.

One day, the prince's wife, who liked the horse, said, "May I ride your horse?"

"Of course, go ahead!"

She mounted the horse, which ran into the ocean with her, and she drowned. Seeing this, all her children—except for the littlest, who was too young—plunged into the water hoping to rescue her, but they too drowned. Then, the sick old father-in-law jumped into the water, and he died also. Only the youngest boy was left, but then the horse returned, ate the child, and ran away. When the prince discovered what had happened, he was absolutely desperate.

"I've lost my wife, my children, my horse, my whole family; I have nothing left. It's better to die!" And so he plunged into the water hoping to drown, but instead of drowning he found himself in the park of his home village with the king and the queen. Confused and trembling, he remembered his beloved wife and children. He explained to his parents what had happened to him, but they said, "Oh, no! Don't be afraid. You fell off the horse, and you fainted here for about an hour. You must rest."

The prince was convinced that his story was real, because he had truly lived it and suffered a lot from it. Finally, after that adventure, the prince realized the illusory nature of ordinary life and totally devoted himself to Dharma. After several years of practice, he became a great master adept.

PART TWO

Section Five

Mahāmudrā and Dzogchen:
The Immediate Path

The Third Karmapa, Rangjung Dorje

I

Mahāmudrā and Dzogchen

Being without intellectual concepts. it is called
the Great Sign, or Mahāmudrā.
Being without extremes, it is called
the Great Middle Way, or Mādhyamika.
As it embraces everything, it is called
the Great Perfection, or Maha-Ati.
May we have the confidence that the experience of one
is the experience of the meaning of all.

—The Third Karmapa, *Mahāmudrā: Boundless Joy and Freedom*

The teachings and practices of mahāmudrā or dzogchen are the heart and quintessence of Dharma. They are the experience of nonduality, the realization of emptiness, the fundamental nature of mind. This realization removes all the veils that obscure mind's nature, the buddha nature. Whatever life we might have led and whatever path we might have taken, if we reach this singular realization, we will have accomplished the consummate result.

Mahāmudrā, "the great seal," or dzogchen, "the great perfection," are truly beyond the distinction between meditation and nonmeditation. It is not really appropriate to name them one way or another. The culmination of all practices, they can conventionally be called the highest form of meditation. Some people make a distinction between dzogchen and mahāmudrā, but this is unnecessary because, fundamentally, they are two names for the same experience. Different lineages simply employ slightly different methods of instruction that lead to the same realization.

Full realization of mahāmudrā or dzogchen completely liberates us from all ignorance. But someone who has "almost" attained this realization and thinks he has understood something that he believes is dzogchen or mahāmudrā is in a very perilous situation indeed. Since he is still subject to ignorance, such a person is in danger of being reborn in the form of some dull-witted and limited creature. It is therefore critical to always follow the lama's instructions faithfully and not arrogantly think one has understood.

In the Kagyu lineage, which primarily transmits mahāmudrā, these different presentations are given several names. For example, in the Karma-Kagyu tradition, mahāmudrā is often the introduction to the three bodies of the Buddha. In the Shangpa-Kagyu tradition of the mahāmudrā reliquary, mahāmudrā is thought of as a reliquary containing the nature of mind. There are many more of these, but essentially they all teach the same thing.

MAHĀMUDRĀ

We can get a kind of traditional definition of mahāmudrā by examining the etymology of this word, which is *chagya chenpo* in Tibetan. *Chagya* is the equivalent of the Sanskrit *mudra* and can be translated as "sign," "symbol," or "seal." The Tibetan *chenpo* is *mahā* in Sanskrit, meaning "great." Thus, "mahāmudrā" is the "great seal" or "great symbol." The sign or seal referred to is the emptiness of all phenomena. The image relates to the experience of mahāmudrā, in which all phenomena, samsara as well as nirvana, are essentially void. More specifically, *cha* is interpreted as "primordial wisdom of emptiness," and *gya* as "not to go beyond" or "not to leave." *Chagya* or mudra refers therefore to the state that never departs from the primordial wisdom of emptiness. Chenpo or "great" is interpreted as the expression that no practice can exceed the understanding that never strays from the essential emptiness of all phenomena. Of all the teachings, it is the best and most profound.

Realization of mahāmudrā is the union of emptiness and compassion: emptiness has a dynamism whose manifestation is compassion.

In the Kālacakra teachings, this realization is designated as the nondual union of fundamental emptiness of all experience and "great bliss" —*mahāsukha* in Sanskrit—which is the fundamental energy of empty mind.

PATH OF MAHĀMUDRĀ

Mahāmudrā can be thought of as comprising three aspects: mahāmudrā as basis, mahāmudrā as path, and mahāmudrā as result. Mahāmudrā as basis or foundation is the nature of our mind, the buddha nature as it is fundamentally present in our mind. Mahāmudrā as path is the practice carried out from the time the lama has introduced to us the nature of mind up until realization. Then, when the practice of mahāmudrā is realized and has become definitively stable, it is mahāmudrā as result. If we consider that mahāmudrā is the actual nature of mind and that this nature has always been there, it may seem easy to realize. But, in fact, it is usually very difficult, because mahāmudrā is extremely profound, and the point is not merely to understand it; it is also vital to be able to practice and cultivate the experience of mahāmudrā until realization has occurred. The difficulty comes from our obscured mind, which has been darkened from beginningless time by the four obscurations we have already discussed: the veil of ignorance, the veil of basic tendencies, the veil of the passions or mental afflictions, and the veil of karma.[144]

To return to an image we have used before, mind in its ordinary state may be compared to the sky obscured by layers of clouds that hide its real nature. These coverings prevent us from recognizing mind's true nature, that is, the buddha nature, *tathāgatagarbha* in Sanskrit. If we recognize it, that is enlightenment, buddhahood, or realization of mahāmudrā. It is the foundation of enlightenment. If mind is not realized, it becomes the ground of all illusions, the basis for samsara. The basic difference between enlightenment and ignorance, between nirvana and samsara, is whether or not we have recognized this buddha nature. So it is a question of unveiling it, discovering it, since everything rests on this recognition.

This discovery is, generally, where all Dharma teachings and meditation practices converge.[145] This is especially what the ngöndro and the Generation and Completion Stage deity yoga practices—extremely profound and efficient for our purification and two accumulations—prepare us for. This is why in the Kham province of eastern Tibet, a realized and very well known lama by the name of Atsom Drupa, each time a disciple came to request a teaching on mahāmudrā or dzogchen, would begin by asking him or her to do 100,000 prostrations, 100,000 Vajrasattva mantra recitations, 100,000 mandala offerings, and 100,000 guru yoga recitations. He would not agree to give the teaching until these preliminaries were completed.

In terms of the path of mahāmudrā, there are several approaches, mainly those of sūtra and those of tantra. Both lead to enlightenment, but they differ in the instructions and methods used to attain the result. The sūtra approach entails many examinations for recognizing mind; it is a rather slow approach. In the tantric approach, the point is also recognition of mind, but particular emphasis is given to blessing or inspiration, which is the active element of the realization. It is the path of "aspiration-admiration" or devotion, which allows for much quicker progress.

2

Transmission and Qualification

Whether we are of greater, middling, or lesser abilities,
the best signs of success are a decrease of self-centeredness
and the easing of mental afflictions.

—Gampopa, *Precious Garland of the Sublime Way*

Mahāmudrā, the essence of the sūtras and tantras and basis of all of the Buddha's teachings, must not be transmitted carelessly or given out indiscriminately. It is a very precious and holy teaching. It must be explained to those who are ready for it, who have the intelligence to understand it and the confidence and enthusiasm to put it into practice.

THE GOLDEN NUGGET

If someone who is fit to understand mahāmudrā makes a deep connection with a qualified lama, true transmission and genuine understanding can take place. This person will be able to benefit greatly from it, which is wonderful and extremely positive. On the other hand, if an unqualified person receives instruction on mahāmudrā, which is secret by nature, no harm will be done, but he will not be helped much; it just would not be particularly useful. There is, however, the danger that this person might get wrong ideas, or else lose any faith he might have had, which would be extremely unfortunate. These teachings, then, have to be given correctly, using good judgment.

The lama who expounds this teaching must be sincerely motivated by concern for others and genuinely wish to help those to whom he transmits it. The teaching must be understood to be a means of obtaining liberation and helping to free all beings from the suffering of cyclic existence. In order to benefit from it, disciples who receive it must truly be able to regard the lama as Buddha Vajradhara and the teaching as a nectar that rids the mind of all impurities. So, if the teaching is understood, this means that it was fit to be received. If not, we must at least keep faith in it, as it can be very beneficial and help certain beings. It is particularly important not to give rise to mistaken ideas. As long as this does not happen, there is no problem. Suppose I have a golden nugget in my hand along with some little stones and seashells, and I toss them all into the audience: someone might find the nugget!

THREE KINDS OF RECEPTIVITY

Mahāmudrā can be extremely difficult or, on the other hand, extremely easy to realize; it depends on the individual. Although we are all basically identical, since we all have the same buddha nature, there are some big differences regarding qualification for the teachings that enable the realization of mahāmudrā. Some beings have a greater receptivity and ability to understand, others have a middling receptivity and capacity, and still others have a lesser receptivity and ability to understand.

All those whose capacity to understand is middling or lesser—the great majority of people—cannot recognize and realize the nature of mahāmudrā at first; they need to approach it gradually, making the preparations we already mentioned.[146] Beings of lesser capacity are people who, on hearing the explanations on mahāmudrā, cannot see what it is about at all. When they try to meditate, they are always in doubt, thinking, "No, it can't really be this," or "I won't succeed, I can't see what it's about." These attitudes indicate the presence of obscurations that can be eliminated with the practice of the accumulations and purification.

Persons of middling capacity who are shown the mahāmudrā understand it to a certain extent but not completely. To arrive at greater receptivity, they too need to practice the accumulations and purification.

Those of highest ability understand the mahāmudrā instantly when their lama shows it to them. Not only do they have keen intelligence that allows them to grasp the teaching's profundity immediately, but they can experience it simultaneously in their mindstream; they know right away what it is about and how to practice it. They feel great joy and obtain results quickly. These persons are naturally very compassionate and very enthusiastic about practice, and they have great faith in their lama and the Three Jewels. Such persons receive all four initiations; the relationship created by this bond, together with heartfelt devotion, establishes the deep connection that transmits blessing. This privileged relationship allows them to quickly understand mahāmudrā and to practice it correctly. The recognition of mahāmudrā then dissolves the darkness of eons of samsaric existence, just as a torch that catches fire can eliminate eons of darkness. For such people, the sole practice of mahāmudrā can be the panacea that fulfills all their needs. But this is possible only in very exceptional cases. The difference between beings of higher, middling, and lesser capacities is not so much a matter of external qualifications—man or woman, strong or weak, having this or that; the difference is that those of higher ability have, in previous lives, already extensively practiced the accumulations of merit and wisdom, and purification, while others have not. But superior ability does not necessarily have to be present from birth: each of us can become a being of highest capacity through ample practice of the accumulations and purification.[147]

THE ENLIGHTENMENT OF INDRABODHI

King Indrabodhi was an example of a person with superior ability, who lived long ago in Buddha Śākyamuni's time in India. A great king, he lorded over a palace and court where he continually enjoyed all the sense pleasures. He was said to have had an entourage of five hundred courtesans by day and five hundred more by night! One day, he was enjoying himself with them on the palace terrace when a flock of five hundred large yellow birds flew through the sky overhead.

"Strange, I've never seen yellow birds that size. Find out about them!" he ordered, his curiosity piqued. A minister who practiced Dharma said, "Your Majesty, those are not birds, but Lord Buddha traveling with his five hundred arhats."

"How wonderful!" said the king. "Invite them to come to the palace, if they would."

"Your Majesty, they live very far away. It would be a long and difficult trip for a messenger, but that surely is not necessary, because Buddha is omniscient. Praying to him is enough for him to come."

The king ordered appropriate preparations to be made and had the palace terrace cleared for Buddha Śākyamuni and his attendants to stay there. A few days later, everything was ready for the great reception, and the king and his court gathered to pray to Buddha to come with his five hundred arhats. The banquet was served. When Buddha arrived with the five hundred arhats, the king prostrated three times before him and said:

"You are truly marvelous! Would you give me a teaching, that I too might obtain the same realization as yours?" Buddha replied, "Certainly!" and taught him the Four Noble Truths, explaining that all life is suffering and especially that since all sense pleasures chain us to samsara, they should be abandoned.

The king, somewhat disconcerted, said, "Yes, I'm sure that's all well and good. But it isn't for me. I'm not going to renounce the sense pleasures just like that. If you don't have any other teachings, I'm afraid I won't be able to practice."

Buddha Śākyamuni, with his clairvoyance, had recognized Indrabodhi's superior capacity, and without letting the five hundred arhats and the entourage see anything, he produced the maṇḍala of the yidam Guhyasamāja for the king alone and gave him the four initiations, simultaneously allowing him to recognize the nature of mind, mahāmudrā.

At the very moment of the initiation, the king attained what in the universal vehicle is called the first bodhisattva level, Sublime Joy. After that, he practiced mahāmudrā in the recognition of his mind's nature, without distraction, over a period of twelve years, continuing all the while to enjoy the pleasures of the five senses and his courtesans.

After twelve years, the king attained the highest realization: the tenth bodhisattva level, the full realization of mahāmudrā. He then began to give the four initiations of Guhyasamāja and the transmission of mahāmudrā to the people of his kingdom. Very soon after that, the land became completely empty, since all his subjects proceeded to the pure lands.

King Indrabodhi was a being of superior ability; that is why he realized mahāmudrā as soon as he received initiation. You might think this is just a story, a sort of legend, because it is difficult to believe that Indrabodhi might have had five hundred courtesans by day and five hundred by night, or that his whole kingdom attained enlightenment. But still, this is a true story, and once again, just as the mind can experience all kinds of joy and suffering and undergo all sorts of ordinary experiences merely by the power of thought, likewise, this same power of mind, when perfectly purified, makes possible things that normally are not. That is also why this story is true and possible.

3

Ngotro: Introducing Mind

If again and again we examine the mind,
which cannot be examined,
We see that which cannot be seen, with total clarity, just as it is.
May the faultless mind, freed from all doubts
about being and not being, recognize itself.

—The Third Karmapa, *Mahāmudrā: Boundless Joy and Freedom*

In terms of practice, mahāmudrā is taught in stages; at each stage, the practitioner meditates on whatever has been transmitted to him, then relates
his experience to the lama. Thus, there is a constant interchange between the
teaching and the practice; the lama gives us instructions, poses questions for
us to examine and meditate on, and afterward we report our experiences to
him. He then questions us, gives us more instructions, and sends us back to
practice. In order to find the correct way to practice, we compare our
meditation and our own observations with his instructions and questions.
Through this vital communication, true understanding based on experience
develops little by little. This whole process serves to make us recognize the nature
of mind; it is "introducing mind," *ngotro* in Tibetan. The nature of mind is presented to us just as a person is presented or introduced to someone. The lama
introduces us to mind and makes us recognize its real nature: what and how it is.

TO SEE MIND

These meditations often begin with contemplation of the mind: "that"
which thinks and experiences what we know. We observe this mind, which
has the ability to think. Where does it come from? Where is it? Where does
it go? We must be able to "see" the way it appears, where it abides, and the
way it disappears.

If we discover how mind comes about, where it is located, and how it disappears, we notice who is experiencing this discovery. We are examining the
mode of existence of the one who is experiencing, the actual disposition of
the mind as experiencer; does it have characteristics as such, in terms of
forms, colors, or anything else?

If, after seriously carrying out this kind of observation, we find that the
mind has form, color, or any other characteristic, we report this to the lama.
Or, we can ask ourselves about "that" which experiences the absence of
characteristics, and we can also see how a mind that is without characteristics

experiences itself. Isn't there someone, with some characteristics, who is there to experience them?

The crucial point is to pursue this experientially, through personal observation during meditation and with the lama, who will give us guidance until we are absolutely certain as to the existence or nonexistence of the mind.

After this preliminary series of observations, we contemplate the mind at rest, the mind in action, and the mind as knower. For example, when the mind is at rest practicing śamatha, how is it abiding? If it is an "open" and "clear" state, what are these like? When the mind moves, when thoughts appear, how does it exist in motion? How do the thoughts appear there? What are the thoughts like? Are mind at rest and mind in motion different or not? In either case, how so? Who knows mind, whether at rest or in motion? How is it known? Is there a difference between mind at rest and mind in motion, and their knower? Or are they identical? In either case, how so? Does either one have characteristics, and if so, what are they? If not, what is this absence of characteristics?[148] We meditate in this way for a time—a few days, a few weeks, few months, or a few years—but we always have to go back and refer to the lama. We bring him our conclusions whenever we have the impression that we have found something, and he tells us what is correct, helps us to overcome our doubts, points out any mistakes we might have made, gives us advice, and asks us new questions. With this relationship, practice becomes sharper and deeper, and we continue like this until we deeply recognize mind's fundamental state, its actual mode, and until we find, beyond any doubt, immediate awareness—in Tibetan, *datarwai shepa*—or ordinary mind, *thamel gyi shepa*.[149]

A PERSONAL RELATIONSHIP

These days, this kind of personal relationship can seem a little difficult because lamas and disciples are often very busy, and it is frequently necessary to give instructions in a hurry. Today, we would have to be able to realize mahāmudrā between half past seven, when we get home, and eight o'clock, the time of the TV news! Or else become a buddha between six and seven o'clock in the morning, before leaving for work!

Understanding the nature of mind is a delicate thing. In order to do it, we need a lama to give us instruction for a long time, and we ourselves must apply these teachings and examine our mind all the time. Equally important are profound devotion to the lama and practicing purification and the two accumulations. Without all these different elements, it is difficult to recognize the nature of mind. To make it possible, there must be, on the one hand, a highly realized lama with genuine ability, and on the other hand, a disciple qualified by devotion and previous practice of the accumulations and purification. When these two come together, the lama can detect the disciple's competence, and the disciple will be receptive to his teaching. Everything is included in this practice then; nothing else is needed. But these days, it is rare to find such qualifications on both sides, so few lamas teach this way.

RINPO DORJE'S DILIGENCE

Rinpo Dorje was a highwayman. One day, he attacked and killed a passing horseman and then proceeded to kill and butcher his mare. The mare was pregnant and about to deliver, so he freed the poor little colt, which stirred deep remorse and compassion in him.

At that point he decided to abandon robbery to practice Dharma, realizing that if he didn't purify his behavior now, he would pay dearly in the most tormenting hells. So, requesting and receiving all the instructions, he settled into a cave and practiced śamatha, vipaśyanā, and mahāmudrā with intense devotion and unflagging energy. His diligence was like that of someone whose hair had caught on fire and was rushing to extinguish it. He never allowed his meditation seat to cool off, and he is known for having reached realization of mahāmudrā in six months!

When he left his cave, he used his robe as a wing and flew away, singing of his realization. He is one of the mahāsiddhas, one of the great Kagyu adepts. To this day, his meditation spot is a place of pilgrimage.

The Seven Shangpa-Kagyu Jewels

4

The Practice of Mahāmudrā

Do not think, nor conceive.
Abide in the natural relaxed state, without contrivance;
With the absence of all projections
is the innate nature attained.
Such is the Way followed by all the Victors of the three times.

—Nāgārjuna, *as cited by Gampopa in* The Jewel Ornament of Liberation

PRELIMINARIES BEFORE A SESSION

Practice is simplified if the body is arranged in certain favorable ways. The first is to sit relaxed with the spine straight.[150] Then, after taking refuge and generating the bodhicitta motivation, each session begins with guru yoga, the yoga of the lama,[151] since the success of practice is linked with receiving blessings. Simply put, we visualize in the space in front of us our root lama in the aspect of Buddha Vajradhara, clear and transparent, with all his characteristics and attributes. He is really present, with his love, compassion, realization, and all enlightened qualities. In essence, he is all the aspects of outer, inner, secret, and suchness refuges. His mind, speech, and body are, respectively, the Buddha, Dharma, and Sangha; yidam, dharma protector, and lama; dharmakāya, saṃbhogakāya, and nirmāṇakāya. In this presence, we recite a prayer that both expresses and fuels our devotion and aspiration. With intense faith, we think and repeat, "For the benefit of all beings, please inspire me to realize mahāmudrā as quickly as possible."

The lama then dissolves into light, which absorbs into us. We thereby receive all his blessings, contemplating that his body, speech, and mind and our own body, speech, and mind become inseparable. We remain absorbed in this state of union for a few moments....

THE MIND OF IMMEDIACY

In itself, the practice of mahāmudrā is extremely simple and easy. There are no visualizations or complicated exercises. There is nothing to do. It is enough just to leave the mind in its natural state, as it is, as it comes, without contrivance. It is extremely simple. In the tradition of mahāmudrā reliquary,[152] it is said that mahāmudrā is:

Too close to be recognized,
Too deep to grasp,

233

Too easy to believe,
Too amazing to be understood intellectually.

Those are the four obstacles that prevent its recognition. Gampopa said:

Still water is clear;
Mind free of strain is happy.

Just as this verse shows, we leave the mind free and relaxed, completely loose, without forcing it in any way. Then, a state of well-being will arise; when mind is not forced, it is naturally peaceful and clear. In this state, the mind does not fix on any outer or inner reference point; instead, it remains free of all fixation, but not controlled.

Nor is there any determination of mind as empty, lucid, or anything else, not even any observation, because to regard the mind as anything, even as empty, would be yet another dualistic perception which would take mind, emptiness, or lucidity as reference points.

But the point is not to stop seeing, because vigilant attention and clarity should not be interrupted. It is necessary to maintain clear seeing. Seeing requires no special effort when there is light; similarly, clear mind does not scatter or sink into darkness or cloudiness. The mind remains translucent, transparent, lucid, detached. Just as the sky is clear and open, so is the mind left as it is in its natural state.

Meditate, leaving the mind in a state of total presence, without looking at the past or projecting to the future; without thinking, "I did this or that, I will do this or that"; let mind just be vigilant, quite simply, without forcing it, without changing anything, within spontaneous nowness, or the mind of immediacy.[153]

If the mind actually remains like this "as it comes from itself, as it is in itself," this is what we call natural mind, *rangbab* in Tibetan. This is also what we call ordinary mind—*thamel gyi shepa* in Tibetan, or "mind of immediacy," *datarwai shepa*. When realized, this is the mind of mahāmudrā.

THE THREE KEY POINTS

The practice of mahāmudrā can be broken down into three essential points: absence of contrivance,[154] absence of distraction,[155] and absence of meditation.[156]

First, the absence of contrivance or constraint: we leave the mind as is, without altering it through any intervention or contrivance whatsoever. We do not try to produce anything or improve on our present state of mind.

Next, the absence of distractions. The first type of distraction occurs when the mind is distracted from the natural ordinary mind (*rangbab, thamel gyi shepa*) by starting to grasp at a form, sound, thought, or anything else. Absence of distraction means absence of fixation. A second type of distraction arises when the mind loses its vigilance, its lucid clarity. Third is the absence of meditation, which means that there is no longer any meditation to do at all. We just leave mind in its natural state, without strain, letting it be the ordinary mind.

MIND'S THREE BODIES

Natural mind, *rangbab*, has a quality of clear transparency in which its three essential aspects exist spontaneously: emptiness, clarity, and unimpededness. Mind's transparency is its essential emptiness; its knowing and luminous nature is its clarity; and the aspects of its enlightened experience are its unimpededness. When mind is in this state of limpid transparency, open and lucid, it is fully aware, in a state of bare awareness—*rigtong* in Tibetan. It is pristine awareness—*rigpa* in Tibetan; unimpeded, experiencing in itself its limitless manifestations in all their aspects.[157] This empty awareness, clear and unlimited, is not far from us. It is our actual face, but like our own face, it cannot perceive itself. This is what we call ignorance, or *marigpa* in Tibetan, which is simply the absence of bare awareness, or *rigpa*. In order to get beyond ignorance, we have to see its empty nature without conceptualizing; then we must accustom the mind to this experience and gradually stabilize it so that it remains free from distraction under all circumstances. This is how practice progresses. But remember that these essential qualities of mind are not anything we have to try to produce; they are mind's very nature and we have only to recognize them.

The mind, being naturally empty, is forever the dharmakāya, the body of emptiness or the Absolute Body of Buddha. Being naturally lucid, it is always the saṃbhogakāya, the Complete Enjoyment Body of Buddha. And since it is naturally unlimited knowledge, it is forever the nirmānakāya, the Manifestation Body of Buddha. So, mind is always by nature the three bodies of the Buddha,[158] naturally and spontaneously free. Nothing could possibly be done to improve their perfection.

The realization of mahāmudrā is called innate primordial awareness[159] because the three aspects of mind's essential nature—emptiness, clarity, and unobstructedness or unimpededness—always exist in it; they are innate.

INTEGRATION AND TRANSMUTATION OF THOUGHTS AND EMOTIONS

When we are just beginning to practice, our mind bubbles and effervesces like a pot of boiling water over a fire. The practice of rangbab teaches us to stop interfering with thoughts and emotions, which is like ceasing to feed the fire; then the boiling will stop on its own.

As beginners, we cannot remain for very long in a state of correct meditation: we are distracted by thoughts and emotions that we fixate on and cling to. We learn, though, not to follow them: simply noting the presence of a thought, we do not follow after it but instead remain alert, in a state of "detached observation" of everything that appears to the mind. We leave the mind as it is, to recognize what is going on within it, and we do not interfere.

"Simply seeing," as we just described, is the state of the detached observer. When we remain in this state of uninvested vigilance, as an impartial witness, thoughts and passions arise and disappear in emptiness like waves rising and falling back in the sea, or like a rainbow that lights up and stretches across space.

In this state of mind, all the thoughts and emotions that arise are no longer either beneficial or harmful. If we can practice this way, whatever arises in our mind will not be a problem, and we will be able to live in a state of continuous meditation in all circumstances. Staying in meditation throughout everything we do, whether praying, reciting mantras, or moving around, working, or sleeping is what is called continual practice. All the accomplished masters of the past followed this same path. In true realization of mahāmudrā, the afflictions adorn the mind rather than disturbing or contaminating it. Negative tendencies are no longer something to reject; they transmute themselves into primordial awareness.

Take the example of the desire between men and women; it is a passionate tendency, but its nature is bliss. It is possible, without either fleeing or following the impulse of desire, to experience its blissful nature which is ultimately "bliss-void."

The same is true of anger. Here again, it is possible, without either expressing or repressing anger, to experience its essence, the dynamic clarity of mind, and to develop the realization of "clarity-void." What is true of desire and anger is also true for pride, envy, and the other mental afflictions, which become transformed through the same meditation.

Desire recognized as bliss-void is transmuted into awareness, or the wisdom of discernment; anger experienced in its essence is transmuted into mirrorlike wisdom, ignorance into primordial wisdom of dharmadhātu, pride into wisdom of equanimity, and jealousy into primordial all-accomplishing wisdom.

Since we have not yet realized these primordial wisdoms, we might doubt the possibility of such transformation. But through effective practice, a profound knowledge of the nature of mind will indeed awaken. Then we will understand that this really is so. When transformation of the emotions is fully completed, the passions are no longer an obstacle. They even become a help. A traditional image is that they become like wood for the bonfire of wisdom; the more you add, the brighter the flame!

THE MAHĀSIDDHA MAITRĪPA

Maitrīpa was a pandit, or scholar, of the great monastic university of Nālanda near Benares. He had received full monastic ordination and kept his 253 vows scrupulously.

At one point, he received tantric instructions from the mahāsiddha Shawaripa. Through practicing those instructions, he attained a high degree of realization. Later on, he took a woman and began to drink while he was still living in the monastery. When the master disciplinarian made routine inspection rounds and Maitrīpa was in his cell drinking with his consort, he would use his powers to transform her into a tantric bell and his beer into a bowl of milk, so that the discipline master never noticed anything amiss. But one day, caught off guard, he was discovered drinking with his consort.

"Whoever breaks the vows and the rules of the monastery must leave," said the master. Maitrīpa was then expelled. He took with him his bamboo cane and a skin which he used as a mat. Going to the Ganges, he put his mat on the water, sat on it with his consort, and rowed away with his cane. At that point, the monks who had expelled him realized he was a mahāsiddha and honored his accomplishments.

Later on, Maitrīpa became Marpa and Khyungpo Neljor's teacher.

5

Experience and Realization

Sovereign is vision that transcends all dualistic grasping.
Sovereign, meditation free of distraction.
Sovereign, action of nonaction.
When there is no more fear or hope,
The goal is won.

—Tilopa, *The Mahāmudrā of the Ganges*

As beginners, it is difficult for us to experience meditation that is really clear and detached. But with the help of our lama, we can learn to leave our mind in its naturally transparent, clear state—vigilant, totally open—and let it simply rest in this way, maintaining just enough acuity to safeguard alertness.

If we meditate regularly this way, our mind will gradually become clearer, more detached and vigilant, and the practice will unfold.

RECOGNIZING, CULTIVATING, STABILIZING

Take again the example of the sky darkened by clouds—an image of the ignorant state of ordinary beings. Space and the sun are there, but space is completely obscured; light cannot shine through. The genuine experiences of meditation that begin to develop are like the slightest opening in the clouds; a small clearing allows a ray of sun to pierce through with some light. We glimpse the emptiness, clarity, or limitlessness of the mind. More and more, the clouds disperse and the sky opens to the sun's brightness. The layers dissolve, uncovering the jewel's brilliance.

What we just said are only words, empty sound. To understand it means to realize emptiness, but that is not easy. We must first receive from our lama the introduction to this practice of recognizing natural mind;[160] then we have to develop it, cultivate it nonstop in all our activities, until the practice definitely stabilizes.[161] These are the steps to realization.

THE FOUR YOGAS

The progression of the realization of mahāmudrā is described as following four yogas, or four levels of approach to unification with the experience of mahāmudrā. Each of these four is divided into three, which makes a total of twelve levels.

The first is unification (*tsechig* in Tibetan). At this stage, after having received initiation into the practice of mahāmudrā and having recognized it, we cultivate "direct mind" without distraction: at first in sitting meditation and then in meditation in action, that is, in all circumstances and activities. As it becomes more stable, we pass through the three levels of unification. When it has become completely stable, day and night, we have reached the superior level of unification. The experience of the next level is not far off.

The second level is called simplicity, or "without thought," because it is beyond all the productions of habitual mind. This level's realization is the direct experience of emptiness. In Mahāyāna classification, this is the Path of Insight, the attainment of the first bodhisattva bhūmi or ground; the beginning of freedom from samsara's illusions.[162]

The third level is called "one taste," as all experiences now have the one taste of mahāsukha,[163] or the great bliss which is mahāmudrā.

The fourth level is nonmeditation. It is the final realization wholly beyond any notion of meditation and nonmeditation. The superior level of absence of meditation corresponds to what the dzogchen tradition calls the experience of the exhaustion of emptiness and is the ultimate state of buddhahood.

CONCLUSION

When we begin to have glimpses of what mahāmudrā practice is, we need to have faith in the teaching of the Three Jewels and to meditate as much as we can, praying to our lama constantly. This way, the practice will advance.

If we do not understand what mahāmudrā practice is about, it is because our mind is still clouded by the many veils of ignorance and mental afflictions, so it is very important to be diligent about the practices of accumulation and purification.

The practice of mahāmudrā is the path that all the lineages' adepts have followed. Through it, all the extraordinary lamas—Milarepa and so many others—reached enlightenment.

MILAREPA'S LAST TEACHING

One day, Milarepa warned Gampopa that the time had come for him to depart. He told Gampopa: "You've received the entire transmission. I have given you all the teachings, as if pouring water from one vase into another. Only one pith instruction remains that I haven't taught you. It's very secret." He then accompanied Gampopa to a river, where they were to part. Gampopa made prostrations to take his leave and started across. But Milarepa called him back: "You really are a good disciple. Anyway, I will give you this last teaching."

Overjoyed, Gampopa prostrated nine times, then waited for the instruction. Milarepa proceeded to turn around and pull up his robe, showing

Gampopa his bottom. "Do you see?"

And Gampopa said, "Uh…yes."

"Do you really see?" Gampopa was not sure what he was supposed to see. Milarepa had calluses on his buttocks; they looked as though they were half flesh and half stone.

"You see, this is how I reached enlightenment: sitting and meditating. If you want to reach it in this life, make the same effort. That is my final teaching. I have nothing more to add."

PART TWO

Section Six

Dharma Practice Today

I
Living Dharma in Daily Life

One who thinks and acts to achieve his own ends is a worldly being.
One who thinks and works for others' welfare alone is a Dharma practitioner.

—Jamgön Kongtrul Lodrö Thaye, *Mind Training in Seven Points*

The crucial point of Dharma practice, the heart of the teachings, as we have said, is the mind.[164] Body and speech proceed from mind; the mind forms the body, which possesses the faculty of speech. Mind is the root of all we are and all we do; it is both the source and the goal of all practices. So, in all our activities, the most important thing is our state of mind, the intention that produces action. Motivation is vital.

RIGHT MOTIVATION

Right motivation is good will, benevolence, compassion, or bodhicitta.[165] If we behave according to the Dharma in our outer activities and gestures but have a bad motivation, we will stray from the Dharma path.

For example, here I am today talking to you, sitting on a high seat, speaking words passed down from the great masters of the past. It's a Dharma situation, and I have all the attributes of a lama. But if I harbored a motivation of selfish interest—wanting fame, money, or anything at all for personal gain—even though all the trappings of Dharma are there, it would have nothing to do with real practice. Our inner attitude and our motivation are the determining elements—they are the most important thing in all circumstances.

ONE TSA-TSA, LOTS OF ENLIGHTENMENT

There was once a man who, out of pure motivation, built a small tsa-tsa (an image of a buddha impressed in clay). The positive karma of making this tsa-tsa established a connection that set him on the path to enlightenment. When he had finished it, he set it at the side of a road. A passerby saw it and, with a motivation just as pure, felt it was improper to leave it lying there, so he placed it up on a wall. This positive gesture made with pure motivation became a cause of enlightenment for him, too. A third person came by. It was raining, and he thought it would be a pity if the tsa-tsa were to be ruined by the downpour, so, with an extremely pure motivation, he covered it with an old shoe he found there. This action was for him as well a cause for reaching enlightenment. Then still another person arrived and, with a very positive state of mind, thought that an old shoe on an object as holy as a tsa-tsa was really inappropriate, so he took the shoe off the tsa-tsa. This gesture as well was a cause for enlightenment.

This story illustrates how our inner attitude and our motivation are the determinants in any circumstance. We must learn to cultivate this right motivation no matter what happens. With it, all situations become a source of practice, of enlightenment, and can be used for making spiritual progress.

Whatever time you can give to Dharma practice—whether a year, a month, a week, or a day—the main thing is the motivation with which you carry it out. It is best if you have a bodhicitta motivation, the mind of enlightenment, an inclination to be of benefit to all beings. This inner attitude is fundamental in that it is the basis of all practice.

Bodhicitta is the philosopher's stone that transforms all activities into the gold of Dharma practice. So when we cultivate the right motivation, which is bodhicitta, absolutely all daily activities become the practice of the six perfections.

DETACHMENT

As long as we remain obsessed with possessions, we will want more and will be in state of constant dissatisfaction and need. Yet by giving, we discover the possibility of real satisfaction, and in this satisfaction we find the capacity for enjoying everything we wish for. One proverb says:

> From possessiveness comes want;
> From nonattachment, satisfaction.

Desire and attachment can take various forms, such as a man's desire for a woman or a woman's desire for a man: they meet, have sex, passions arise, problems follow. This lasts for a certain time, then a new relationship begins, and so forth. Episodes of desire and troubles keep repeating themselves over and over. We can have attachment for things or for near and dear ones. Desires bring only dissatisfaction: if you have a house, you want a second one; if you have two, you want three. If you have a thousand dollars, you want ten thousand, a hundred thousand, a million, a billion...mind is insatiable.

THE KING AND THE WISH-FULFILLING GEM

At the time of Buddha Śākyamuni, a monk found himself in possession of a marvelous jewel that granted any wish—all the gold, silver, and precious stones you could ask for. The lucky owner thought: "I am a monk and have no need of all these riches. Better to give this jewel to a poor person. But there are so many of them, why favor one over another? Buddha is omniscient. He will tell me whom to give it to." So, going to Buddha, he explained his difficulty and asked him to designate a fitting recipient. Buddha Śākyamuni recommended that he give it to the king of that area, a very wealthy and powerful monarch. The monk made the offering, and the king accepted it, inquiring about the reason for the gift. The monk explained, "I thought I should give this gem to a poor person, but not knowing whom to choose, I asked Buddha Śākyamuni. He advised me to bring it to you."

The king thought that was quite strange, since there probably was no one on earth richer than he. So he went to Buddha Śākyamuni for an explanation. The king asked why Buddha had chosen him when the monk had asked which poor person would best be provided for with the gem.

"It's true," Buddha said. "Without a doubt, there is no one wealthier than you in the world; but there is also no doubt that there is no greed as great as yours. That is why I told the monk to give you the gem."

Dissatisfaction can make the wealthiest into the neediest! So it is essential to be contented, to be satisfied and happy with what we possess now, and not constantly follow our desires. Otherwise, even if we had a house made of solid gold and all the wealth in the world, we would only get attached to it, and at the hour of our death we would not be able to take a single bit of that gold with us. Instead, we would leave with the attachment that would cause us to be reborn as a hungry ghost.

THE SIX PERFECTIONS IN DAILY LIFE

The first perfection is generosity, of which there are four types:[166] material things, love, protection, and Dharma. We can practice these at every moment. We must help the poor and those in need by generously giving to them. If we can specifically help someone who is practicing Dharma, the gift is especially profound and more precious, because it helps that person to reach enlightenment as well. Giving develops positive karma, which is the source of well-being and wealth; this is something very real. Personally, I have always given or used for the Dharma everything I had. When I arrived from Tibet, I had almost nothing, and the little that I did have, I gave to help monks. But somehow I was able to build a monastery where now reside a hundred monks, for whom I am responsible and help. I have also been able to build stupas and do many things—not by doing business or other sorts of enterprises, but by virtue of the Dharma, the virtue of giving.

Using wealth as best we can to help Dharma practitioners and all those in need constitutes an enormous positive activity. Helping to contribute to or bring about a project dedicated to Dharma brings benefits and profits far greater than those that a bank funds because this kind of positive activity can provide benefits for all future lives as well as for this one!

Of all gifts, teaching Dharma is the most profound, but its value depends on the motivation with which it is done. We must perceive the beings we give it to as our parents, thinking that from beginningless time they have been wandering in samsara, experiencing unfathomable suffering, and we must perceive that if they continue this way they will suffer endlessly. With deep compassion, we must wish to transmit to them the instructions that will help them to free themselves from their misery and attain enlightenment. It is only with such a motivation that we can practice giving Dharma properly. When this is possible, it is the most valuable and effective gift of all. Better to make a gift of genuine Dharma than to give material objects to many people. Why? Because material giving, though very useful, has a very limited scope, since it is short-lived; at best, it will help the recipient only during this life. But the gift of Dharma helps for this life and all future lives as well. And, if someone can attain enlightenment through the gift of Dharma, this one person will in turn be able to help an immeasurable number of beings. This is why the gift of Dharma has a broader significance.

The second perfection is discipline or restraint. It is possible to train ourselves at all times to stop the ten negative actions and cultivate the ten positive ones. Developing this outer discipline with a correct motivation, which is the inner discipline, will transform everything without exception into Dharma practice. Life brings all sorts of difficulties, but the biggest problems are the inner ones: they come from our aggressive and angry attitude, our desires and attachments, and our lack of insight. So in all our life situations and circumstances, we must practice the discipline of working with the passions or afflictions. This is the innermost level of morality. It is developed in sitting meditation and in action.

The third perfection is patience. Conflicts, harsh words, aggression, and anger often arise with our neighbors, family, or spouse. These are real and serious problems, because these attitudes can spoil all the positive things we may do. Aggression is the source of so much misery. Let's take the example of a married couple. If your husband or wife is aggressive, be patient, forbear, and disregard it; do not respond to aggression with anger. If you live together, of course you want to be happy. But marital disputes are the source of pain and problems that can undermine your happiness. These days, the world situation is difficult. Many people fear a conflict, even a third world war, which would be a terrible thing. Nevertheless, if such a war occurred, it would be played out over a few years, months or perhaps only weeks or days. It would not last very long. But your conflicts with your spouse last a whole life! If your spouse attacks you, it is because he thinks you are mean and he is nice, or she is right while you are wrong. It is important to see that the responsibility is shared.

You need two hands to clap—one is not enough! Anyway, try to live harmoniously. Do not let this situation become a source of antagonism and negative actions; instead, use it to accomplish positive actions.

Let's consider the different forms of the next perfection, meditation. Realization of the four fundamental ideas,[167] śamatha-vipaśyana,[168] the practices of lojong and tonglen,[169] deity yoga such as that of Chenrezig which includes the essentials of all the Vajrayāna meditations—all of these allow us to use every situation as practice.

There are twenty-four hours in a day. If you can give half an hour a day or even less to the practice of sitting meditation, you will derive immeasurable benefits. By meditating in this way, you will learn to develop a kind mind and get rid of ill will.

The perfection of effort or energy is vital for all practices. You know how to do many things: drive a car, get on a plane. There are so many things you do automatically which you had to learn, and took time to learn. Think about the number of years you went to school and learned a job for a purpose restricted to this life. In Dharma, it is important to understand that advancing toward enlightenment and attaining of buddhahood cannot happen without enthusiastic perseverance or effort. Whatever the practice, we must first listen to the instruction and then apply it energetically. We should dedicate more time and energy to the practice of Dharma than to our worldly studies, because its benefits are much more far-reaching; they exceed the limited framework of this life.

Finally, there is the perfection of wisdom. It is vital to understand that all the things we aspire to, all the situations we normally focus on, do not have true reality. They are basically like an illusion or mirage. They are unreal. If we understand the transitory and fleeting nature of our perpetual desires, they will become less compelling. All suffering and all emotions originate in our mind, whose basis is emptiness. Seeing this, we will realize that the afflictions as well are fundamentally empty and unreal. And understanding their lack of solidity, their unreality, we will be able to deal with them freely, without entanglement.

Lastly, if you understand the meaning of mahāmudrā meditation and can put it into practice, you will attain transcendent knowledge, which, of all things, is the most useful and wonderful.

A DAY OF PRACTICE

How should we live each day? Refuge is our first link with the Dharma. It is the starting point of all practices, and it is important to begin our day by simply reciting the refuge formula, thereby turning toward enlightenment and the Three Jewels every day, without fail. At the same time, with the proper motivation, we make the different offerings to the Three Jewels: water, flowers, incense, and so on. Then we generate the mind of enlightenment, or bodhicitta. We remember all the beings who are suffering in samsara and think: "May I do something to really help them. Today especially I will be careful to maintain a positive state of mind, and I will try to help others no matter what the day brings." Every morning we impress upon our mind a motivation of good will and compassion. We try to bring bodhicitta into all situations. Bodhicitta is the philosopher's stone that transforms all our actions, even the most trivial and ordinary, into true Dharma practice. It sanctifies all our activities.

When something fortunate or wished-for happens to us, we should be happy and recognize it as a blessing from the lama and the Three Jewels. If something difficult or undesirable occurs, we should understand it to be a result of past negative karma. We should think, "May I purify this negative karma." Whatever circumstances we encounter, we can accept them and integrate them into our practice. They will all become the foundation for a positive state of mind oriented toward enlightenment.

The best thing to do for our family and our children is to act in such a way that their minds will turn toward Dharma and Dharma practice. But even if this does not work out the way we wish, we must still love them and help them as much as we can.

Concerning our family, spouse, possessions, and wealth, we should be careful to avoid attachment and not fixate on things and situations, thinking, "This is mine. It should be like this." Such an attitude is unproductive in deal- ing with others. It only creates problems and misery for us. Nonattachment is essential in all situations; things and events have only relative value and are fundamentally illusion.

At the end of the day, we should remember to look at the good things we have done and dedicate them with the wish that this will contribute to the happiness and enlightenment of all beings. We should also be sorry about the negative attitudes we have had and really resolve to watch those delicate areas where we have had difficulty maintaining a positive attitude. Dedication mag- nifies the benefits of positive actions and prevents them from being lost. One bad thought, one moment of anger, or another negative tendency can nullify the positive effects of a series of positive actions, whereas once dedicated, those bene- fits cannot be lost or damaged. One drop of water can quickly evaporate, just like the good results of an action. Dedicating good deeds is like putting that drop of water into the ocean: it will remain there as long as the ocean does not dry up.

So, if we take refuge and generate bodhicitta in the morning, and dedicate the merits as we just explained in the evening, and vigilantly practice positive actions with a good motivation in between, avoiding harmfulness, ill will, and attachment, this is the important thing.

2

The Study and Practice of Dharma

At the beginning, gain knowledge of Dharma,
Be like a starving man before a good meal;
In the middle, gain understanding of mind like one finding a precious jewel;
In the end, develop an understanding of nonduality
like the collapse of the charlatan's greatest deception.

—Gampopa, *Garland of the Supreme Way*

How to Listen to Dharma

It is very important to listen to Dharma properly, or respectfully and without the wrong attitude. There are three such wrong attitudes; the first is listening with a closed mind, like an upside-down pot that will not retain what is poured into it. Secondly, not only should we receive the teaching, but also retain it and keep it in mind. If we forget the teaching right after hearing it, we are like a leaky pot. The third kind of wrong attitude is to listen while overcome with negativity. Listening to the Dharma with a disturbed mind is like eating scrumptious food that has been mixed with poison: it is good at first, but later the poison makes us ill.

Having an attitude of respect and faith means receiving the Dharma joyfully and attentively, and regarding the lama who transmits the teaching not as an ordinary being but as Buddha himself. Also, we should not think of our fellow listeners the way we normally might; instead, we should recognize that each of them has buddha nature. We also should think that the sounds of the teaching are the union of sound and emptiness and that they possess the sixty qualities of a buddha's speech. This attitude is helpful for opening us to blessings and repelling disturbing emotions.

When we request a teaching, it is appropriate to see ourselves as patients suffering from the illness of ignorance and its associated afflictions, and to see the lama who gives the instruction as our doctor, while the Dharma itself is the medicine that cures our ills.

Furthermore, our motivation for listening to and practicing the Dharma must be to realize enlightenment for the sake of all beings. For any Dharma activity, bodhicitta is the indispensable preliminary.

Practice in Daily Life

Right Dharma practice can be accomplished at every moment and in any circumstance, whether we are walking, eating, working, or doing anything else. All daily activities are an opportunity to overcome negativity and cultivate goodness: an opportunity to dedicate ourselves to the Dharma. Moreover, we can use our body, speech, and mind for something positive every single instant.[170] When we bear in mind the value of human life, the truth of impermanence, the faults of samsara, and karmic causation,[171] we will find we really can simplify our life, renouncing frivolous activities and completely devoting ourselves to practice. It is important for us, who are always so busy, always coming and going, to be able to stop and give ourselves a break, a moment's respite just for spiritual practice.

IN A DHARMA CENTER

People who live in a Dharma center are in a privileged and especially favorable situation. That is because they live close to the Dharma and to the lama, from whom they can receive instruction on a regular basis. Life in a Dharma center is organized so that all activities are practice oriented. In this context, the disturbances of everyday life are reduced or nonexistent. The environment is very conducive to Dharma study and practice.

Most people, however, cannot live in a Dharma center. But you do have vacations, and every week there is a weekend. If you could use that free time for more intensive practice, that would be wonderful. Go to a center and listen to teachings, meditate, do retreats, ask questions, and put an end to your doubts. This is what a Dharma center is for.[172]

ON RETREAT

Doing a retreat means withdrawing from all forms of distraction and outer disturbances for a period of time; it could be for a few days of vacation or any amount of time that is available. In a retreat situation, our mind is insulated from all distractions, so we can dedicate ourselves completely to practice and devote all our energy to the retreat.

Because of its isolation and silence, retreat offers the best conditions for practicing meditation in general, but it is especially useful for training in śamatha-vipaśyanā. The goal of retreat is to minimize distraction, but, as always, practice depends on us, on our own inner attitude. Doing a retreat without the proper motivation prevents us from fully benefiting from it. Without energy or discipline, retreat in and of itself cannot accomplish anything. If we went to live like a wild animal on the remotest mountaintop, with neither energy nor the right motivation, we would cultivate nothing but our pride. But if we have the proper motivation and determination, a retreat is an ideal situation for practicing meditation and for making rapid progress.

THE THREE-YEAR RETREAT

In Tibet, there were many hermits like Milarepa who gave up all ordinary activity and meditated in caves. This kind of practice is wonderful, but the hermetic tradition has waned as the times have degenerated. That is why some great lamas such as Jamgön Kongtrul Lodrö Thaye instituted the three-year retreat as a good context for practice. This tradition has arisen out of their efforts.

In the West, the Dharma has just begun to spread. It has been only a few years since it was introduced here, and the door is just beginning to open. Looking at the Western lifestyle, I have noticed that Westerners are very busy people, extremely involved in the world through their work and very engrossed in their daily activities. It seems to me that practicing in a retreat center would be good for Westerners, since it would enable them to devote themselves completely to practice for three years. They would derive incredible benefits from this. I myself have done this retreat, and I have also served as a retreat master (*drubpön* in Tibetan), so I am very familiar with its potential; I think it can be very productive. I started one of the first three-year retreat centers in France, and since then, several other centers have been created in Canada, Sweden, the United States, and other parts of France. Kagyu and Nyingma retreat centers have been founded by other lamas as well.

In Tibet, many people devoted themselves to monastic life, but very few did retreats. Those who undertook three-year retreats did so on their own initiative, out of their own personal motivations. If ordination was a way to get out of the cyclic rut of worldly life and to rise above it to some extent, doing a retreat was like taking a further step, making a deep commitment to putting the teachings into practice. Becoming a lama was held in high esteem.

Westerners who choose to undertake a three-year retreat do it out of their own motivation even more so: nobody makes them do it—neither king, president, nor parents. It truly comes from their own aspiration, from their own wonderful inner motivation. Considering impermanence, it is never a mistake to renounce outer things in order to give ourselves completely and profoundly to Dharma practice.

This kind of retreat is the best way to practice Dharma intensively for three years, without worldly cares or distractions. This period offers the most favorable conditions for devoting all the energies of body, speech, and mind to the most important tantric practices: sādhana of the yidams, yogas of Niguma, the Five Golden Teachings, mahāmudrā, and so forth. If you are considering doing a three-year retreat in the future, you must prepare yourself well for it. If you can actually follow through on it, it will give extraordinary meaning to your human life.

Because I have observed that it is difficult to keep monastic vows in the West, I have asked those who wish to do a three-year retreat to keep the vow of celibacy only for the duration of the retreat. During this time, retreatants live as celibates, immersing themselves fully in the practice. Afterward, those who wish to do so can receive monastic vows, and the others can resume lay lives.

Even if you do not continue in total commitment to the Dharma once the retreat is over, you will still have used all your energy in a very positive pursuit during that time, and that alone is an extraordinary achievement.

A three-year retreat offers the opportunity to get well acquainted with Dharma and with tantric practices. Afterward, we can follow up by doing lengthy solitary retreats and eventually attain buddhahood in this very life.

TIBETAN LANGUAGE STUDY

Generally speaking, learning Tibetan is not mandatory for practicing the Dharma well, but in order to engage in deep commitment to Dharma, such as a three-year retreat, knowledge of Tibetan is extremely important because it allows us to understand the practice texts and the traditional Tibetan commentaries. If I tell people who are going to do the retreat to learn Tibetan, it's not because I am Tibetan—and anyway, being from Kham, I do not particularly consider myself Tibetan, and I speak in a dialect that no one can understand! Anyway, what you need to know, what is important, is the classical Dharma Tibetan.

In Tibet, we didn't have the conveniences of the West—the means of transportation, the cars, the machines. Practically speaking, there were only three occupations: farming, animal husbandry, and commerce. But on the other hand, an enormous number of people were involved with Dharma study and practice. When Westerners introduced material comforts to Tibet, the Tibetan language was not at all adapted to modern life. It did not have the words to accommodate modern science and technology. In the West, there is a similar situation in terms of Dharma, but reversed. Tibetan is a traditional language that has a very rich vocabulary for meditation and spiritual practices—a vocabulary without any equivalent in Western languages. When Western scientists go to Tibet to share their knowledge, they should teach in their own language, at least initially. Some Tibetans could learn from them; and then later on, adequate terminology could be devised and translated into Tibetan. Here, we have the reverse situation. In order for Dharma to be properly understood in the West, there must be Westerners who are willing to master the Tibetan. Of course, my wish is that in the future, everything will be translated correctly. Once the totality of Dharma is adequately translated into Western terminology, there will be no need for Tibetan. But for now, anyone wishing to study the Dharma deeply, and particularly anyone preparing for a three-year retreat, will reap great benefit from the study of Tibetan. If you study regularly, a little bit every day, you will quickly become knowledgeable.

THE RACE BETWEEN THE LOUSE AND THE FLEA

Once upon a time, someone suggested that a flea and a louse have a race and offered a prize to the winner. They were to run and deposit a load of grass at the finish line. The flea accepted happily, because it knew that it could go faster than the louse. The louse also accepted because it knew that by going along steadily and energetically, it could finish first. The signal was sounded. The flea made a great leap forward but spilled its load and had to pick it up before attempting its next leap. With each great leap, the flea would spill its whole load, and it wasted a lot of time picking up all the grass it kept dropping. Although it was able to jump quite far, it was making little progress. On the other hand, the louse, though it advanced slowly, did not drop anything or stop. Guess who was the winner?

MONASTIC DISCIPLINE

Why become ordained? Why do a three-year retreat? Because these are favorable situations for thorough and efficient Dharma practice, since they provide the optimal framework for practice. Monastic life is solitary,[173] which offers the independence for total dedication to practice. Without spouse or children, without financial or family problems, we have none of the usual sources of worry and much more freedom to study and practice Dharma.

Our usual circumstances involve many completely consuming situations that drown us in passions and afflictions, and we have little inclination to practice. The general tendency of everyday life is toward conflict-ridden emotions rather than enlightenment. Ordinary life is inclined more toward the passions. Our activities are like timber on a mountainside which can go down easily but is not so easy to bring back up. This is why monastic discipline is so useful and valuable. But of course it is not without renunciation and its own difficulties.

BUDDHA ŚĀKYAMUNI'S GREAT DEPARTURE

In his youth as a prince, Buddha Śākyamuni was destined to rule. It had been prophesied that he would become either a buddha or a universal monarch. His father, who held him in high regard, loved him deeply and wished he would become such a king. But the future Buddha perceived the suffering of beings, the suffering of birth, sickness, old age, and death. He understood that kingship and the power that accompanies it are not an ultimate way of benefiting beings, so he decided against becoming a king and chose instead to dedicate himself to spiritual life. His father, aware of young Siddhartha's intentions, tried to keep him from leaving the palace by placing him under guard. However, with the help of divine beings, the future Buddha succeeded in escaping one night with his horse and groom. Once he had left the palace grounds, he removed his royal ornaments, cut his hair, and took up the ascetic life, dedicating himself completely to religious practice.

Through his renunciation, he became fully awakened—a buddha—and gained the ability to help countless beings. Buddha Śākyamuni taught:

> One hundred lives as a universal monarch
> Are insignificant when compared
> To a single life that's truly dedicated to Dharma.

The life of a king is always oriented to samsara, while commitment to the Dharma opens onto enlightenment.

BEYOND ATTACHMENT

At the moment, we have all sorts of fixations on what we see, hear, taste, smell—everything we experience. Our experience of ourselves and of the outer world is the result of these fixations, which are the source of all our delusions. Understanding the nature of mind frees us from them and the suffering they cause.

But fixations exist in various areas of the Dharma as well. Lama, buddha, yidam really do exist, and it is because of them that we can receive their blessings, realize the attainments, and realize mind's nature. Nevertheless, their true existence is not material like that of crystal, gold, iron, or stone. Their essence is emptiness, their nature lucidity, and their appearance the expression of unobstructed wisdom. It is vital for us to think of them this way, and not think that they exist as something physical.174 Understanding them like this, we can have real faith in them, join our mind with theirs, and remain absorbed. Some people go astray in their practice; they have faith in the lama, the Buddha, and think that they actually exist and have form, hearing, sense of taste, and so on. This point is extremely important to understand, but these days such understanding is rare.

There is a famous saying:

> If we become attached to them,
> There is no greater fetter than the divine states.
> If we fixate on them,

There is no greater obstacle than the attainments. If we become attached to divinity, it will hold us captive, and we will remain bound by it. Likewise, if we are attached to attainments in practice, they become huge obstacles.

Attachments to the things of this world are like straw chains; attachment to things of the Dharma are like chains of gold; their value is not the same, but the straw ones are easier to break.

PATRIARCHS OF THE LINEAGE: DIFFERENT STYLES OF PRACTICE

Above all, do not consider it impossible to practice correctly without being ordained, or outside a three-year retreat. This would be a huge mistake. Not everybody has to become a monk or nun or do that kind of retreat. It is quite possible to reach enlightenment in other ways.

In the tantric tradition, there were many accomplished sages, such as Tilopa, Nāropa, and others, who were not monks and never did such retreats. Some even reached enlightenment while acting in eccentric and nonconformist ways. These "mad yogis" [175] indulged in all manner of outrageous behavior, but they reached enlightenment nonetheless.

In the Kagyu tradition, there were many lineage holders who were very different from one another. After Tilopa and Nāropa[176] came Marpa the Translator, a family man and a farmer who was involved in all kinds of activities; his neighbors considered him proud and quick-tempered. He had a rather bad reputation and was allegedly hard to get along with. But he had realized the teachings—while leading quite an ordinary life he attained enlightenment. It is he who started the Kagyu lineage in Tibet.

Marpa's principal disciple was Milarepa,[177] who was not a monk either, but a lay practitioner. The life he chose, however, was different from his teacher's—he abandoned all mundane activities and went to meditate alone in mountain caves. He lived like a wild animal fleeing people. Through his practice, he too attained enlightenment.

Milarepa's main disciple was Gampopa, who had been a husband and father and practiced the Dharma as a layman. He had a very beautiful wife and children. Then one day, his wife became ill, and both knew she would soon die. Exceedingly grief-stricken, Gampopa asked her not to remain attached to him. He pledged never to remarry, but to become a monk and devote himself to Dharma; he touched a Dharma book to his head and made her that promise. She died soon after, and Gampopa kept his word. At first, he received ordination and monastic education in the Kadampa lineage. He carefully kept all the precepts and was an outstanding monk. Later, he met Milarepa,[178] became his disciple, practiced at his side, and gained realization. He himself became a Kagyu lineage holder. Gampopa's four main disciples were the originators of the four main branches of the Marpa-Kagyu lineage.

Among these, there was Tusum Khyenpa, the first Karmapa. Then, in his lineage were great lamas like the Karmapas, the Shamarpas, the Situpas, and others who manifested enlightened activity and worked for the welfare of beings through what might be called their royal or princely positions.

Milarepa had other disciples as well, in particular three men and four women, the Pusum Moshi, who weren't monastics and who, in their lives as lay hermits, also reached enlightenment.

Within the lineage, there has been every possible style in approaching the path.[179] The most important thing is the state of mind and the quality of practice. The outer status—ordained, married, hermit, or parent—is not the determinant. You can reach enlightenment in any context.

Kyabje Kalu Rinpoche

Epilogue: *The Great Ship of Liberation*

Immense wishes linked to the cycle of teachings of the glorious Shangpa-Kagyu, composed by Kyabje Kalu Rinpoche.

I. INVOCATION

Vajradhara and the two dākinis of innate wisdom,[180]
Khyungpo Neljor, root and lineage lamas,
Cakrasaṃvara, Hevajra, Guhyasamāja, Mahāmāyā,
Vajrabhairava, Hayagrīvā, and the other yidams,[181]

Dākinis of the five classes, Mahākāla and Remati,
Four lieutenants and myriad oath-bound ones,[182]
May the Three Jewels and the Three Roots, all refuges,
Look upon me from the realm of the invisible.

By the power of the truth of your compassionate love,
And by the power of all the good done throughout the three times,
Please fulfill all these wishes quickly in this life and those to come.

II. THE COMMON PRELIMINARIES[183]

This precious human life, endowed with leisure and fortune, and so hard
    to obtain,
May I not waste it but extract its essence.

Knowing that it is subject to change—
Impermanent and unstable,
May I stay centered on the present and not waste any time.

Convinced of the results of all actions,
Good or bad, great or small,
May I keep the discipline of karmic law.

Perceiving the suffering
Of the three conditioned worlds,
May I have no attachment for the things of samsara.

III. REFUGE[184]

Now, in future lives, and in the bardo,
May I always be under the protection of the
Three Jewels and the Three Roots.

IV. BODHICITTA[185]

Toward all mother beings of the six realms,
As many in number as space is vast,
May I, from the depths of my being,
Awaken love and compassion.

V. FAVORABLE CONDITIONS

Having gathered all favorable conditions,
May I practice undistracted in a hermitage[186]
And attain the goal of experiences and realizations.

In all my lives may I be guided
By sublime lamas endowed with all good qualities.[187]

And toward my root lama,[188]
Living manifestation of all buddhas,
May I, from the depth of my heart,
Generate genuine devotion.

VI. GENERATION STAGE[189]

May the innate, ever-present
Maṇḍala of the deity be recognized;
May its luminous appearance be stable.

And may I see, as soon as I practice,
The lama, yidam, ḍākini, or dharmapala.

VII. THE FIVE GOLDEN TEACHINGS[190]

By the yoga of tummo,
May bliss and fierce heat blaze within the body
And the meditation of bliss and emptiness
Be stable in the mind.

By the yoga of illusory body,
May illusion be uprooted,
Which grasps as real
The dreams and hallucinations
That are all phenomena.

In dream yoga, at night, without effort,
Within the lucid dream,
May I practice training, multiplication,

Projection, transmutation,
And uncovering objective appearance.

By the yoga of clear light,
In the darkness of sleep's ignorance,
May I recognize the superficial and profound clear lights.

May I master the yogas of transferring consciousness:
dharmakāya, lama, yidam, clear light, and celestial realms.

And by the yoga of the bardo,
And the practices of the three bodies' spontaneous appearance
Of nonmigration and such,
May I achieve the three bodies in the intermediate state.

The four obstacles self-liberated;
The four bodies, spontaneously present,
May the essential state of mahāmudrā be thus realized in this life.

By the practices of integration, based on devotion to the lama,
On forms as deities and sounds as mantra,
And on appearances as illusions and dreams,
May all situations become part of the path.

With the venerable dākinis, who enjoy the space
That is bliss and voidness,
May I, in the realization of utpatti and sampanna,
Travel in celestial enjoyment.

Seeing that in itself body is inanimate
And mind is free of birth and death,
May I realize the fruit of the path:
The state that is deathless and beyond migration.

VIII. THE PROTECTOR'S ACTIVITY[191]

From the perfect vision of the face of the lama protector,
May the supreme accomplishment
Of the four activities be attained.

Through the activities of pacifying,
May all beings abandon every suffering
And become buddhas.

Through the activities of magnification,
May all qualities,
Long life, blessings, powers, experiences,
Realizations, and the others well up like summer floods.

By the activities of power,
May all the forces of the triple world and triple existence
Be gathered for the sublime good
Of the teachings and of beings.

By the activities of destruction,
May the powers of wrathful mantra blaze up
To free the enemy who accumulates the ten misdeeds.

IX. THE SIX PERFECTIONS[192]

May all bad actions that we have done be purified,
Both those that go against the natural discipline
And those that are against vows.

By giving material goods, Dharma, or protection,
May I establish all beings in happiness.

May I always be able to keep all my vows:
Those of personal liberation, bodhisattva vows,
And the commitments of Vajrayāna.

With patience, may I be able to bear
My body's being cut up into a thousand pieces
Even for a hundred eons, to benefit a single being.

With enthusiasm equal to Buddha Śākyamuni's,
May I practice for the sake of all
The sublime path of liberation.

Through the meditations of śamatha and vipaśyanā,[193]
May the experience of dharmakāya,
The mind in itself, the clear light,
Free of all concept, be firm and immutable.

And may I, like Mañjuśrī, with transcendent wisdom,
Perfectly know all the phenomena of samsara and nirvana.

May I reach the very end of the instructions I practice:
Whether sūtra or tantra,[194] whether old or new traditions.

X. Wishes for Bodhisattva Activity

May I always have a beautiful body and voice,
Long life, fame, power, and wealth.

By the grace of the Buddha's teachings in general,
And those of the Shangpa lineage,
May I be like the six ornaments of the world[195]
And the founders of the eight vehicles of practice.[196]

When I die, may I, without interruption of the essential,
Guide beings with rainbow lights and precious relic pills.

On leaving this world,
May I be reborn in Sukhāvatī[197]
In the presence of Khyungpo and his children,
And all at once obtain the ten bhūmis,[198]
Reaching perfect, unsurpassable enlightenment.

Not remaining in the extremes of becoming or abiding,[199]
May I, for the good of beings, become the equal
Of all the victorious ones and their children.

And whoever might have had a connection with me,
Through seeing, hearing, thinking, contact, nourishment, or Dharma,
May they form my first circle of disciples.

May I cause a shower of Mahāyāna and Vajrayāna teachings to rain on them.
May my very being finally establish all beings
In the state of buddhahood.

As long as we are not yet established in that state,
May there be no obstacle, for even a moment,
To our Dharma practice.

May the beings of the six realms
Have all my goodness and virtue,
And having obtained them,
May they forever be happy.

May all the suffering, negative actions,
And obscurations of beings melt into me,
That I might experience their pain.[200]

And by the powers that result from this,
May none among them ever experience any more suffering.

XI. DEDICATION

By the grace of the Three Jewels and Three Roots,
By the power of the dākinis, dharmapalas, and other protectors,
By the immutable truth of the ultimate,
And by the power of infallible dependent arising,
May all these wishes be realized quickly according to their thoughts.

May all their virtues be bestowed upon my mothers of old, as numerous
    as space is vast.
Free of all suffering, endowed with supreme bliss,
May all of us together attain the state of buddhahood.

This prayer was given in the year of the male earth dragon, 1928, by he who is at the end of the glorious Shangpa lineage: Karma Rangjung Kunkhyab

May it result in great benefit for beings—Mangalam.[201]

Notes

1. Besides Jamgön Kongtrul Lodrö Thaye, mentioned here, there were Jamyang Khyentse Wangpo (1820–1892) and Mipham Rinpoche (1846–1912).

2. *Khenpo* in Tibetan.

3. *Rimé* in Tibetan. For more about the Rimé movement, see the Biographical Note (p. xv).

4. Concerning these meditations, see Ngotro: Introducing Mind, and The Practice of Mahāmudrā, in Mahāmudrā and Dzogchen (pp. 229 and 233).

5. For more on meditation and the nature of mind, see Śamatha-Vipaśyanā, in The Mahāyāna (p.151), as well as The Practice of Mahāmudrā, in Mahāmudrā and Dzogchen (p. 233).

6. The subject-object dichotomy is indeed a veil covering pure mind, but we must understand this point precisely in order to avoid serious mistakes. At the ordinary level—relative and relational—a dualistic perception in terms of subject and object is normal and even indispensable for the construction of what we call the I or the ego, the being conscious of its acts, of others, and of the world around it and capable of interacting harmoniously with them. In the context of positive references and relationships, the structure and functioning of the I-ego constitutes what Dharma calls the development of benevolent activity. This is based on practicing right (nonegocentric) action within the context of karma (see Karma and Outer Discipline, in The Hīnayāna, p.109). This development of benevolent activity is a prerequisite that cannot be bypassed in the "development of direct awareness" through which dualistic illusions are transcended. In fact, a realization of the second depends on the quality of the first. (See The Two Accumulations, in The Mahāyāna, p. 141).

7. We use "passion" in its ancient sense signifying all movements or attitudes of mind, positive or negative, including obscurity and mental dullness.

8. For more about karma, see the rest of this chapter.

9. See also, Karma, Interdependence, and Emptiness, in Mind, Reality, and Illusion (p. 43).

10. See also, The Karma of Meditation, in The Hīnayāna (p. 121).

11. See also, The Components and Results of Actions, in The Hīnayāna (p.117).

12. On the precious human rebirth, see also, The Common Preliminary Practices, in The Vajrayāna (p. 197) and Human Life: Using It Well, in The Transformations of Mind (p. 85).

13. See also, The Karma of Meditation, in The Hīnayāna (p. 121).

14. See also, Death and the Continuity of Mind, in The Transformations of Mind (p.48).

15. About this idea, see also, Faults of Samsara, in The Vajrayāna (p. 200).

16. See also, Openness, in Mind, Reality, and Illusion (p. 21).

17. See also, Karma and Freedom: The Game of Illusion, in Mind, Reality, and Illusion (p. 31).

18. See also the description in The Twelve Links of Dependent Origination, in The Transformations of Mind (p. 71).

19. Often the wrong understanding of emptiness leads Westerners to nihilistic conceptions of Dharma.

20. The different bardos are detailed in the following chapters.

21. See, The Eight Consciousnesses and the Five Principal Elements, in The Transformations of Mind (p. 67).

22. See, The Eight Consciousnesses and the Five Principal Elements, in The Transformations of Mind (p. 67).

23. See also, Inner Dissolution, in The Transformations of Mind (p. 57).

24. See the following chapter, The Eight Consciousnesses and the Five Principal Elements, in The Transformations of Mind (p. 67).

25. See The Nature of Mind, in Mind, Reality, and Illusion (p. 21).

26. See, The Bardo of Emptiness, in The Transformations of Mind (p. 59).

27. As mentioned earlier in The Bardo of Becoming, in The Transformations of Mind (p. 61). Its subtle form is an appearance that counts as only half the form aggregate.

28. About tendrel, see, Karma, Interdependence, and Emptiness, in Mind, Reality, and Illusion (p. 43).

29. See above, Karma, Interdependence, and Emptiness, in Mind, Reality, and Illusion (p. 43).

30. See, The Two Truths, in Mind, Reality, and Illusion (p. 41).

31. See above, The Six Realms, in Mind, Reality, and Illusion (p. 37).

32. See also, Impermanence and Death, in The Vajrayāna (p. 198).

33. See, The Practice of Mahāmudrā, in Mahāmudrā and Dzogchen (p.233).

34. See, Deity Yoga, in The Vajrayāna (p. 209).

35. See, The Bardo of Becoming, in The Transformations of Mind (p. 61).

36. See, Enlightenment and the Three Bodies of the Buddha, in The Mahāyāna (p. 167).

37. See, The Stages of Realization, in The Mahāyāna (p. 163).

38. See, The Two Accumulations, in The Mahāyāna (p. 141).

39. See, Bodhicitta and the Bodhisattva Vow, in The Mahāyāna (p. 127).

40. See, The Five Aggregates of Individuality, in The Transformations of Mind (p. 50).

41. See above, The Bardo of Birth to Death, in The Transformations of Mind (p. 65).

42. See also, The Common Preliminary Practices, in The Vajrayāna (p. 197), for more on the precious human rebirth.

43. See, Dharma: A Practice of Unveiling, in Mind, Reality, and Illusion (p. 29).

44. For the specifics of the three vehicles, see also, The Path of Transmutation, in The Vajrayāna (p. 173).

45. The Theravada, referred to by some as the southern tradition at the time of its main geographical expansion, has a more marked Hīnayāna component than Mahāyāna Buddhism or the Buddhism of the "north." However, the Theravada tradition has a Mahāyāna dimension in that it teaches love and compassion as essential virtues, just as the Mahāyāna tradition has a Hīnayāna dimension, in the discipline on which is founded. It is very important

to distinguish Theravada, Mahāyāna, and Vajrayāna from the three vehicles or levels of practice noted in the Vajrayāna tradition: namely, Hīnayāna, Mahāyāna, and Vajrayāna.

46. See above, One Mind, Two States, in Mind, Reality, and Illusion (p. 19).

47. Major monastic ordination includes 253 vows divided into five categories. The basic vows are similar to those of minor monastic ordination (see following note). Other vows are added that regulate the way of life.

48. Minor monastic ordination includes ten main vows based on the five lay vows (the fifth is celibacy). In addition to those, the following are added: not to sing; not to dance; not to make music unless it is religious; not to wear ornaments, jewelry, or perfume; not to use high chairs or beds; not to eat after noon; and not to accept gold or silver. They are broken down into thirty-three subdivisions.

49. The five upasaka or lay vows are: not to kill, not to steal, not to lie, not to take intoxicants, and not to engage in sexual misconduct. The fifth one may be a vow of celibacy. It is possible to take one or more of the five vows.

50. See below, Karma and Outer Discipline, in The Hīnayāna (p.109).

51. Though such realizations free us from samsara, they are not considered to have the same qualities and implications as the realizations gained through the Vajrayāna.

52. For more on the qualities of a buddha, see, Enlightenment and the Three Bodies of the Buddha, in The Mahāyāna (p. 167).

53. See, Dharma: A Practice of Unveiling, in Mind, Reality, and Illusion (p. 29).

54. See also, Outer, Inner, and Absolute Refuges, in The Vajrayāna, (p. 190).

55. See, Karma and Freedom, in Mind, Reality, and Illusion (p. 32).

56. See, The Six Realms, in Mind, Reality, and Illusion (p. 37).

57. See, The Karma of Meditation, in The Hīnayāna (p. 121).

58. See, The Six Realms, in Mind, Reality, and Illusion (p. 37).

59. See, The Game of Illusion, in Mind, Reality, and Illusion (p. 31).

60. For example, anger or hatred that results in the killing of a wise, compassionate, and enlightened being is far more aggressive than if the killing involved an ordinary being. In addition, killing an enlightened being is much more wrongful than killing a mosquito!

61. For more on this expression, see, The Two Accumulations, in The Mahāyāna (p. 141).

62. See, The Common Preliminary Practices, in The Vajrayāna (p. 197).

63. The first two are negative karma and positive karma. See, Karma and Outer Discipline, in The Hīnayāna (p. 109).

64. For a general presentation of meditation, see, Śamatha-Vipaśyanā, in The Mahāyāna (p. 151).

65. With regard to these states, see also, Śamatha-Vipaśyanā, in The Mahāyāna (p. 151).

66. For more on karma in general, see, Karmic Causality, in The Vajrayāna (p. 201).

67. See, The Six Perfections, in The Mahāyāna (p. 143).

68. In the preceding two chapters (pp. 127–136).

69. See, Mind, Reality, and Illusion (pp. 15–44) as well as below, Transcendent Wisdom, in The Mahāyāna (p. 146).

70. By "self," we mean an autonomous, self-sufficient, and static entity. If things and beings give the impression of existing by themselves, or being self-existent, a closer examination indicates that they do not in fact exist as such. This lack of self-existence is called nonself. In our usual experience, we distinguish a self belonging to a subject or person, which is the apparent entity that I am, the "me" or my usual identity, and the self of objects, or the self-entities that are all the objects of the outer world. The fictional and deceptive appearance of these two selves, their lack of true existence, is called the twofold selflessness. This dual nonself is the emptiness of all phenomena; everything lacks a self, or its own inherent existence.

71. The ultimate fusion of emptiness and compassion expresses itself in a buddha's compassion without reference. See, Compassion, in The Mahāyāna (p. 131).

72. See, Dharma: A Practice of Unveiling, in Mind, Reality, and Illusion (p. 29).

73. On everyday practice of the perfections, see, The Six Perfections in Daily Life, in Dharma Practice Today (p. 247).

74. See, The Three Roots, in The Vajrayāna (p. 189).

75. See, Enlightenment and the Three Bodies of the Buddha, in The Mahāyāna (p. 167).

76. See, Enlightenment and the Three Bodies of the Buddha, in The Mahāyāna (p. 167).

77. See, Śamatha-Vipaśyanā, in The Mahāyāna (p. 151).

78. See, The Karma of Meditation, in The Hīnayāna (p. 121).

79. See, The Stages of Realization, in The Mahāyāna (p. 163).

80. On mind and its manifestations, see, Mind, Reality, and Illusion (pp. 15–44).

81. See also, Emptiness: Twofold Selflessness, in The Mahāyāna (p. 137).

82. In this chapter, only Mahāyāna meditations are discussed. See below for those unique to Vajrayāna, in the two sections The Vajrayāna (pp. 173–217) and Mahāmudrā and Dzogchen (pp. 221–241).

83. Vipaśyanā in Sanskrit, lhag-thong in Tibetan.

84. See, Mahāmudrā, in Mahāmudrā and Dzogchen (p. 222).

85. See, Meditation, in The Mahāyāna (p. 146).

86. About birth in these states, see, The Karma of Meditation, in The Hīnayāna (p. 121).

87. See also, From Life to Life: Transitions and the Bardo, in The Transformations of Mind (p. 53).

88. See above, A Brief Meditation, in Mind, Reality, and Illusion (p. 24). In this short meditation, mental tranquillity corresponds to śamatha, and knowledge of mind's empty, lucid, and unobstructed nature to vipaśyanā.

89. See, What Is Mind? in Mind, Reality, and Illusion (p. 15), and also Ngotro: Introducing Mind, in Mahāmudrā and Dzogchen (p. 229).

90. See also, The Practice of Mahāmudrā, in Mahāmudrā and Dzogchen (p. 233).

91. See also, Integration and Transmutation of Thoughts and Emotions, in Mahāmudrā and Dzogchen (p. 235).

92. The ten bodhisattva bhūmis; their classification intersects with that of the five paths, given in the preceding chapter.

93. See, Mind's Veils, in Mind, Reality, and Illusion (p. 27).

94. See, Śamatha-Vipaśyanā, in The Mahāyāna (p. 151).

95. The ten perfections are the six mentioned in The Six Perfections, in The Mahāyāna (p. 143), plus those of method, wishes, power, and primordial wisdom. These last four are not explained in this work.

96. For the mind's three bodies, see, Mahāmudrā, in Mahāmudrā and Dzogchen (p. 222).

97. See, The Three Vehicles: Complementarity and Unity, in The Different Approaches of Dharma (p. 97).

98. Sukhasiddhi and Niguma are two primordial wisdom ḍākinīs, gurus to Khyungpo Neljor, the founder of the Shangpa-Kagyu lineage, of which Kyabje Kalu Rinpoche was the principal heir.

99. The Tibetan terms for initiation, scriptural transmission, and instruction are, respectively, *wang*, *lung*, and *tri*.

100. For more about tendrel, see, Karma, Interdependence, and Emptiness, in Mind, Reality, and Illusion (p. 43).

101. On devotion, see, Guru Yoga, in The Vajrayāna (p. 206).

102. See, The Role of the Root Lama, in The Vajrayāna (p. 184).

103. See, Enlightenment and the Three Bodies of the Buddha, in The Mahāyāna (p. 167).

104. Generation Stage: *utpattikrama* in Sanskrit, *kye-rim* in Tibetan; Completion Stage: or *sampannakrama* in Sanskrit, *dzog-rim* in Tibetan.

105. See, Deity Yoga, in The Vajrayāna (p. 209).

106. See, Beyond Attachment, in Dharma Practice Today, (p. 256).

107. See, The Path of Discipline (p. 103) and Karma and Outer Discipline (p. 109), in The Hīnayāna.

108. For more on these four ideas, see, The Common Preliminary Practices, in The Vajrayāna (p. 197).

109. See, The Six Perfections, in The Mahāyāna (p. 143).

110. See, Śamatha-Vipaśyanā, in The Mahāyāna (p. 151).

111. See, Tonglen, in The Mahāyāna (p. 132).

112. See, The Ngöndro, in The Vajrayāna (p. 203).

113. See, Deity Yoga, in The Vajrayāna (p. 209).

114. See, The Subsequent Practices, in The Vajrayāna (p. 213).

115. See, Transmission and Qualification, in Mahāmudrā and Dzogchen (p. 225).

116. See, Mahāmudrā and Dzogchen: The Immediate Path (pp. 221–241).

117. See also, Human Life: Using It Well, in The Transformations of Mind (p. 85).

118. See also On the Urgency of Practice, in The Transformations of Mind (p. 87).

119. See also, The Bardo of Becoming, in The Transformations of Mind (p. 61).

120. See, On the Urgency of Practice, in the Transformations of Mind (p. 87).

121. See also, Human Life and Its Problems, in The Transformations of Mind (p. 81).

122. See, The Six Realms, in Mind, Reality, and Illusion (p. 37).

123. See, The Game of Illusion, in Mind, Reality, and Illusion (p. 31).

124. See, Karma and Outer Discipline, in The Hīnayāna (p. 109).

125. See, The Components and Results of Actions, in The Hīnayāna (p. 117).

126. In the context of the five Hundred Thousand, we generally count the refuge prayer and the prostrations separately. In certain other cases, the practice of generating bodhicitta, performed together with the recitation of the refuge prayer, is also counted.

127. We have not described here the specific details of each of the ngöndro practices because their study requires a particular transmission, and descriptions of them can be found in other published works.

128. See also, Refuge and the Three Jewels, in The Hīnayāna (p. 105).

129. See also, Outer, Inner, and Absolute Refuges, in The Vajrayāna (p. 190).

130. Prostration is the symbolic refuge gesture expressing the abandonment of self-cherishing individuality; we thereby open ourselves up to the enlightened qualities of the Three Jewels and the Three Roots.

131. See, Karma, Interdependence, and Emptiness, in Mind, Reality, and Illusion (p. 43).

132. See the section, Generosity, in The Mahāyāna (p. 143).

133. See also, Transmission and Blessing, in The Vajrayāna (p. 183).

134. See also, Preliminaries Before a Session, in Mahāmudrā and Dzogchen (p. 233).

135. See, The Three Roots, in The Vajrayāna (p. 189).

136. The primordial wisdom aspect is *jnanasattva* in Sanskrit; *yeshepa* in Tibetan. The aspect endowed with forms is *samayasattva* in Sanskrit, *damtsigpa* in Tibetan.

137. See, The Path of Transmutation, in The Vajrayāna (p. 173).

138. This is why the Shangpa-Kagyu lineage is sometimes called the lineage of the Seven Jewels, referring to these seven masters. See illustration on p. 232 with a description of each at the end of this work.

139. The better-known six yogas of Nāropa parallel those of Niguma.

140. See also, Liberating Practices in the Different Bardos, in The Transformations of Mind (p. 75).

141. On the bardos, see, The Transformations of Mind (p. 47–88).

142. See, the following chapter, Mahāmudrā and Dzogchen, (p. 221).

143. See, On Retreat, and The Three-Year Retreat, in Dharma Practice Today (pp. 252, 253).

144. See, Mind's Veils, in Mind, Reality, and Illusion (p. 27).

145. See, One Mind, Two States, in Mind, Reality, and Illusion (p. 19).

146. See, Progression in Vajrayāna, in The Vajrayāna (p. 193).

147. See also, Progression in Vajrayāna, in The Vajrayāna (p. 193).

148. See also, What Is Mind?, in Mind, Reality, and Illusion (p. 15).

149. See also, The Practice of Mahāmudrā, in Mahāmudrā and Dzogchen (p. 233).

150. See, Insight Practice, in The Mahāyāna (p. 154).

151. See, The Ngöndro, in The Vajrayāna (p. 203).

152. See, The Five Golden Teachings, in The Vajrayāna. (p. 213).

153. *Datarwai shepa*: the different translations of this Tibetan term evoke a quality of immediate awareness and knowing which belongs to the mind in this state.

154. *Ma-cho*

155. *Ma-yen*

156. *Mi-gom*

157. See also, A Brief Meditation, in Mind, Reality, and Illusion (p. 24).

158. See also, Enlightenment and the Three Bodies of the Buddha, in the Mahāyāna (p. 167).

159. Innate primordial awareness; *lhenchig kyepe yeshe* in Tibetan.

160. See preceding chapter.

161. Introduction, cultivation, and stabilization of this practice are *ngotro, kyongwa,* and *tenpa* in Tibetan.

162. See above, The Stages of Realization, in The Mahāyāna (p. 163).

163. See, The Practice of Mahāmudrā, in Mahāmudrā and Dzogchen (p. 233).

164. See One Mind, Two States, in Mind, Reality, and Illusion (p. 19).

165. See, Bodhicitta and the Bodhisattva Vow, in The Mahāyāna (p. 127), and Compassion, in The Mahāyāna (p. 131).

166. See, The Six Perfections, in The Mahāyāna (p. 143).

167. See, The Common Preliminary Practices, in The Vajrayāna (p. 197).

168. See, Śamatha-Vipaśyanā, in The Mahāyāna (p. 151).

169. See, Tonglen, in The Mahāyāna (p. 132).

170. See the preceding chapter.

171. See, The Common Preliminary Practices, in The Vajrayāna (p. 197).

172. See p. 320 for information on Dharma centers founded by Kalu Rinpoche.

173. See, The Path of Discipline, in The Hīnayāna (p. 103)

174. See, Outer, Inner, and Absolute Refuges, in The Vajrayāna, (p. 190).

175. *Nyonpa* in Tibetan.

176. See the anecdote, Nāropa Meets Tilopa, in The Vajrayāna (p. 185).

177. See the anecdote, The Crimes and Tests of Milarepa, in The Mahāyāna, (p. 147).

178. See the anecdote, Gampopa Meets Milarepa, in The Vajrayāna (p. 178).

179. See also above, The Story of Sukhasiddhi, in The Vajrayāna (p. 175).

180. The two dākinis of innate wisdom are Niguma and Sukhasiddhi; see, The Story of Niguma, in The Vajrayāna (p. 213), and The Story of Sukhasiddhi, in The Vajrayāna (p. 175).

181. These are the main yidams or meditational deities of the Shangpa-Kagyu lineage; see, Deity Yoga, in The Vajrayāna (p. 209).

182. These two lines allude to the main Shangpa protector deities; see, The Three Roots, in

The Vajrayāna (p. 189).

183. See, The Ngöndro, in The Vajrayāna (p. 203).

184. See, Refuge and the Three Jewels, in The Hīnayāna (p. 105) and The Three Roots, in The Vajrayāna (p. 189).

185. See, Bodhicitta and the Bodhisattva Vow, in The Mahāyāna (p. 127).

186. See, On Retreat, in Dharma Practice Today (p. 252).

187. See, The Guide and Spiritual Direction, in The Vajrayāna (p. 177).

188. See, The Role of the Root Lama, in The Vajrayāna (p. 184).

189. See, Deity Yoga, in The Vajrayāna (p. 209).

190. On the Five Golden Teachings, see, The Subsequent Practices, in The Vajrayāna (p. 213).

191. See, The Three Roots, in The Vajrayāna (p. 189).

192. See, The Six Perfections, in The Mahāyāna (p. 143).

193. See, Śamatha-Vipaśyanā, in The Mahāyāna (p. 151).

194. About sūtra and tantra, see, Buddhadharma, in The Unity of the Different Traditions (p. 7).

195. The six ornaments of the world are the six best-known Indian masters; see "Six Ornaments" in the glossary of terms.

196. The eight vehicles are the eight main lineages of Tibetan Buddhism.

197. See, Wishes to Be Reborn in a Pure Land, in The Transformations of Mind (p. 77).

198. The ten bhūmis are the ten bodhisattva grounds; they correspond to the five paths. See, The Stages of Realization, in The Mahāyāna (p. 163).

199. That is, without abiding in the extremes of samsara or nirvana.

200. This and the previous stanza allude to the practice of tonglen. See, Compassion, in The Mahāyāna (p. 131).

201. Mangalam means "May everything be auspicious."

List of Stories and Anecdotes

List of Illustrations

For more information on the persons depicted in the illustrations,
please refer to the glossary of proper names and the index.

Also known as the Wheel of Life. The six Tibetan letters symbolize the six realms; the twelve outer panels depict the links of dependent origination. The three animals in the center represent the three mental poisons.

Illustrates the correspondence between the twelve interdependent factors and the four great bardos.

The image depicts the first masters of the Marpa-Kagyu lineage. In the center, Marpa the Translator, who introduced the lineage teachings to Tibet; above him, Vajradhara; upper left and right, respectively, Tilopa and Nāropa, Marpa's Indian predecessors; at the lower left and right, respectively, Milarepa and Gampopa, his successors; between them, the first Karmapa, Gampopa's main disciple. More about their lives can be found in stories and anecdotes listed in the back of the book.

The Five Golden Teachings are usually depicted by a tree whose roots are Niguma's six yogas; the trunk is the mahāmudrā reliquary; the branches are the three methods of integration; the flowers are the red and white dākinis; and the fruit is faultless immortality.

The drawing illustrates the first seven masters of the Shangpa-Kagyu lineage. They are known as the Seven Jewels because, for seven consecutive generations, each of them was the only lineage holder (see The Story of Niguma, p.213). Khyungpo Neljor's two main masters, Rāhula and Dorje Denpa, are also added.

In the upper center, Vajradhara; above left, Niguma; at the center, Khyungpo Neljor; underneath him, Mochopa; at the lower right, Kyergangpa; and to the left, Nyentonpa. These are the first six jewels in order. Upper right is Rāhula; and beneath Niguma, Dorje Denpa. Under Rāhula, Sangye Tonpa, the Seventh Jewel who spread the teachings widely.

This image is a reproduction of a thangka made in the first half of the century at Pelpung monastery. It depicts, at the center, Kyabje Kalu Rinpoche, surrounded by Shangpa-Kagyu, Dakpo-Kagyu, and Nyingma lineage lamas, representatives of the Rimé, or impartial, movement.

Glossary of Terms

ENGLISH	TIBETAN	SANSKRIT
abbot	mkhan po	upādhyāya
abhiṣeka, *see* initiation		
accumulation of merit	bsod nams tshogs	puṇyasambhāra
accumulation of wisdom	ye shes tshogs	jñānasambhāra
accumulation; collection	tshogs	sambhāra
action	las	karma
action, harmful	sdig pa'i las	pāpa
action, negative	mi dge ba'i las	akuśala
action, positive	dge ba'i las	śubha
action, see karma		
activity, enlightened	phrin las	karma
adept	grub thob	siddha
aggregate	phung po	skandha
aggression; hatred	zhe sdang	dveṣa
analysis; investigation	dpyod pa	vicāra
animal	dud 'gro	tiryañc
aspect	rnam pa	ākāra
attachment	'dod chags	rāga
bardo of being	srid pa bar do	
bardo of birth and death	skye shi bar do	
bardo of dreaming	rmi lam bar do	
bardo of emptiness	chos nyid bar do	
bardo of meditation	bsam gtan bar do	
bardo of the moment of death	'chi kha bar do	
being	srid pa	bhava
believing faith	yid ches pa'i dad pa	abhisampratyaya
blessing; spiritual influence	byin rlabs	adhiṣṭhāna
bodhicitta	byang chub kyi sems	bodhicitta
bodhisattva	byang chub sems dpa'	bodhisattva
Bön	bon	
buddha	sangs rgyas	buddha
buddha nature	de bzhin gshegs pa'i nying po	tathāgatagarbha

ENGLISH	TIBETAN	SANSKRIT
cakra	'khor lo	cakra
cause	rgyu	hetu
children of the Buddha	rgyal sras	jinaputra
clear light	'od gsal	prabhāsvara
compassion	snying rje	karuṇā
Completion Stage	rdzogs rim	sampannakrama
composed, composite	'du byas	saṃskṛta
concentration	bsam gtan	dhyāna
conception; perception	'du shes	saṃjñā
conceptuality	rnam rtog	vikalpa
Conqueror	rgyal ba	jina
consciousness	rnam shes	vijñāna
conventional truth	kun rdzob bden pa	saṃvṛtisatya
cyclic existence	'khor ba	saṃsāra
dākini	mkha' 'dro ma	ḍākinī
definition	mtshan nyid	lakṣaṇa
definitive meaning	nges don	nitārtha
demi-god	lha ma yin	asura
demon	bdud	māra
dependent origination	rten cing 'brel 'byung	pratītyasamutpāda
desire realm	'dod khams	kāmadhātu
desire; attachment	'dod chags	rāga
Dharma	chos	dharma
dharma body	chos sku	dharmakāya
Dharma protector	chos skyong	dharmapāla
dharmadhātu	chos dbyings	dharmadhātu
dharmata	chos nyid	dharmatā
discipline	'dul ba	vinaya
discursive thought	rnam par rtog pa	vikalpa
drop	thig le	bindu
dzogchen	rdzogs chen	mahāsandhi
effort; exertion	brtson 'grus	vīrya
element	'byung ba	bhūta
Emanation Body	sprul sku	nirmāṇakāya
emptiness, openness	stong pa nyid	śūnyatā
empty	stong pa	śūnya
Enjoyment Body	longs sku	saṃbhogakāya
enlightenment	byang chub	bodhi
eon; cosmic cycle	bskal pa	kalpa
equanimity	btang snyoms	upekṣā
essence	ngo bo	svabhāva

ENGLISH	TIBETAN	SANSKRIT
feeling; sensation	tshor ba	vedanā
five constituents	khams nga	pañcadhātu
Foe Destroyer	dgra bcom pa	arhat
forbearance; patience	bzod pa	kṣānti
form	gzugs	rūpa
Form Body	gzugs sku	rūpakāya
form realm	gzugs khams	rūpadhātu
formless realm	gzugs med khams	arūpyadhātu
foundational consciousness	kun gzhi rnam shes	ālayavijñāna
fruit; result	'bras bu	phala
full lotus posture	rdo rje dkyil krung	vajrāsana
fully ordained monk	dge long	bhikṣu
ganacakra	tshogs kyi 'khor lo	gaṇacakra
gathering purification	tshogs bsags sgrib sbyang	
Generation Stage	skyed rim	utpattikrama
generosity	byin pa	dāna
geshe	dge ba'i bshes gnyen	kalyāṇamitra
god	lha	deva
grasping	'dzin pa	grāha
grasping at duality	gnyis 'dzin	
great adept	grub thob chen po	mahāsiddha
great bliss	bde ba chen po	mahāsukha
great compassion	snying rje chen po	mahākaruṇā
ground, stage	sa	bhūmi
happiness	bde ba	sukha
hell	dmyal ba	naraka, niraya
Hīnayāna	theg pa dman pa	Hīnayāna
hungry ghost	yi dvags	preta
ignorance	gti mug	moha
ignorance	ma rig pa	avidyā
illusion	'khrul pa	bhrānti
impermanence	mi rtag pa	anityatā
impurity; stain	dri ma	mala
individual	gang zag	pudgala
individual liberation	so so thar pa	prātimokṣa
infinite consciousness	rnam shes mtha' yas	vijñānānantya
initiation; empowerment	dbang	abhiṣeka
inner heat	gtum mo	caṇḍālī
insight	lhag mthong	vipaśyanā
intermediate state	bar do	antarābhava
interpretable meaning	drang don	neyārtha

ENGLISH	TIBETAN	SANSKRIT
jealousy	phrag dog	īrsyā
joy	dga' ba	muditā
kālacakra	dus 'khor	kālacakra
kapala	ka pa' la	kapāla
knowledge	chos mngon pa	abhidharma
limitless space	nam mkha' mtha' yas	ākāśānantyā
love	byams pa	maitrī
lucidity faith	dang ba'i dad pa	prasāda
lucidity; clarity	gsal ba	prabhāsvara
mahāmudrā; great seal	phyag rgya chen po	mahāmudrā
mandala	dkyil 'khor	mandala
mantra	sngags	mantra
master	slob dpon	ācārya
master of retreat	sgrub dpon	
meditation	sgom	bhāvanā
meditational deity	yi dam	istadevatā
meditational peace	zhi gnas	śamatha
mental affliction	nyon mongs pa	kleśa
mental fabrications	spros pa	prapañca
mental stability	bsam gtan	dhyāna
method; means	thabs	upāya
Middle Way	dbu ma'i lam	madhyamaka
mind	sems	citta
mind training	blo sbyong	
morality	tshul khrims	śila
motivational factors	'du byed	samskāra
mudra	phyag rgya	mudrā
natural condition	rang babs	
nature	rang bzhin	svabhāva
neither perception nor non-perception	'du shes med 'du shes med min	naivasamjñānāsamjñā
nirvana	mya ngan las 'das pa	nirvāna
noble; superior	'phags pa	ārya
nothingness	ci yang med pa	ākimcanya
novice monk	dge tshul	śrāmanera
obstruction	sgrib pa	āvarana
offering	mchod pa	pūja
omniscient	rnam pa thams cad mkhyen pa	sarvākārajñāna
one taste; indistinguishable	ro gcig	ekarasa
One Thus Gone; Buddha	de bzhing gshegs pa	tathāgata
oral instruction	man ngag	upadeśa

ENGLISH	TIBETAN	SANSKRIT
ordinary being	so so skyes bo	pṛthagjana
ordinary mind	tha mal gyi shes pa	
Path of Accumulation	tshogs lam	sambhāramārga
Path of Meditation	sgom lam	bhāvanāmārga
Path of No More Learning	mi slob lam	asaikṣamārga
Path of Preparation	sbyor lam	prayogamārga
Path of Seeing	mthong lam	darśanamārga
path; way	lam	mārga
peace	zhi ba	śānti
perfection of wisdom	shes rab kyi pha rol tu phyin pa	prajñāpāramitā
permanence	rtag pa	śāśvata
person	mi	manuṣya
pledge being	dam tshig sems pa	samayasattva
preliminary	sngon 'gro	abhimāna
pride	nga rgyal	
primordial wisdom	ye shes	jñāna
propensity	bag chags	vāsanā
purification	sgrib sbyang	
quality	yon tan	guṇa
reading transmission	lung	āgama
reality	chos nyid	dharmatā
realization	rtogs pa	adhigama
recollect; remember	dran pa	smṛti
refuge	skyabs	śaraṇa
ritual bell	dril bu	ghaṇṭa
root	rtsa ba	mūla
Sangha	dge 'dun	saṃgha
self	bdag	ātman
self-conscious; self-knower	rang rig	svasaṃvedanā
self-grasping	bdag tu 'dzin pa	ātmagrāha
self-grasping	ngar 'dzin	ahaṃkāra
selflessness	bdag med	nairātmya
sense power	dbang po	indriya
sensitivity, unobstructed intelligence	ma 'gags pa	
sentient being	sems can	sattva
single-pointed concentration	ting nge 'dzin	samādhi
six realms	'jig rten gyi khams drug	ṣallokadhātu
skillful means	thabs mkhas	upāyakauśalya
Solitary Realizer	rang sang rgyas	pratyekabuddha
space	nam mkha'	ākāśa
spiritual friend	dge ba'i bshes gnyen	kalyāṇamitra

ENGLISH	TIBETAN	SANSKRIT
stupa	mchod rten	stūpa
subtle channel	rtsa	nāḍī
subtle wind	rlung	prāṇa
suchness	de bzhin nyid	tathatā
suffering; unsatisfactoriness	sdug bsngal	duḥkha
sutra	mdo	sūtra
taking and giving	gtong len	
tantra	rgyud	tantra
tantra vehicle	rdo rje theg pa	Vajrayāna
tantric meditation	sgrub thabs	sādhana
ten powers	stobs bcu	daśabala
thought; conceptuality	rtog pa	kalpanā
Three Jewels	dkon mchog gsum	triratna
to reflect	bsam pa	cintā
to show the nature of	ngo sprod	
transcendent wisdom	shes rab	prajñā
transference of consciousness	'pho ba	
treatise	bstan bcos	śāstra
truth	bden pa	satya
Truth Body	chos sku	dharmakāya
tsa-tsa	tsha tsha	
two truths	bden pa gnyis	satyadvaya
ultimate truth	don dam bden pa	paramārthasatya
universal vehicle	thegs pa chen po	Mahāyāna
vajra	rdo rje	vajra
vehicle	theg pa	yāna
view	lta ba	dṛṣṭi
vigilance	shes bzhin	samprajanya
virtue	dge ba	śubha
vow	dam tshig	samaya
wisdom being	ye shes pa	jñānasattva
wisdom of immediacy	da ltar ba'i shes pa	
wish; prayer; aspiration	smon lam	praṇidhāna
yearning faith	'dod pa'i dad pa	abhilāṣa
yoga	rnal 'byor	yoga
yogi	rnal 'byor pa	yogi
Zen	gzan	

Glossary of Proper Names

See also body of text after referring to index.

Abhidharma (Tibetan: chos mngon pa; Sanskrit: abhidharma)
One of the three collections of Buddha's teachings which comprise the *Tripiṭaka,* or the Three Baskets, contained in the *Kangyur.* The two other collections are the vinaya and the sūtras.

Akaniṣṭa (Tib. 'og min; Skt. akaniṣṭa)
Name of the realm of dharmadhātu, "the sphere of reality," which is the pure field of Vajradhara.

Amitābha (Tib. 'od dpag med; Skt. amitābha)
Among the five victorious ones ruling the five buddha families, he belongs to the *padma* or lotus family. In particular, he is the master of Chenrezig (Skt. Avalokiteśvara) and resides in Dewa Chen (Skt. Sukhāvatī).

Ānanda (Tib. kun dga'o; Skt. ānanda)
Cousin and personal assistant of Buddha Śākyamuni. He recited the sūtras at the Council of Vaiśali at the time of the first compilation of the Canon.

Āryadeva (Tib. 'phags pa'i lha; Skt. āryadeva)
(End of third century C.E.). One of the Six Ornaments, he was Nāgārjuna's principal disciple, continuing his teaching of Madhyamaka and composing, in particular, the Four Hundred (Catuḥśataka).

Asaṅga (Tib. thog med; Skt. asaṅga)
(ca. 310–390 C.E.) One of the two Indian masters called the Two Supremes (mchog gnyis); the other is Nāgārjuna. Born in Puruṣapara, the capital of Gandhāra, he lived for twelve years at Nālandā. Author of the *Abhidharmasamuccaya* and brother of Vasubandhu, he was, along with his brother, one of the founders of the Yogācāra school. He is well known for his meditation practice on Maitreya, who transmitted to him the Five Teachings of Maitreya (byams chos sde lnga).

Atiśa (Tib. jo bo rje; Skt. atīśa)
(982–1054 C.E.) Dīpaṅkaraśrījñāna Atiśa (jo bo rje mar me mdzad) was a superior of Vikramaśila University. He was invited to Tibet in 1042, where he taught for the remaining twelve years of his life. Recipient of two great transmission lineages of the Buddha's word—Widespread Activity (rgya chen spyod rgyu) from Maitreya-Asaṅga, and Profound View (zab mo'i lta rgyud) from Mañjuśri-Nāgārjuna—he established the tradition of the graduated path teachings with his text *Lamp on the Path to Enlightenment* (*Bodhipathapradīpa; byang chub lam sgron*), which became the prototype of the lam-rim, whose treatises present from an instructional perspective the stages on the path to enlightenment. He composed over a hundred works included in the *Tengyur* and assisted in the translation into Tibetan of numerous others. He founded the Kadam lineage, which became a fundamental component in the second spread of Buddhism in Tibet and in the forms it took there in the Kagyu, Sakya, and Gelug schools.

Atsom Drupa (Tib. a 'dzom 'brug pa)
(1842–1924) Also called Natsho Rangdröl (snga tshogs rang grol). One of Mipham Rinpoche's principal disciples

Bardo Thödrol (Tib. *bar do thos grol*)
The Tibetan Book of the Dead.

Ben (Geshe) (Tib. 'ben)
A great Kadam master of the eleventh and twelfth centuries.

Bodhicaryāvatāra (Tib. *spyod 'jug*; Skt. *bodhicaryāvatāra*)
A famous work by Śāntideva whose title literally means "the introduction to the life of a bodhisattva." A long poem in ten chapters which explains the bodhisattva path, the different aspects of bodhicitta, and the six pāramitās.

Brahmā (Tib. tshangs pa; Skt. brahmā)
Major deity whose state corresponds to one of the levels of the world of pure form.

Buddha Śākyamuni (Tib. sa kya thup pa; Skt. śākyamuni)
(Fifth century B.C.E.: 566–476 or 558–468 B.C.E.) The fourth Buddha of our era (skal pa) who, like his predecessors, manifested himself in the twelve works. He initiated the Buddhist teachings transmitted up until the present.

Cakrasaṃvara (Tib. 'khor lo sdom pa; Skt. cakrasaṃvara)
One of the principal meditational buddhas or deities (yidams) of the anuttarayogatantra. He is especially popular in the Kagyu lineage practices.

Candrakīrti (Tib. zla ba grags pa; Skt. candrakīrti)
(ca. 600–650) One of the main exponents of the Madhyamaka-Prāsaṅgika school. His principal works are *Introduction to the Middle Way* (*Madhyamakāvatāra, dbu ma la 'jug pa*) and *Clear Words* (*Prasannapadā, tshig gsal*).

Chang Chub Chö Ling (Tib. byang chub chos gling)
Kagyu monastery located in Bhutan. Kyabje Kalu Rinpoche became its director at the invitation of the royal family and at the instigation of the Karmapa. Kyabje Kalu Rinpoche remained there several years, developing the monastery and having two retreat centers constructed. Afterward, he left for India, where he founded Sonada monastery.

Chenrezig (Tib. spyan ras gzigs; Skt. avalokiteśvara)
The buddha of compassion. He is the patron and protector of Tibet and also a meditational deity, whose practice is very widespread. See Amitābha.

Chogyur Dechen Lingpa (Tib. mchog gyur bde chen gling pa)
(1829–1870) Great tertön (revealer of teachings stemming from Guru Rinpoche), he was, along with Kongtrul, Khyentse, and Mipham Rinpoche, one of the main creators of the Rimé movement.

Dagpo-Kagyu (Tib. dvags po bka' rgyud)
This lineage dates back to Marpa Lotsawa (1012–1099), who made three journeys to India and studied at the feet of numerous masters, the principal one being Nāropa. Marpa's principal disciple, Milarepa (1040–1123), was one of the most famous yogis and poets of all Tibet. Milarepa's two principal disciples were Rechungpa and Gampopa. The patronymic of the Dagpo lineage is one of Gampopa's names. Gampopa's four principal disciples made up the four major branches of the school (see Kagyu). The main branch is the Karma-Kagyu, or Kamtshang-Kagyu, lineage, founded by the first Karmapa, Tusum Khyenpa (1110–1193). In addition to the Karmapas, his lineage is primarily made up of the Shamarpas and the Taï Situpas.

Dalai Lama (Tib. ta la'i bla ma)
The lineage of Dalai Lamas dates back to Gendun Drub (1391–1474), one of the closest disciples of Je Tsongkhapa (1357–1419), who initiated the Gelug school. Gendun Drub founded Tashi

Lhunpo monastery at Shigatse. His work was continued by Gendun Drub, followed by Sönam Gyatso, who received from the Mongol emperor Altan Khan the title "Dale Lama" (ta la'i bla ma), or Dalaï Lama, signifying "ocean" with reference to his wisdom. The title was applied retroactively to his two predecessors. A grandson of Altan Khan, Yönten Gyatso, was the fourth Dalai Lama. His successor, Lobsang Gyatso (1617–1682), known as the Great Fifth, relied on his Mongol allies to emerge victorious in power struggles between provinces and Tibetan schools. They established him as the supreme authority of all Tibet, of which he was in great part the unifier and organizer. It was he who had the Potala palace built at Lhasa. The lineage of Dalai Lamas has continued without interruption up to the present fourteenth holder of the title: His Holiness Tenzin Gyatso, born in July 1935. The Dalai Lamas are emanations of Chenrezig, the buddha of compassion, who is the patron and protector of Tibet.

Damema (Tib. bdag med ma)
Wife of Marpa. Her name means "egoless."

Darmadode (Tib. dar ma ldo sde)
The son of Marpa and Damema.

Dewa Chen (Tib. bde ba can; Skt. sukhāvatī)
Realm of Amitābha and Chenrezig. The practices and wishes associated with them direct the mind at the time of death to be reborn there, liberated from samsara.

Dharmakīrti (Tib. chos kyi grags pa; Skt. dharmakīrti)
(ca. 600–660) One of the Six Ornaments. Logician who elucidated and expanded the work of Dignāga. He is the author of the works on logic called *Seven Treatises* (*tshad ma sde bdun*).

Dignāga (Tib. phyogs kyi glang po; Skt. dignāga)
(Fifth–sixth centuries) One of the Six Ornaments and the most distinguished Mahāyāna logician. His most important work is without question the *Compendium of Valid Cognition* (*Pramāṇasamuccaya*; *tshad ma kun las btus pa*, or, *tshad ma mdo*).

Dorje Denpa (Tib. rdo rje gdan pa; Skt. vajrāsana, abhayā)
One of Khyungpo Neljor's masters. See Shangpa-Kagyu.

Drom Tönpa (Tib. 'brom ston pa)
(1004–1064) Atiśa's principal disciple. See Kadampa.

Gampopa (Tib. sgam po pa)
(1079–1153) Also called Dagpo Lhaje (dvags po lha rje), literally, the physician from Dagpo. The village and mountain of Gampo, which he was named after, are located in the Dagpo region of southeastern Tibet. Gampopa was trained in the Kadam tradition. He then met Milarepa and became his principal disciple. He was the founder of the Dagpo-Kagyu monastic order whose principal disciple was Tusum Khyenpa, the first Karmapa. His transmission fused the Kadam spiritual current with the Mahāmudrā, received from Milarepa. Among other works, he composed *The Jewel Ornament of Liberation* (*dvags po thar rgyan*) a lam-rim text which is the basic manual of traditional Kagyu studies.

Gelug (Tib. dge lugs)
The Gelug school is one of four main Tibetan Buddhist schools, initiated by Tsongkhapa Lobsang Drakpa (1357–1419), who founded Ganden monastery near Lhasa. At first the school was known as that of the Gandenpas and, later, of the Gelugpas.

Gönpo Chadrupa (Tib. phyag drug pa)
Name of the six-armed aspect of Mahākāla, who is the Dharma protector (dharmapāla) mainly

in the Shangpa-Kagyu and Gelug lineages. "The six-armed protector of primordial wisdom" is a wrathful emanation of Chenrezig, the buddha of compassion, who manifests himself in a dynamic and powerful form in order to subjugate illusions and obstacles.

Guhyasamāja (Tib. gsang ba 'dus pa; Skt. guhyasamāja)
Name of a deity (yidam) and tantra of the father lineage in anuttarayogatantra. He is part of the maṇḍala of deities of the five tantras (rgyud sde lha lnga). See Shangpa-Kagyu.

Guṇaprabha (Tib. yon tan 'od; Skt. guṇaprabha)
One of the Six Ornaments.

Gyaltsen (Lama) (Tib. rgyal mtshan)
Kyabje Kalu Rinpoche's lifelong assistant and father of his reincarnation.

Hayagrīva (Tib. rta mgrin; Skt. hayagrīva)
Name of a deity (yidam) practiced in different schools. In the Shangpa lineage, his origin dates back to Kyergangpa, who received his revelation from Guru Rinpoche.

Hevajra (Tib. kye rdo rje; Skt. hevajra)
Name of a deity (yidam) and tantra of anuttarayoga. He belongs to the maṇḍala of the deities of the five tantras (rgyud sde lha lnga).

Indrabhūti (Tib. Indra bhuti; Skt. indrabhūti)
One of the eighty-four mahāsiddhas; king of Oḍḍiyāna.

Jamgön Kongtrul Lodrö Thaye (Tib. 'jam mgon kong sprul blo gros mtha' yas)
(1813–1899) Extremely brilliant in his youth, recognized by the eleventh Situpa Pema Wangcho Gyelpo (1886–1952) as a tulku, he undertook, with other great masters—among them Jamyang Khyentse Wangpo, Mipham Rinpoche, Chogyur Dechen Lingpa and Dza Patrul—a great revival movement known as the Rimé, the impartial approach. This movement was based on the spiritual experience and fundamental unity of the different traditions, beyond their specific formulations. Jamgön Kongtrul Lodrö Thaye left an immense heritage in the form of five treasures: *The Encyclopedia of Traditional Knowledge* (*shes bya mdzod*) in four volumes; *The Treasury of Precious Terma* (*rin chen gter mdzod*) in sixty-three volumes; *The Treasury of Kagyu Tantras* (*bka' brgyud sngags mdzod*) in eight volumes; *The Treasury of Essential Instructions of the Eight Practice Lineages* (*gdams ngag mdzod*) in ten volumes; and *The Treasury of Vast Words* (*rgya chen bka' mdzod*) in ten volumes—his personal writings.

Jamgön Kongtrul Lodrö Thaye played an essential role in many lineages, compiling teachings and allowing for their continuous transmission. In the second generation, he had several emanations, the best known being Pelpung Kongtrul, Pelden Khyentse Öser (1904–1953), who became a link in the transmission of the Kamtsang-Kagyu lineage; Sechen Kongtrul Padma Drime (1901–1960), who was Trungpa Rinpoche's (1939–1987) root lama, and Kyabje Kalu Rinpoche, who was recognized especially as the emanation of the enlightened activity of Jamgön Kongtrul. In the third generation, Pelpung Kongtrul Chöki Senge Tenpe Gocha (1954–1992), disciple of the sixteenth Karmapa, was particularly well known; he taught in the West.

Jamyang Khyentse Wangpo (Tib. 'jam dbyangs mkhyen brtse dbang po)
(1820–1892) Emanation of the omniscient Jigme Lingpa (1730–1793), one of the most eminent figures of the Nyingma tradition. He was a great Nyingmapa and Sakyapa master, inspirer and director of the Rimé movement. Afterward, he had different tulkus recognized in several schools, in particular:

Dilgo Khyentse Rabsel Dawa (1910–1991) who taught and founded centers in the West connected to the Nyingma school. He was friend, master, and disciple of Kyabje Kalu Rinpoche.

Beri or Pelpung Khyentse Karma Khyentse Öser (1896–1945) whose tulku is Bero Khyentse Rinpoche (born in 1947), disciple of the sixteenth Karmapa. He has taught in the West and now resides in Bodhgaya.

Jonang (Tib. jo nang)
Name of a school whose philosophical viewpoint and practices date back to Yumo Mikyö Dorje, a great master of Kālacakra who established, in accordance with his teachings, the perspective of great Madhyamaka, or Yogācāra-Madhayamaka-Shentong. This view goes beyond the divergences between dialectical Prāsaṅgika and the Yogācāra experience, and is a synthesis of the two great Mahāyāna philosophical perspectives. Kunpang Thuje Tsöndru (1243–?), a holder of the lineage, established its seat in the Tsang province at Jomonang monastery which gave the school its name. His great disciple, the omniscient Dölpo Sherab Gyaltsen (1292–1361), greatly spread the Madhyamaka Shentong perspective in the provinces of Ü and Tsang. He composed numerous works including *The Ocean of Definitive Meaning* (*ri chos nges don rgya mtsho*) which explains the Madhyamaka Shentong perspective. The lineage continued without interruption; among its members there were Jonang Kunga Drölcho (1495–1566), who received revelations from Niguma, and particularly the omniscient Jetsün Drolwe Gönpo, known by the name of Taranatha (1575–1634), who founded the monastery of Taten Puntsoling. In the seventeenth century, political problems caused the Jonang monasteries to become Gelug, but the teachings of the school continued to be transmitted and practiced while being incorporated into other lineages, and particularly to the Shangpa-Kagyu transmission.

Kadampa (Tib. bka' gdams pa)
The Kadam school was founded by Atīśa (982–1054). His disciple Dromtön (1004–1064) founded Radreng monastery in North Lhasa in 1056. This became the source of his teachings. The school did not survive independently mostly because the majority of Kadampas, being hermits, did not construct monasteries, but the Kadam school did profoundly influence the other schools. In particular, the Gelugpas call themselves the new Kadampas, and the Dagpo-Kagyupas say that their transmission is the confluence of the mahāmudrā and Kadam teaching traditions.

Kagyu (Tib. bka' brgyud)
The Kagyu school has two main branches: Shangpa-Kagyu (shangs pa bka' brgyud) and Marpa-Kagyu (mar pa bka' brgyud). The Marpa-Kagyu branch has continued in the Dagpo-Kagyu (dvags po bka' brgyud) transmission, which stems from Dagpo Lhaje, or Gampopa. The Dagpo-Kagyu lineage itself includes the four main branches founded by the four disciples of Gampopa. The two better-known branches are the Karma-Kagyu, or Kamtshang-Kagyu, founded by the first Karmapa Tusum Khyenpa (1110–1193) and the Drikung-Kagyu, founded by Kyobpa Jigten Sumgön (1143–1217). Gampopa's third disciple, Phagmo Drupa (1110–1170), founded the Phagdru-Kagyu lineage. He had eight principal disciples who originated the eight schools of the secondary branch. Among the eight, the best known is the Drukpa-Kagyu school, founded by Ling Repa (1128–1189).

Kālacakra (Tib. dus 'khor; Skt. kālacakra)
Name of a tantra and deity (yidam) of anuttarayogatantra. The teachings of the Kālacakra tantra (literally, "cycles of time") were requested by the king of Shambhala and played a fundamental role in the perspectives and practices of the Vajrayāna.

Kamtshang-Kagyu (Tib. kam tshang bka' brgyud)
See Dagpo-Kagyu.

Kangyur (Tib. *bka' 'gyur*)
A collection, often in 108 volumes, that constitutes the base of the Buddhist canon in the

Tibetan tradition. The *Kangyur* (literally, "translation of the words of Buddha") is divided into several sections, of which the main ones are the *Tripiṭaka,* or Three Baskets, (sde snod gsum) and the tantras (rgyud).

Karma-Kagyu (Tib. kar ma bka' rgyud)
See Dagpo-Kagyu.

Karmapa (Tib. karma pa)
The first Karmapa, Tusum Khyenpa (1110–1193), was the disciple of Gampopa (1079–1153) and founded Tsurphu monastery. The succession of Karmapas is at the heart of the Karma-Kagyu, or Kamtshang-Kagyu, lineage. From the second, Karma Pakshi (1204–1283) to the fifth, Deshin Shekpa (1384–1415), the Karmapas were spiritual guides of the emperor of China. The Third Karmapa, Rangjung Dorje (1284–1339), was a remarkable scholar and adept who also played an important role in the Nyingma lineage. The lineage of Karmapas proceeded without interruption until the seventeenth century. The sixteenth Gyalwang Karmapa was Rangjung Rigpe Dorje (1924–1982); his fame caused him to be more generally recognized as the head of the Kagyu school as a whole. The seventeenth Karmapa was recognized by His Holiness the Dalai Lama and by Taï Situpa in the person of an eight-year-old child who was enthroned at Tsurphu monastery in Tibet in September 1992. Karmapa signifies "he who translates enlightened activity into works." The Karmapas are recognized as emanations of Chenrezig, the buddha of compassion.

Karma Rangjung Kunkhyab or Karma Rangjung Thrinley Kunkhyab Zangpo (Tib. kar ma rang byung 'phrin las kun khyab bzang po)
Kyabje Kalu Rinpoche's monastic name, given to him by the eleventh Taï Situpa at Pelpung at the time he took ordination from him. It literally means "omnipresent nature."

Kham, Khampa (Tib. khams, khams pa)
The Khampas are inhabitants of Kham, which is, along with Amdo, one of the two principal regions of eastern Tibet.

Kharak Gomchung (Tib. kha rag sgom chung)
Kadampa master of the eleventh century, he was the disciple of Gönpapa (aranyaka), abbot of Radreng monastery, and of Potowa (po to ba, 1031–1105), the famous yogi. He received the dzogchen teachings and attained the rainbow body.

Khyungpo Neljor (Tib. Khyung po rnal 'byor)
(978–1128, or 990–1139) Tibetan initiator of the Shangpa lineage. See Shangpa-Kagyu.

Kyergangpa (Tib. skyer sgang pa)
(Late twelfth, early thirteenth centuries) Lama of the Shangpa lineage. See Shangpa-Kagyu.

Lama Norbu Töndrup (Tib. nor bu don grub)
He was a lama of Pelpung monastery. His realization brought him the name *drubpön,* master of retreat, given by the eleventh Taï Situpa, a responsibility he would assume over many years, during which time Kalu Rinpoche met him. He became Kalu Rinpoche's root lama and transmitted to him the Shangpa lineage. Having been designated as his best disciple, Kalu Rinpoche succeeded him as drubpön at Pelpung. At death, Lama Norbu manifested the signs of the rainbow body, characteristic of ultimate realization.

Lawapa (Tib. la ba pa; Skt. lva va pa)
Some say, in accordance with a prophecy and ancient texts, that Lawapa and Indrabhūti, the king of Oḍḍiyāna, are the same person. In some transmissions, Lawapa is the master of

Indrabhūti, as well as of Virūpa. Niguma declared him, along with herself, to be the only other holder of the teachings that she transmitted to Khyungpo Neljor.

Mahāmāyā (Tib. sgyu 'phrul chen mo; Skt. mahāmāyā)
Meditational deity (yidam) and tantra of anuttarayogatantra. See Shangpa-Kagyu.

Maitreya (Tib. byams pa; Skt. maitreya)
The future Buddha; he will manifest at the beginning of the next cosmic cycle. His teaching will follow that of Śākyamuni, when the latter's has disappeared.

Maitrīpa (Tib. mi tri pa; Skt. maitrīpa)
(1007–1078) Mahāsiddha and great scholar of Vikramaśila university; contemporary of Atiśa, he was one of Marpa's and Khyungpo Neljor's principal masters.

Mañjuśrī (Tib. 'jam dpal dbyangs; Skt. mañjuśrī)
The Buddha of wisdom and intelligence.

Māra (Tib. bdud; Skt. māra)
He is the lord of the world of the passions, the demon who sustains and animates them.

Marpa Lodrapa (Tib. mar pa lho brag pa)
See Marpa the Translator.

Marpa-Kagyu (Tib. mar pa bka' brgyud)
Name of the lineage introduced to Tibet by Marpa the Translator. See Dagpo-Kagyu.

Marpa the Translator (Tib. mar pa lo tsa' ba)
(1012–1097) Tibetan initiator of the Marpa-Kagyu lineage. See Dagpo-Kagyu.

Mila Chepa Dorje (Tib. mi la bzhad pa rdo rje)
See Dagpo-Kagyu.

Milarepa (Tib. mi la ras pa)
(1052–1135) See Dagpo-Kagyu.

Mipham Rinpoche (Tib. mi pham rgya mtsho)
(1846–1912) Mipham Gyatso. One of the best-known masters of the Nyingma school, he was a major artisan in the Rimé movement, along with Kongtrul, Khyentse, and Dechen Chogyur Lingpa.

Namkhe Nyingpo (the bodhisattva Ākāśagarbha) (Tib. nam mkha'i snying po; Skt. ākāśagarbha)
Literally, "the essence of space." He is one of the eight great bodhisattvas (nye ba'i sras chen brgyad).

Nāgārjuna (Tib. klu sgrub; Skt. nāgārjuna)
Indian master; one of the Two Supremes. He lived six hundred years and his activity places him mainly in the second and third centuries C.E. He was born to a Brahman family in the region of Vidarbha in southern India. As a youth, he studied and mastered all the traditional sciences, both ordinary and special, the *Tripiṭaka,* and the four classes of tantra. At Nālanda, he took monastic ordination from the mahāsiddha Saraha and soon became abbot of the university. A physician of great talent, he healed Mucilinda, king of the nāgas, who, in gratitude gave him the texts of the *Prajñāpāramitāsūtra* in 100,000 verses. This text had been entrusted to him by Ānanda, Buddha Śākyamuni's principal disciple, to be revealed in the future. This is how he was given the name Nāgārjuna. The Tibetan canon counts 180 works attributed to him. He composed numerous texts based on the *Prajñāpāramitāsūtra,* but his main contribution was the

Madhyamaka, with the *Six Collections of Logic* (*dbu ma rigs tshogs drug*), which became his fundamental texts.

Nālanda (Tib. Nālanda; Skt. Nālanda)
Well-known Buddhist university. It was founded near the middle of the fifth century (earlier according to some sources), under the first Kumāragupta. It produced numerous great masters, among them Asaṅga and Vasubandhu.

Nanda (Tib. nanda)
Half brother of Buddha Śākyamuni; son of King Śuddhodana (father of Buddha Śākyamuni) and his second wife, Mahāprajāpatī, who educated the young Buddha Śākyamuni after the death of Mahāmāyā, first wife of the king and mother of Buddha Śākyamuni.

Naro Bönchung (Tib. na ro bon chung)
A famous Bönpo master who was a rival of Milarepa.

Nāropa (Tib. na' ro pa; Skt. nāropa)
(1016–1100) He was chancellor of Nālanda University when he left in search of true realization with Tilopa, who subjected him to twelve major tests before his enlightenment. He was a mahāsiddha and the Indian master of Marpa the Translator, who initiated the Marpa-Kagyu lineage.

Niguma (Tib. ni gu ma; Skt. niguma)
One of two primordial wisdom ḍākinīs, inspirer of Khyungpo Neljor. See Shangpa-Kagyu.

Nyentönpa (Tib. gnyan ston pa)
A master of the Shangpa lineage. See Shangpa-Kagyu.

Nyingma (Tib. rnying ma)
"The old school." Originating from the first spread of Dharma in Tibet, it developed after Padmasambhava starting in the eighth century.

Oḍḍiyāna (Tib. o rgyan; Skt. oḍḍiyāna)
Legendary country, domain of the ḍākinīs, kingdom of the king Indrabhūti, and Padmasambhava's birthplace. Some situate it between present-day Afghanistan and Kashmir. It is the origin of numerous Vajrayāna teachings.

Ogmin (Tib. 'og min; Skt. akaniṣṭa)
See Akaniṣṭa.

Padmasambhava (Tib. gu ru rin po che; Skt. padmasambhava)
Introduced Dharma to Tibet under the reign of King Thrisong Detsen (790–858). He spread the teaching and hid numerous instructions in the form of treasures destined to be revealed at a later date. He is venerated as the second buddha, prophesied by the first, Buddha Śākyamuni.

Patrul Rinpoche (Tib. rdza dpal sprul o rgyan 'jigs med chos kyi dbangpo)
(1808–1987). One of the greatest Tibetan masters of the nineteenth century and an important architect of the Rimé movement, he is known in the West for the translation of his work *The Path of Great Perfection.*

Pelpung (Tib. dpal spungs)
Principal Kagyu monastery of old Tibet. See Situpa.

Raga Āse (Āraga) (Tib. ra ga a' sras (a' ra ga); Skt. raga Āse (āraga))
Also known as Karma Chame (or Karma Araga, 1613–1678). A meditator and adept of both

the ancient and new traditions, he remains famous in particular for his texts addressed to hermits on retreat (*ri chos zhal gdams*) and those associated with Chenrezig and Sukhāvatī (*bde ba can gyi mon lam*). At death he manifested the rainbow body.

Rāhula (Tib. ra hu' la; Skt. rāhula)
One of Khyungpo Neljor's masters. See Shangpa-Kagyu.

Rangjung Dorje (Tib. rang byung rdo rje)
The Third Karmapa was a remarkable scholar and adept who gathered together the teachings on mahāmudrā and dzogchen. He was an important link in the Kamtshang-Kagyu and Nyingma lineages; he was Dölpopa Sherab Gyaltsen's master and taught Longchenpa, one of the dzogchen tradition's most important masters.

Rechungpa (Tib. ras chung pa)
(1083–1161) He was, with Gampopa, one of Milarepa's principal disciples. See Dagpo-Kagyu.

Remati (Tib. re ma ti; Skt. remati)
Mahākāla Chadrupa's partner.

Rimé (Tib. ris med)
Tibetan name of the "impartial movement," or impartial approach. See Jamgön Kongtrul Lodrö Thaye and the Biographical Note.

Rinpoche (Tib. rin po che)
Literally, "very precious." Honorific term of address.

Sādhujyoti (Tib. legs pa'i skar ma; Skt. sādhujyoti)
An unbelieving and defiant monk-servant of Buddha Śākyamuni.

Sakya (Tib. sa skya)
One of four principal schools of the Tibetan tradition founded by Könchok Gyelpo (1034–1102). His special teaching is the Lamdre, "the way and the fruit."

Śākyamuni (Tib. Sha' kya thub pa; Skt. Śākyamuni)
See Buddha Śākyamuni.

Śākyaprabha (Tib. sa skya 'od; Skt. śākyaprabha)
One of the Six Ornaments.

Sangye Tönpa (Tib. sangs rgyas ston pa)
A master of the Shangpa lineage. See Shangpa-Kagyu.

Śāntideva (Tib. zhi ba lha; Skt. śāntideva)
(ca. 685–763) One of the principal masters of the Madhyamaka-Prāsaṇgika school, following Buddhapālita (470–540) and Candrakīrti (ca. 600–650). Two of his works, *Introduction to the Life of a Bodhisattva* (*Bodhicaryāvatāra, spyod 'jug*) and *The Compendium of Instructions* (*Śikṣāsamuccaya, bslab pa kun btus pa*), are among the Mahāyāna's most famous.

Saraha (Tib. mda' bsbun zhabs; Skt. saraha)
Without a doubt the best known of the Indian mahāsiddhas; an arrow maker, he lived in the seventh century and composed three cycles of songs which remain famous: the dohas of the king, of the queen, and of the people. He is the originator of the distant lineage of mahāmudrā.

Śāriputra (Tib. sha' ri'i bu: Skt. śāriputra)
Śāriputra and Maudgalyāyana were initially disciples of one of the six great religious masters during the time of Buddha Śākyamuni. They left him to follow the Buddha and became his

principal listeners, Śāriputra being the most distinguished in transcendent wisdom and Maudgalyāyana in working wonders. They both died shortly before Buddha Śākyamuni's passing.

Śawaripa (Tib. sha ba ri pa; Skt. śavaripa)
One of the eighty-four mahāsiddhas. Initially a hunter, he was converted by an emanation of Chenrezig. After twelve years of meditation, he attained the realization of mahāmudrā.

Shamarpa (Tib. zhva dmar pa)
The lineage of Shamarpa tulkus, literally, the "holders of the red hat," began with the first Shamarpa Drakpa Senge (1283–1349), who was a disciple of the Third Karmapa, Rangjung Dorje. The Shamarpas played an important role in the Karma-Kagyu lineage between the births of the Karmapa. Between 1792 (the date of the death of the tenth Shamarpa) and 1964 (when the thirteenth Shamarpa was enthroned), there was not, for political reasons, an officially recognized Shamar tulku. His Holiness the Sixteenth Karmapa recognized the thirteenth Shamarpa in the person of Chöki Lodrö, born in 1952. He resides in India and teaches in the West. The Shamar tulkus are recognized as emanations of Buddha Amitābha.

Shangpa-Kagyu (Tib. shangs pa bka' brgyud)
The Shangpa lineage was established in Tibet by the scholar-adept Khyungpo Neljor (ca. 990–1139). Initially, he studied and practiced the Bön and dzogchen traditions; later he went to India in search of teachings. From there he brought back the quintessence of the instructions of 150 masters, among whom the five most important were: the primordial wisdom ḍākinīs Niguma and Sukhasiddhi, Maitrīpa, Abhayā (or Vajrāsana, Dorje Denpa), and Rāhulaguptavajra. He attained realization of and transmitted the Five Golden Teachings and the Five Ultimates, or the ultimate result of the five principal tantras of anuttarayogatantra through the sādhana of the *Deities of the Five Tantras* (*rgyud sde lha lnga*), which are brought together in one single maṇḍala consisting of Guhyasamāja, Mahāmāya, Hevajra, Cakrasaṃvara, and Vajrabhairava. This practice, which comes from the *Ocean of Jewels Tantra* (*rin chen rgya mtsho'i rgyud*) and which was transmitted to him by the mahāsiddha Vajrāsana, constitutes the basis of the Shangpa initiation system.

Khyungpo Neljor established his headquarters at Shang Shong (zhang zhong) in the Shang (shangs) valley of central Tibet, west of the Tsang province. The name "Shangpa" was given to the school that developed after him; he lived to the age of 150. He founded over one hundred monasteries, gave teachings, and performed many miracles. He had innumerable disciples, of whom the main one was Mochopa (rmog lcog pa, c. 1117–?), followed by Kyergangpa (skyer sgang pa, c. late twelfth century, early thirteenth; lived 73 years), Nyentön Rigonpa (gnyan ston ri gong pa, early thirteenth century; lived 72 years), and Sangye Tönpa (sangs rgyas ston pa, thirteenth century; lived 72 years); they constituted, with Vajradhara, Niguma, and Khyungpo Neljor, the first seven masters of the lineage, or the Seven Jewels. The instructions that had until then only been transmitted orally and secretly were spread by Sangye Tönpa. They were put down in writing by his successors: Samdingpa Chöndrup (d. 1319), Japa Gyaltsen Bum ('jag chen rgyal mtshan 'bum, 1261–1334), and Serlingpa Tashipel (1292–1365). He had a disciple, Khedrup Tsangma Shangtön (1234–1309); this lineage is said to be distant, and it has continued without interruption within the Kagyu, Nyingma, Sakya, and Gelug schools. Two other lineages, known as "close" and "very close," stemmed from direct revelations from the primordial wisdom ḍākinī Niguma. Their origins are, respectively, the mahāsiddha Thangtong Gyelpo (thang stong rgyal po, 1361–1485) on the one hand, with the Thangluk lineage following, and, on the other hand, Jonang Kunga Drölcho and Taranatha (Drölwai Gönpo, 1575–1634) followed by the lineage called Jonangluk. These different lineages converged in Jamgön Kongtrul Lodrö Thaye in the nineteenth century. He transmittd them to Tashi Chöpel, who transmitted them to Norbu Töndrup, who in turn transmitted them to Kyabje Kalu Rinpoche, who was the hierarch of this lineage and established its principal seat at Sonada monastery in India, near Darjeeling.

The principal teachings transmitted by the Shangpa lineage consist of five cycles:

1. From Niguma, particularly the Five Golden Teachings (gser chos sde lnga), which present in a coherent and concise entirety one of the highest and most profound methods for realization;
2. From Sukhasiddhi (six yogas and mahāmudrā);
3. From Maitrīpa (Mahākāla Chadrupa);
4. From Abhayā (deities of the five tantras); and
5. From Rāhula (joint practice of four deities).

These teachings constitute the heart of the transmission and practices for the three-year retreat in Shangpa centers.

Siddhartha (Tib. don grub; Skt. siddhārtha)
Name that King Śuddhodana gave his son, the future Buddha Śākyamuni.

Situpa (Tib. ta'i si tu pa)
The lineage of Situpas began with Situ Drogön Rechen (1088–1158) who received the Kamtshang-Kagyu lineage transmission from the first Karmapa Tusum Khyenpa. He was the master of Gyalse Pomdrapa, who was, in turn, master of the second Karmapa Karma Pakshi. The lineage of Situpas passed from Drogön Rechen to two yogis, first to Neljor Yeshe Wangpo, and then to Rigowa Ratnabhadra. Next, it passed to Chöki Gyaltsen (1377–1448), a disciple of the fifth Karmapa Deshin Shekpa, and the first to hold the honorific title of Situ Tulku which he received from the emperor of China. The lineage continued without interruption, playing an essential role between several Karmapas. The eighth Taï Situpa Chöli Jungne, also Chöki Nyingje or Tenpe Nyingje, was known in particular as Situ Penchen, the great scholar. He founded Pelpung monastery in 1727; this would become the largest Kagyu monastery in Tibet. The twelfth Taï Situpa, (fifteenth in the lineage since Drogön Rechen) Pema Nyingje Wangpo, was recognized by His Holiness the Sixteenth Karmapa. He was born in 1954 and established his headquarters at Sherab Ling in India; he gives frequent teachings in the West. He has recognized the seventeenth reincarnation of the Karmapa, Ugyen Thrinley Dorje, whom he enthroned at Tsurphu monastery in September 1992. The Taï Situpas are emanations of Maitreya, the buddha of love, who is the next Buddha to come.

Six Ornaments (Tib. rgyan drug)
These are the six principal Indian Buddhist masters: Nāgārjuna (klu sgrub) and Asaṅga (thogs med), originators, respectively, of the lineages of the Profound View (zab mo lta rgyud) and Widespread Activities (rgya chen spyod rgyud); they are called the Two Supremes (mchog gnyis). The four others are: Āryadeva ('phags pa lha), Vasubandhu (dbyig gnyen), Dignāga (phyogs glang) and Dharmakirti (chos grags). In some cases, the Two Supremes are not counted among the Six Ornaments, so two other masters having particular importance in the vinaya transmission are added: Śākyaprabha (shakya 'od) and Guṇaprabha (yon tan 'od).

Sossaling (Tib. so sa gling)
Name of the charnel ground where Khyungpo Neljor met Niguma.

Subāhu (Tib. labs bzang; Skt. subāhu)
One of the first ten disciples of Buddha, son of a notable Indian family.

Sukhasiddhi (Tib. bde ba'i dngos grub; Skt. sukhasiddhi)

One of two primordial wisdom ḍākinīs, inspirers of Khyungpo Neljor. See Shangpa-Kagyu.

Sukhāvatī (Tib. bde ba can; Skt. sukhāvatī)
The pure realm of Amitābha and Chenrezig.

Taktungu (Tib. rtag tu ngu; Skt. sadāprarudita)
Master who remains famous for his extraordinary energy and self-sacrifice in his quest for the prajñāpāramitā teachings.

Tenzin Gyatso (Tib. bstan 'dzin rgya mtsho)
The lineage of Dalai Lamas has continued without interruption up to the present fourteenth holder of the title, His Holiness Tenzin Gyatso, born in July 1935.

Tengyur (Tib. *bstan 'gyur*)
Literally, "translation of the commentaries." The *Tengyur* (over 200 volumes) consolidates the commentaries on the *Kangyur* written by Indian masters. Together the *Kangyur* and *Tengyur* constitute the canon of the Tibetan Buddhist tradition.

Thogme Zangpo (Tib. thogs med bzang po)
(1295–1369) Kadampa master, author of the *Thirty-Seven Practices of Bodhisattvas* and of a teaching on lojong, among others.

Tilopa (Tib. ti lo pa; Skt. tilopa)
(988–1069) Mahāsiddha who originated the "close" mahāmudrā transmission of the Karma-Kagyu lineage. His successor was Nāropa. See Dagpo-Kagyu.

Tuṣita (Tib. dga' ldan; Skt. tuṣita)
Name of the divine state in which the buddhas find themselves prior to manifesting in our world.

Tusum Khyenpa (Tib. dus gsum mkhyen pa)
(1110–1193) First Karmapa; disciple of Gampopa. See Dagpo-Kagyu.

Two Supremes (Tib. mchog gnyis)
See Six Ornaments.

Vairocana (Tib. bai ro tsa na)
Tibetan translator who, from 810 C.E. on, worked at Samye, the first monastery founded in Tibet by the king Thrisong Detsen (790–858). He was one of Padmasambhava's principal disciples and played a very important role in the Nyingma transmissions.

Vairocana (Tib. rnam par snang mdzad; Skt. vairocana)
The Victorious One of the buddha family.

Vajrabhairava (Tib. rdo rje 'jigs byed; Skt. vajrabhairava)
Meditational deity (yidam) and tantra of anuttarayogatantra. See Shangpa-Kagyu.

Vajradhara (Tib. rdo rje chang; Skt. vajradhara)
Meditational deity of the dharmakāya, the primordial awakening; inspirer of the revelations of numerous lineages.

Vajrasattva (Tib. rdo rje sems dpa'; Skt. vajrasattva)
Meditational deity whose practice is particularly associated with purification.

Vajrayoginī (Tib. rdo rje rnal 'byor ma; Skt. vajrayoginī)
Female deity, consort of Cakrasaṃvara. Her practice is very important in the Kagyu tradition.

Vasubandhu (Tib. dbying gnyen; Skt. vasubandhu)
(ca. 350) One of the Six Ornaments, great scholar of the Vaibhāṣika and Sautrāntika schools, author of the *Abhidharmakośa*. Later on, he was converted to the Mahāyāna by his brother Asaṅga and became, along with him, one of the founders of the Yogācāra school; he was abbot of Nālanda.

Vikramaśila (Tib. rnam gnon tshul; Skt. vikramaśila)
Famous monastic university of eastern Bihar, founded by the king Dharmapāla in about the year 800. It progressed until the decline of Nālanda and remained in existence until the Muslim invasions of the thirteenth century. Atīśa was its chancellor before coming to Tibet.

Vinaya (Tib. 'dul ba; Skt. vinaya)
"Discipline." Collection of instructions and precepts of the discipline taught by Buddha Śākya-muni. The vinaya is one of the Three Baskets of the *Kangyur*.

Virūpa (Tib. bi ru' pa; Skt. virūpa)
One of the eighty-four mahāsiddhas. He remains famous for his miracles, which included having stopped the course of the sun to postpone payment of his drinking debts.

Index

progressive, 213
quick, 174
universal (*see* Mahāyāna)

Patience, 248
perfection of, 143, **145**

Patrul Rinpoche, 177, 183, 189, 292

Peace, 43
in meditation, 152

Pelpung, xv, 277, **292**, 295

Perceptions, 41, **50**, 61

Perfections, 143, 147
daily, **247**
the six, **143**, 264
transcendent, 128

Phases of meditation
Completion Stage, **211**
Generation Stage, **211**

Phenomena, 41, 222

Phenomena, luminous, 59

Philosopher's stone, 127, 246

Phonetic transliteration, xxiv

Phowa. *See* Yoga of transference

Physical posture
for meditation, xvii, 154

Physician, 287

Pig, 73

Poisons, three mental, 73

Potter, 72

Power(s), 23
Buddha's ten, 168
miraculous, 164
of refuge, 168

Practice, 253
a day of, 249
at each moment, 252
continual, 236
cultivation of a, 239
framework for, 255
heart of, 4, 245

in a Dharma center, 252
in ordinary life, 246, 247, **249**, 256
styles of, 257–258
subsequent, **213**
urgency of, **87**
without delay, 88

Practices of integration, 263
common preliminaries, 193, 195, **197**
of dzogchen, 194
of familiarization with a yidam, 194
of lojong, 194
of mahāmudrā, 195, **233**
of śamatha, 194
of vipaśyanā, 194
unique preliminaries (*see* Ngöndro)

Pratyekabuddha, 104

Prayers, xix, 12, 77, 204, 233, 272n. 126

Presence, 234
total, 155, 234
See also Datarwai shepa

Presenting the nature of mind. *See* Ngotro

Pride, 28, 37, 39
transformed, 169, 236

Primordial wisdom(s), 19, 67, 164
afflictions transmuted into, 236
all-accomplishing, 236
innate, 235
mirrorlike, 236
of discernment, 236
of emptiness, 222
of equanimity, 236
of the dharmadhātu, 236
the five, 169, 189

Principal elements, **67**
the five, 67

Principle
feminine, 57
masculine, 57
red feminine, 58, 64
white masculine, 58, 64

Procreation. *See* Sex

Production. *See* Projection

Professor, 178

Wisdom Publications

WISDOM PUBLICATIONS, a not-for-profit publisher, is dedicated to making available authentic Buddhist works for the benefit of all. We publish translations of the sutras and tantras, commentaries and teachings of past and contemporary Buddhist masters, and original works by the world's leading Buddhist scholars. We publish our titles with the appreciation of Buddhism as a living philosophy and with the special commitment to preserve and transmit important works from all the major Buddhist traditions.

If you would like more information or a copy of our mail order catalog, and to keep informed about our future publications, please write or call us at:

WISDOM PUBLICATIONS
361 Newbury Street
Boston, Massachusetts, 02115, USA
Telephone: (617) 536-3358 • Fax: (617) 536-1897

The Wisdom Trust

AS A NOT-FOR-PROFIT PUBLISHER, Wisdom Publications is dedicated to the publication of fine Dharma books for the benefit of all sentient beings and dependent upon the kindness and generosity of sponsors in order to do so. We have many excellent manuscripts waiting for benefactors. One hundred per cent of any donation made to the Wisdom Trust Fund will be used exclusively for the project for which it was intended. If you would like to make a contribution to Wisdom to help us continue our Dharma work, or to receive information about opportunities for planned giving, please contact our Boston office.

Thank you.

Wisdom Publications is a non-profit, charitable 501(c)(3) organization and a part of the Foundation for the Preservation of the Mahayana Tradition (FPMT).

Guesar (CDR) and The Dharma Files

KYABJE KALU RINPOCHE founded Dharma centers throughout the world, such as the Institut Karma Ling in France. These centers continue to operate under the direction of qualified lamas who transmit the practice of the teachings contained in this work.

Luminous Mind: The Way of the Buddha was generated from a Dharma transmission program called The Way of Buddha, which was sponsored by Guesar (CDR).

To receive information on future programs and the location of centers, please contact:

Guesar (CDR)
Hameau de Saint Hugon
F-73110, Arvillard (Savoie)
France

Tel: (33) 79 25 54 90
Fax: (33) 79 25 78 08

The Dharma Files

The Dharma Files are reference documents. Each issue addresses a particular theme, which is explained by different masters and illustrated by translations from the tradition. This triannual publication of the Institut Karma Ling is available by contacting: Dharma, 73110, Arvillard, FRANCE (Tel: 79 25 54 90, fax: 79 25 78 08).

Issues available:

1. Deaths, Rebirths, and Immortality (January 1988)
2. & 3. Compassion and Wisdom
4. Meditation
5. The Bodhisattva
6. Homage to Kyabje Kalu Rinpoche
7. Mahāmudrā, Ultimate Mental Practice
8. Dharma and Contemporary Thought
9. Introduction to Tantric Buddhism
10. Foundations of Buddhism
11. Alchemy of Emotions
12. The Spiritual Guide
13. Taking Refuge
14. Spiritual Journey in Daily Life
15. Traditional Images and Symbols
16. Inner and Outer World
17. Interdependence (May 1993)

Other Books from Wisdom

ADVICE FROM A SPIRITUAL FRIEND
Geshe Dhargyey and Geshe Rabten
Translated and edited by Brian Beresford

Based on practical Buddhist verses of thought transformation composed centuries ago, this profound wisdom reaches out to all types of people from all walks of life. No matter what your spiritual orientation, you will benefit from this sage advice on how to develop the skills that lead to contentment and happiness.
Special two-color printing, inc. Tibetan texts, 176 pp. 6 x 6, paper,
ISBN 0-86171-107-6
B017 $14.95

AWAKENING THE MIND
Basic Buddhist Meditations
Geshe Namgyal Wangchen

The profoundly effective methods of meditation presented here have helped people overcome their problems for centuries. Based on the teachings of the Tibetan saint Tsong Khapa, these techniques help replace depression, anger, and other forms of mental pain with the qualities of tranquility, compassion, and wisdom. *15 line drawings, 272 pp., 5 3/8 x 8 1/2, paper,*
ISBN 86171-102-5
B039A $14.95

CREATION AND COMPLETION
Essential Points of Tantric Meditation
Jamgön Kongtrul

Jamgön Kongtrul, a master practitioner and one of Tibet's most prolific writers, composed this text as a guide to the effective practice of tantric Buddhist meditation. Usually passed from teacher to student by oral transmission, these powerful meditation techniques are presented here in Sarah Harding's excellent translation.
"[This]is an exceptionally important text that is very beneficial to read and to possess. It will answer all questions and resolve all doubts about Vajrayana practice." —Venerable Thrangu Rinpoche *Tibetan text included, 144 pp., 6 x 9, paper, ISBN 0-86171-105-X*
B105 $14.95

DRINKING THE MOUNTAIN STREAM
Songs of Tibet's Beloved Saint, Milarepa
Translated by Lama Kunga Rinpoche and Brian Cutillo

Milarepa, Tibet's renowned and beloved saint, wandered the terrain of eleventh-century Tibet guiding countless followers along the Buddhist path. Milarepa's songs and poems are bold and inspiring, his language direct and immediate. Lama Kunga Rinpoche and Brian Cutillo render a faithful translation of this rare collection. *8 b&w illustrations, 192 pp., 6 x 9, paper,*
ISBN 0-86171-063-0
B063 $14.95

ENLIGHTENED BEINGS
Life Stories from the
Ganden Oral Tradition
Compiled and translated by Janice D. Willis

Jan Willis provides a wealth of information about the worlds in which six mahamudra masters from the Geluk school of Tibetan Buddhism studied, practiced, meditated, and became enlightened beings in their lifetimes.
"[The life stories] offer a dimension of understanding not seen in other literature. A fascinating addition to any library of Buddhist thought." —*Small Press*
8 line drawings, 1 color plate, 318 pp., 6 x 9, paper, ISBN 0-86171-068-1
B068 $18.00

HOW TO MEDITATE
A Practical Guide
Kathleen McDonald

What is meditation? Why practice it? How do I do it? The answers to these often-asked questions are contained in this down-to-earth book, written by a Western Buddhist nun with solid experience in both the practice and teaching of meditation.
"This book is as beautifully simple and direct as its title." —*Yoga Today*
224 pp., 5 1/4 x 8 1/2, paper, ISBN 0-86171-009-6
B009A $12.95

INTRODUCTION TO TANTRA
A Vision of Totality
Lama Yeshe

"As lucid an explanation of Buddhist tantra as you are likely to find. ...a classic." — Philip Glass, composer

"No one has summarized the essence of tantra with such clarity, coherence, and simplicity as well as Thubten Yeshe does here."—*Religious Studies Review*
176 pp., 5 1/4 x 8 1/2, paper, ISBN 0-86171-021-5
B021 $14.95

THE MEANING OF LIFE FROM A BUDDHIST PERSPECTIVE
The Dalai Lama
Translated and edited by Jeffrey Hopkins

The Dalai Lama presents the basic world view of Buddhism while answering some of life's most profound and challenging questions. He bases his explanation on the twelve links of dependent-arising as depicted in the famous Buddhist image of the wheel of life.
114 pp., 6 x 9, paper, ISBN 0-86171-096-7
B096 $12.50

MEDITATION ON EMPTINESS
Jeffrey Hopkins

One of the world's foremost scholar-practitioners of Tibetan Buddhism offers a clear exposition of the view of emptiness. In bringing this remarkable philosophy to life, he describes the meditational practices by which emptiness can be realized and shows that, far from being merely abstract, these teachings can be vivid and utterly practical.
"One of the great classics of the study of Buddhism in the West. Few subsequent works on the subject can be said to equal it in profundity and accessibility. "
—José Ignacio Cabezón, Professor of Philosophy, Iliff School of Theology
992 pp., 5 1⁄4 x 8 1⁄2, paper ISBN 0-86171-110-6
B014P $29.95

THE TANTRIC PATH OF PURIFICATION
The Yoga Method of Heruka Vajrasattva
Lama Yeshe
Compiled and edited by Nick Ribush

This powerful purification practice has proven to be especially effective for Western practitioners. Lama Yeshe cuts through misconceptions and challenges us to act.
280 pp., 6 x 9, paper, ISBN 0-86171-020-7
B020 $15.00

TRANSFORMING PROBLEMS INTO HAPPINESS
Lama Zopa Rinpoche

"This book should be read as the words of a wise, loving parent whose sternness underlines the importance of what is being taught. A masterfully brief statement of Buddhist teachings on the nature of humanity and human suffering....Zopa Rinpoche [is] a wise and inspiring teacher."
— Utne Reader
104 pp., 6 x 9, paper, ISBN 0-86171-038-X
B038 $11.95

THE WARRIOR SONG OF KING GESAR
Douglas J. Penick
Foreword by Sakyong Mipham Rinpoche
Introduction by Tulku Thondup Rinpoche

This is an epic tale of the legendary Tibetan warrior king, Gesar of Ling. The saga of Gesar's life—from the harsh circumstances of his youth to his climactic days of battle against the enemies of the four directions—is an interweaving of scenes ranging from the gritty and human to the mystical and wondrous.

Many of Asia's most inspiring and sacred teachings have to do with courage: the bravery to face the inner and outer obstacles that prevent us from finding true freedom. This traditional story has been recreated by visionary bards in Central Asia for centuries. In a modern rendition, Douglas Penick brings us the unbroken heritage of spiritual warriorship embodied by the life of the enlightened warrior-sage Gesar, King of Ling.

DOUGLAS J. PENICK was born in 1944 and is a graduate of Princeton University. He studied with the Venerable Chogyam Trungpa Rinpoche from 1971 until his death in 1987. Mr. Penick lives in Boulder, Colorado. *176 pp., 6 x 9, paper, isbn 0-86171-113-0*
B113 $16.95

THE WORLD OF TIBETAN BUDDHISM
An Overview of Its Philosophy and Practice
The Dalai Lama
Translated by Geshe Thupten Jinpa
Foreword by Richard Gere

"A lucid and profound yet eminently readable introduction to this subject." —*Library Journal*
"Suitable for beginners…as well as more advanced practitioners of the Buddhist way." —
Publishers Weekly
224 pp., 6 x 9, cloth, ISBN 0-86171-100-9
B097H $25.00
224 pp., 6 x 9, paper, ISBN 0-86171-097-5
B097A $14.00